Erich Przywara, S.J.

Erich Przywara, S.J.

His Theology and His World

Thomas F. O'Meara, O.P.

Foreword by Michael A. Fahey, S.J.

University of Notre Dame Press
Notre Dame, Indiana

Manufactured in the United States of America

Library of Congress Cataloging-in-Publication Data
O'Meara, Thomas F., 1935–
Erich Przywara, S. J. : his theology and his world / Thomas F.
O'Meara ; foreword by Michael A. Fahey.
p.   cm.
Includes bibliographical references and index.
ISBN 0-268-02763-3 (alk. paper)
1. Przywara, Erich, 1889–1972.   I. Title.
BX4705.P736 O44 2002
230'.2'092—dc21
2001006422

Contents

Foreword

English-speaking readers will be especially grateful to Professor Thomas F. O'Meara, O. P., for providing not only a comprehensive theological commentary on the diverse writings of Erich Przywara, S. J. (1889–1972) but also fascinating biographical details about this major German Catholic theologian. In our academic settings, Przywara is scarcely known, much less read. This is explained in part by his complex German prose and by the unwieldy methodology he chose for his principal publications. Whereas the writings of Karl Rahner, Romano Guardini, Karl Adam, and Augustin Bea were translated quickly and were widely read on this side of the Atlantic, Przywara's works have gathered dust on our library shelves.

I am honored to have been asked by Professor O'Meara to preface his valuable study with some introductory reflections, especially from the viewpoint of one who has just completed fifty years as a Jesuit. Reading this book has afforded me many insights and has steered me toward the original sources I should have read long ago. Perhaps this present monograph will encourage translators to produce an English collection of at least Przywara's less formidable writings.

O'Meara describes how he first came into contact with Przywara's work in the early 1960s while he was editing essays on Paul Tillich by various authors. Arriving in Munich in 1963, he paged through some of Przywara's theological writings without having the time or courage to delve into them. Now, some forty years later, after having established himself as an expert in the complexities of nineteenth- and twentieth-century German Catholic intellectual life, especially its philosophy and theology as represented by Schelling, Rahner, and others, and after having acquired a fond appreciation for Munich and Bavarian culture, he shares the fruits of his recent reading of Przywara's thickest tomes and thinnest book reviews. His two important contributions to earlier German theology, *Romantic Idealism and Roman Catholicism: Schelling and the Theologians* (1982) and *Church and Culture: German Catholic Theology, 1860–1914,* prepared him for understanding the *Sitz im Leben* of this later esoteric Catholic theologian. His breadth of vision makes this study readable and reliable. For example, he explains why, in the aftermath of Bismarck's *Kulturkampf,* religious orders such as the Society of Jesus had been banned from territorial German lands and how Przywara's novitiate training (1908–1910) was done in exile in Exaten, The Netherlands. Later Przywara was assigned as part of his formation to teach briefly in a Jesuit secondary school in Austria. Finally, he pursued theological studies for ordination from 1917 to 1921 at the extraterritorial German Jesuit theologate across the border in Valkenburg, The Netherlands. After his ordination and a shift in the political scene, Jesuits and other religious were allowed to take up apostolic work in the Fatherland. For Przywara this facilitated his appointment to the Munich-based editorial offices of the Jesuit monthly journal of culture and thought, *Stimmen der Zeit.*

That a Dominican scholar should undertake a major exposition of a Jesuit theologian is neither unprecedented nor disadvantageous. To list only one other example, the challenging task of translating into French the volume *Method in Theology* of Bernard Lonergan, S. J., was tackled by a team of French-Canadian Dominican theologians from Montreal. O'Meara's Dominican understanding of the theology of grace rooted in the writings of Thomas Aquinas and in a variety of Thomisms handed down both accurately and distortedly (in the latter case sometimes by Jesuits), allows him to identify pitfalls in the way Jesuit theology has sometimes been distorted into what O'Meara calls "the Baroque mechanics of actual grace and mortal sins pushing and pulling a neutral human person from day to day."

Munich in the 1920s was a cultural mecca, rich in artists and musicians, including Ibsen and Rilke, Thomas Mann, Kandinsky, Schoenberg, Richard Strauss, and Mahler. Eugenio Pacelli (the future Pius XII) had already arrived in Munich to take up the post of apostolic nuncio in 1917 until 1925 when he moved on for another four years in Berlin. But below the surface of freedom and exhilaration there was also unrest, insecurity, and confusion caused partly by the negative effects of the Treaty of Versailles. When the rise of National Socialism was later criticized it was done delicately and indirectly.

In those days, it would have been impossible for a member of a religious order to teach at a German university. That exclusion has been described as a deprivation, but in fact, in my judgment, it proved to be a stroke of luck for Przywara. His editorial assignment allowed for a relatively placid pace of living. He read voraciously in the arts, history, philosophy, and theology. His readings as a member of the editorial team of *Stimmen der Zeit,* where he was assigned from 1922 to 1941 (although the journal was closed down by the Gestapo in 1937), included titles by many Jewish, Protestant, and agnostic authors. Few university professors then or now have the leisure to read uninterruptedly such hefty tomes. Yet he had the time to assimilate, write, lecture in academic circles, and preach in church settings. He had no secretary, no electric typewriter, no computer, no Internet access, but he managed nonetheless. His lively Jesuit community included several persons whose interests paralleled his own, men of specialized intellectual interests. He accepted speaking engagements in various parts of the country, taking advantage of the excellent German train service of his day. His circle of friends and colleagues, as O'Meara indicates, was unusually large.

Przywara never experienced the harsh restrictions that were earlier and later meted out by Rome to theologians in France, Italy, Great Britain, and the United States, during the Modernist era and the rise of the *nouvelle théologie.* O'Meara describes the theologian's contacts with Pacelli and his need from time to time to clarify puzzling points he had delivered in public statements (especially remarks critical of the institutional church). Although his writings and radio addresses were carefully scrutinized and occasionally challenged by his Roman or Jesuit superiors, he wrote and spoke without harassment.

Przywara was a pre–Vatican II Catholic theologian, not in the sense that his writings were hostile to developments that occurred at the council. Still his direct influence there was negligible. Sadly, for at least the last ten years of his life, he suffered from a debilitating mental illness, perhaps schizophrenia or perhaps Alzheimer's. His voice grew silent as he needed specialized nursing care in a series of various countryside locations isolated from his community and admirers.

O'Meara correctly observes, as have other commentators, that Przywara's theology was colored by Jesuit spirituality, especially as embodied in the *Spiritual Exercises* of Ignatius Loyola. This spirituality of course is shared by a number of streams of Christianity and is certainly not gnostic or arcane. But it did project a recognizable accent. Ignatian spirituality, to be sure, was not his only spiritual wellspring. Cardinal Newman's vision of the Church continued to inspire him all his life.

O'Meara describes Przywara's theology of creation, grace, and redemption as seen through Ignatian prisms. Przywara drew inspiration from his celebration of daily Mass. Besides being a theologian, he perceived himself as a *Seelsorger* and he treasured opportunities to help out in parishes and to preach. His own annual Ignatian retreats, based on an abbreviated version of the *Spiritual Exercises,* kept alive the Ignatian themes. In 1925 he wrote an idiosyncratic study of Jesuit spirituality entitled *Majestas Divina: Ignatianische Frömmigkeit* (translated into English only in part by Thomas Corbishley some forty-six years later!). From 1938 to 1940 he labored tirelessly on a three-volume work, *Deus Semper Major,* a 1053-page commentary on the *Spiritual Exercises* that went into a second edition in 1964.

From the spiritual legacy of Ignatius Loyola, Przywara learned "to find God in all realities." He learned not to be afraid of philosophers who thought differently from himself. He found elements of truth in Nietzsche, Husserl, Heidegger, and many other suspect philosophers. He found intimations of grace in novels by Julien Green, Graham Greene, and Gertrud von Le Fort. Much like Gerard Manley Hopkins he experienced that the world was charged with a divine "inscape." Another Ignatian characteristic that he experienced is the possibility and desirability of being a "contemplative in action." In order to offer, in response to divine grace, "greater glory to God" (*ad majorem Dei gloriam*), he attuned himself to Ignatius's "discernment of spirits," searching to appreciate how God was speaking to him through his feelings and desires. He had an acute sense of Ignatius's "Rules for Thinking with the Church" (*sentir con la Iglesia*), although he did not identify every decision or choice of action by church leaders to be purely and simply the mind of the Church. In an article written in 1929 titled "Papst König" he warned of the dangers of papalism as when the pope exclusively names all bishops and cardinals, and confines the exercise of universal jurisdiction to Vatican offices (an "ecclesial office-machine") thereby ignoring the inner grace-life of individuals. Finally in Ignatius's notion of election which he called *Wandlung,* he recognized the importance of what Lonergan later identified as intellectual and moral conversions. However, Przywara also recognized that the Suppression of the Society of Jesus from 1773 to 1814 had cut off from Jesuits' collective memory certain spiritual traditions that needed reappropriation. Some of the original Ignatian insights had been clouded by some problematic restoration efforts of Jan Roothaan, the Superior General who held office from 1829 to 1853.

Przywara had a theology that was deeply inculturated (although the term would have been unfamiliar to him). But it was an inculturation that identified largely with the German intelligentsia. Unlike more recent embodiments of Ignatian spirituality by Jesuits such as Ignacio Ellacuría or Jon Sobrino, associated with El Salvador's Universidad Centroamericana José Simeón Cañas (the "UCA"), Przywara's *Wandlung* did not lead to a theology of liberation. Przywara's existential and personal dimension of salvation remained, as this book argues, rather abstract. Furthermore, his exploration of divine and human freedom remains rather tentative.

Because of his wide reading and his contact with a number of Protestant thinkers including Karl Barth, Przywara ranks as a German pioneer in ecumenism. He shared the vision of his co-Jesuit Max Pribilla who published as early as 1929 a pioneering work titled *Um die kirchliche Einheit,* a far-sighted account of the Faith and Order Movement and the Life and Work Movement. Before the council Przywara published in 1956 his important *Gespräch zwischen den Kirchen.* Although not as active an ecumenist as his contemporary, Father— later Cardinal—Augustin Bea (1881–1968), Przywara still promoted various principles that paralleled Vatican II's Decree on Ecumenism, *Unitatis redintegratio.* O'Meara notes his public dialogue with Paul Tillich, his public discussions with Karl Barth at the University of Münster in 1929, his contacts with the Una Sancta Movement, and his close association with ecumenical pioneers such as Hans Asmussen and Otto Karrer.

More surprising to readers who have stereotypical perceptions of German Catholics' attitudes to Jews in the period between the two World Wars, is Przywara's close contacts with Jewish thinkers. Despite the fact that Berlin was a more favorable setting for exchange between Christians and Jews than Munich, he carried on respectful dialogue. For him a Jewish philosopher was not automatically a Bolshevist Jew. His favorite Jewish dialogue partner was Leo Baeck, but he also was familiar with the writings of Martin Buber and others.

Like Ignatius Loyola he had extensive contacts with women. He relied on the advice of the Jewish (later Catholic) philosopher Edith Stein, as well as the novelist Gertrude von le Fort. While not a full fledged feminist in today's sense, he resisted the view that women fulfilled their identity simply by their responsibilities with *Kinder, Küche,* and *Kirche.*

Przywara does not fit into the mold of those French theologians who renewed theology via *ressourcement,* a return to the sources of Scripture, the Fathers of the Church, and liturgical renewal. Yet his contributions to Christian life and spirituality, his call for participation in the eucharistic liturgy, and his ecclesiology will probably be more appreciated in this century than his metaphysical studies on the analogy of being.

In 1555, finally acquiescing to the entreaties of his early companions, Ignatius of Loyola agreed to dictate to his secretary, Fr. Louis Gonçales da Cámara, an autobiographical account of his life prior to his moving definitively to Rome. He described himself in that narrative simply as "the pilgrim" and his story was *The Pilgrim's Tale.* The metaphor of pilgrim which Vatican II applied to the Church itself, is an Ignatian image that Erich Przywara adopted himself when he described himself as a "dust-surrounded messenger." O'Meara's account of his life and thought will inspire those who, amid interludes of joy and exhilaration, as well as suffering, disappointment, and setbacks, press on along the way to God.

MICHAEL A. FAHEY, S.J.

Emmett Doerr Professor of Theology
Editor in Chief, *Theological Studies*
Marquette University, Milwaukee

Preface

"From everywhere it is just a single step into the metaphysical."
—Robert Musil

"One must not forget Father Erich Przywara. For the Catholics of Germany in the twenties, thirties, and forties he was one of the keenest minds. He had a great influence on all of us when we were young." So Karl Rahner recalled his fellow Jesuit in 1965.[1] Few taking up this book, however, have heard of Erich Przywara. Nonetheless, Karl Neufeld calls him "a pioneer of a conscious and comprehensive analysis of the age,"[2] and Friedrich Wulf describes him as "one of the most important Catholic theologians in the German-speaking area in recent times,"[3] while for Martha Zechmeister he is "someone whose lectures and writings gave decisive impetuses for a Catholic restoration, a precursor of Vatican II."[4]

In the summer of 1962, as I was looking for writings by Catholics on the thought of Paul Tillich for the volume *Paul Tillich in Catholic Thought,* I came across very few European Catholics who had taken note of the Protestant theologian after his emigration. Tillich had left Europe in 1933, and the subsequent geographical markers in his career would be in America: Union Theological Seminary, Harvard University, and the University of Chicago. I found a curiosity, however: a European Jesuit with an unusual name who had an essay in an American book honoring Tillich's seventieth birthday in 1959, *Religion and Culture: Essays in Honor of Paul Tillich.* In that volume Erich Przywara's ideas stood apart from the usual themes of existence, faith, and word preferred by the other contributors. He described the theological sources and roots of Tillich's thought, naming it a Christian grammar moving amid four "root terms": *ke-rygma, mysterium, kairos,* and *oikonomia.* That interpretation of faith un-folded from a *kairos* centered on an economy of revelation in cultural moments of time.[5] Who was this perceptive reader of Tillich, writing from a theological stance so different from that of American Protes-tants? A mysterious figure of some exotic Slavic origin? Perhaps a vic-tim of Hitler or Stalin? Who was the Jesuit Erich Przywara?

The next year in Munich, pursuing doctoral studies, I came across Przywara's lengthy writings treating phenomenology, idealism, and scholastic analogy, because some of his works had just appeared in three volumes of a new edition. But they were too much for me: their topic of analogy seemed passé, while their language of idealism was foreign. Evidently he had carried on earlier in the twentieth century a conver-sation with issues in modern philosophy, and, at the same time, like Romano Guardini, he had written on spirituality, liturgy, and literature. I did not know of meetings in the 1920s by Catholics who had been culturally engaged with modernity decades before Vatican II. I once asked Karl Rahner about Przywara in 1965, and he responded briefly and sadly that he was still alive but was ill and mentally not in contact with the world around him. He died in 1972 at the age of eighty-three.

There are a number of dissertations and monographs on Przywara in German, some of them of considerable scope and insight, and a few studies in Spanish, Italian, and French; in English there are less than a dozen articles and one book. Consequently the identity and impact of the Jesuit is not easily accessible to the English-speaking world. The following chapters offer no more than an introduction to the life and career of a Catholic cultural theologian of breadth and originality. The author, little more than a surveyor of Przywara's hundreds of books and articles, presents this intellectual biography of a philosopher-theologian as a stimulus to further research and interpretation.

This book is, too, a contribution to an awareness and understanding of German Catholic theology in the past century and a half; to the ap-preciation of how philosophers and theologians prepared for Vati-can II. Erich Przywara is, along with Romano Guardini, Paul Schanz, A. D. Sertillanges, Pierre Teilhard de Chardin, and Joseph Maréchal, a Roman Catholic who broke out of the confines of Tridentine decrees and myopic papal mandates. In the years after Bismarck's *Kulturkampf,* Catholic intellectuals strove, without compromising the role of the church and the history of revelation, to express in theology, philosophy, art, literature, and liturgy some of the thought-forms of the time. New approaches and the longing for a vital Catholicism were present in German Catholicism before and after World War I.

The following presentation looks at Przywara's philosophical theology and its historical context. It will not repeat the numerous expositions of the analogy of being other than to summarize analogy's prominent but not exclusive role. Attention is paid to three areas: sources and contemporaries, underlying theological approaches, and the three areas of church, liturgy, and spirituality.

My special thanks to Martha Zechmeister, who gave generously of her information and insight; to Lisa Amend at the Bavarian State Library in Munich, who helped me extensively with research, and to Dr. Timothy Nelsen, director of the Dokumentationsbibliothek of Davos, Switzerland. I thank Robert Krieg, who encouraged this project when its weight and abstraction seemed too burdensome. I am particulary grateful to Michael Fahey, S. J., who contributed many suggestions for the text and a Foreword.

Chapter 1

Erich Przywara

His Age and His World

Erich Przywara was a German Jesuit whose ideas and writings influenced Catholic intellectuals and church movements in the twentieth century. A thinker, a writer, a contemplative of the unseen, from 1920 to 1960 he carried on a wide-ranging conversation with the creators and issues of modern philosophy and culture, mainly in Germany and Austria. He was a critic of philosophies of disbelief but also of a Catholicism of simplistic devotions and cultivated ignorance. Knowledgeable in patristic and medieval theologies, he was an interpreter of modern directions. He published his first essays on the Christian life as the First World War came to its bloody end, and four decades later he wrote a book on what might be expected from the coming council, Vatican II.

The theologian drew to himself men and women from every walk of life, counseling students, advising Benedictines, teaching Protestants, corresponding with intellectuals. He found sources for his ideas in figures as diverse as the French philosopher Léon Brunschwicg to the British novelist Graham Greene.[1] Beginning in the 1920s countless publications and innumerable journeys to give lectures placed him at the center of vital movements in society and the church: one of his Jesuit colleagues wrote of him in the 1920s, "What would have been unthinkable a decade earlier is now reality: a German Jesuit published in journals like *Logos* and *Kantstudien* without, in these distinguished journals, the letters "S. J." being seen as a drawback."[2] Some have compared him to Origen or Thomas Aquinas, calling him a seer and a herald; he was not a researcher or professor, and certainly not a pompous academic or ambitious ecclesiastic. Choosing not to condemn the cultural world in which he worked as a theologian, he was a missionary, one seeking God's deep, primal revelation not among African tribes but in horizons of European culture. Today, thirty years after his death, he might appear as a speculative Romano Guardini or as an anticipation of Karl Rahner.

Yet, few English-speaking Catholics know Erich Przywara: a few philosophers and theologians may recognize the name, connecting him with analogy or Cardinal Newman. In the United States, James Collins, an almost solitary observer of philosophical directions in Europe, wrote in 1942 an article on Przywara's publications describing them as "notable both as an indication of the role of Catholic thinkers in the general cultural movement and for their own intrinsic value as a speculative achievement,"[3] while decades later Friedrich Wulf explained his "meteoric rise" in intellectual circles in the 1920s.[4] In the last fifty years in America one dissertation and a few articles have been published.[5]

It is interesting that just as Thomas Mann was fashioning for his novel *The Magic Mountain* the Jesuit Leo Naphta, an unconvincing hybrid of Jew, Marxist, Jesuit, and Catholic, Erich Przywara, Jesuit and cultural observer, was beginning his career.[6]

Why is Przywara little known outside of Germany? The main reason is the linguistic and intellectual formats. The language is not always abstract but it is at times metaphysical, rhetorical, even poetic or idiosyncratic. The intuitive leaps and the assembly of ideas and implications, at times like blank verse, can inspire but they can also confuse; links based upon words and terms run through varied fields (the Bible or a particular metaphysics) and different topics (Aristotelian natural philosophy or Chalcedon's Christology).[7] Sometimes what is specifically Christian is not easy to uncover, and the works as the decades pass repeat the same ideas.

German scholars have never lost sight of his importance and have composed over the past forty years a stream of articles, dissertations, and monographs giving a true overview of his work. Karl Neufeld begins an insightful essay commemorating the one hundredth anniversary of Przywara's birth:

> After World War II in the wider world there was silence. Not only his name but his person made an approach difficult. He could not be fitted in, and the context for understanding him lay far back in history. His figure reflected neither the university professor nor the

scholar: he did not present himself as a thinker, researcher, or private scholar but also not as a charismatic founder of an intellectual or spiritual movement. Przywara remained a person *sui generis*, although his figure and image was not the result of a self-willed individual but a consequence of the situation he decided to engage when he entered the Society of Jesus persecuted by the *Kulturkampf.* Without that background his person, destiny, role, and contribution must remain a puzzle. Above all he was a witness to a time.[8]

To one of his articles, one looking at recent philosophical and theological publications, he gave the title "A Walk through Time."[9] He had been a witness to time whose own several times have run their course, although they are prelude and parent of our time.

LIFE AND WORKS

Erich Przywara was born on October 12, 1889, in Kattowitz in the German Oberschlesien (Upper Silesia) which lies today within the borders of Poland. His father Mathias Przywara, originally from a Polish farming community, was a successful merchant, while his mother, Bertha Peiker, was from a German family of civil servants. One of three boys, he was born the same year as Martin Heidegger and Adolf Hitler and three years after Paul Tillich and Karl Barth.

Przywara was very conscious of his geographical origins, of how history and subjectivity met in the place where a person was born and grew up. He wrote about Silesia, of that world near to where the three realms of Austria, Russia, and Germany met. He wrote about the impact his *Heimat* had on him: an intersection of East and West, a small city filled with different ethnic and religious groups, young men and women raised in deeply Catholic families attending state schools.[10] He attended the *Gymnasium,* preparing his lessons while working in his father's store. Favorite courses of the gifted student were not in science or history but in music, particularly in the choral compositions of Johann Sebastian Bach and Franz Liszt: "'Music as form,'" he wrote a decade or so later, "is the real birthplace of what later I took up as 'polarity' . . . , the center of my thinking."[11]

Years of schooling concluded with a comprehensive exam, the *Abitur,* leading to the possibility of further studies at a university. Przywara decided to join the Society of Jesus. Entering the Jesuits in June of 1908 was a move that required independence and courage: it meant exile because the Society, due to the anti-Jesuit laws of July 4, 1872, was still forbidden in the German Reich. A classmate from days at schools, Franz Sladeczek, was also entering the Society, and the two young men went for their novitiate in 1908 to Exaten, Holland, one of the two novitiates of the German Jesuit province in exile.

Why were the Jesuits and other religious orders kept out of Germany? After the successful Franco-Prussian war Bismarck had decided to drive the Catholic church out of the public life of the new Reich. This involved removing the religious orders from the schools and hospitals they conducted. In July 1871, the Catholic section of the *Kultusministerium* was dissolved; Catholic church life was to be directed by Protestant offices in the bureaucracy administering church affairs. As their institutions were taken over by the state, the Jesuits, like most religious orders, even those caring for the sick, were dissolved or exiled. The Prussian bishops, followed by all but a few clergy and laity ("State-Catholics"), adopted a plan of passive resistance to the measures involving the clergy and church institutions. An attempt to replace an episcopal church with a congregational form completed the alienation of Catholics from the government. Soon most dioceses lacked bishops and over a quarter of the Catholic parishes became empty. The battle then stagnated; Bismarck could foresee no victory but refused to compromise with Pius IX lest such a step appear to be a new Canossa. Within a few days of his election in February 1878, Pope Leo XIII wrote to Kaiser Wilhelm I to initiate a rapprochement.[12] The Kulturkampf ended with a truce between Berlin and Rome which pleased neither side but which restored church operations. Financial normality for the Catholic dioceses came in 1891; bishops' elections (involving not only Rome but the local chapters of canons) were permitted; the Redemptorists returned in 1894. In 1902 a Catholic theological faculty was established at Strassburg, and in 1904 the law expelling and imprisoning the Jesuits—a symbol and slogan of the entire Kulturkampf—was withdrawn. Rudolf Lill concludes: "So the Kulturkampf must be evaluated, along with the persecution of the socialists, as the most severe mistake of Bismarck in international politics.... The needed evolution of civil structures and the integration of Catholics into the national state were foolishly delayed. Relationships with the church as well as between Germany and Poland were injured."[13] The Kulturkampf isolated German Catholics, and they reacted around the time of World War I, as groups forced into a ghetto usually do, by depending on their own powers, by professing civil loyalty, and by viewing the outside world as hostile.[14]

Thus while Catholic writers and teachers were in danger of being rejected by the antimodernist measures of the Vatican after 1910 for any thinking that was not blandly neo-medieval, they were accused by the state of being un-German.

Przywara's novitiate (1908–1910) was followed by years of study and formation, first by philosophical studies (1910–1913) in Valkenburg in Holland. In 1911 his mother died, an unhappy event which occasioned a manifestation of the unhealthy spirituality which at that time could touch religious orders. The young Jesuit, when asked whether his presence was necessary at her deathbed and funeral, did not insist that he travel back to Schlesien (Silesia). That austerity, encouraged by his superiors and typical of a discipline in religious life suited to neither grace nor nature, haunted him later.[15] The Jesuits inserted between their philosophical and theological education for future priests an internship in ministry, and Przywara spent some years teaching music at the college preparatory school of Stella Matutina at Feldkirch in the Vorarlberg of Austria (1913–1917). In 1915 he published with Josef Kreitmeier a hymnal, and in 1917 essays which had been published in devotional journals were gathered together in a first book on the Eucharist as related to daily work; the volume ran through four editions in four years.[16] The gaining of a doctorate in philosophy and a ministerial internship led on to four years of theology in Valkenburg from 1917 to 1921; his free time he dedicated to the thought of Augustine and Newman. A popular collection of excerpts from the English thinker appeared in print in 1922 as did a book of reflections on the parables of Jesus.

Ordination to the priesthood came in 1920, and, returning home to Kattowitz to celebrate his first Mass at the end of the great war, he saw the devastation and suffering of the years of battle. Perhaps that experience also prompted a personal, lifelong attention to the realities behind words and symbols; real life and humanity place demands upon speculative philosophy and theology. Certainly Przywara sensed that European culture and history were at a crossroads. (One recalls that at the same time, in 1919, Paul Tillich was facing large classes of war veterans at the University of Berlin and offering them a new theology with faith touching existence, some objectivity in revelation, and a dialogue between culture and religion.) In 1921 Przywara spent the period of the Jesuits' second novitiate, the tertianship, back in Exaten during which he prepared notes on Ignatian spirituality for later writings on the *Spiritual Exercises.*

The future theologian's education was done in Jesuit theologates constrained not only by Prussian persecution but by Rome's anti-modernist campaign. During those years the Vatican had a kind of secret police intent on detecting any employment of modern ideas in philosophy and theology, particularly among seminary professors (they had circulated suspicions about Angelo Roncalli, the future Pope John XXIII). Valkenburg was unusual in that it was a rare center of philosophical dialogue between modernity and the Middle Ages, between Kant and Aquinas. Bernhard Gertz sums up: "He [Przywara] expressed gratitude to significant Jesuit figures encountered in his early years. He said he owed his attitude toward the relationship of church to culture and state to those teachers from whom he learned 'to study in pure objectivity (without pastoral or apologetic secondary goals) each author (regardless of how anti-Christian or anti-religious), to understand them better than they understood themselves, and thus to begin a dialogue with them.'"[17] Independent study of Augustine and Aquinas during his Jesuit formation led to the person of Newman and also to the spirituality of the Carmelites. "Understanding the neo-scholastic education which Przywara had does not explain the 'Przywara phenomenon.' It seems that during his formation those studies were fruitful which transcended the scope of what was normal or even led it in a different direction."[18]

What would this gifted young Jesuit priest, already a published author and a serious student of Christian intellectual currents, do? Surely enter upon an academic career in the German universities, or teach in a Jesuit *Gymnasium.* That was not so easy: the Jesuits had only recently reentered Germany, and there was the century-old prejudice that members of the theology faculties would be drawn overwhelmingly from the diocesan clergy, not from members of religious orders. Gustav Wilhelmy writes, "Despite his achievement and first successes, Przywara, as he himself observed, was someone for whom a position was not easily found or decided upon. He already had had some difficulties with censors who wanted more documentation for his ideas. Provincial authorities sent him to the editorial staff of the Jesuit journal, *Stimmen der Zeit,* whose offices were near the Munich University and the Bavarian State Library."[19] From 1922 to 1941 he served on the staff of that periodical whose goal was the expression of Catholic faith and spirituality amid German philosophy, art, and religion. The editorial direction for the journal had come to Munich at the end of the war when the effects of the laws against the Jesuits were ending, and the periodical was being transformed from *Stimmen aus Maria Laach,* a journal published outside of Germany but aimed at influencing religious and cultural life in Germany during and after the Kulturkampf. In the twenty years before 1941 he published countless reviews and studies: for instance, in the year 1925 there are three reviews, three overviews of books, and fourteen articles; the topics range from surveying contemporary philosophy to evaluating the careers of the neo-Kantian Paul Natorp and the neo-scholastic Clemens Bäumker. During the same twenty years Martha Zechmeister finds three hundred and forty-four lectures, some to large assemblies like the first international congress on the thought of Thomas Aquinas in Rome, or to Catholic lay intellectuals on Augustinianism and Romanticism in terms of the role of Catholicism in today's world.[20]

Przywara did not become a professor, not at the beginning of his ministry or later; he never taught in a seminary nor did he belong to the theology faculty of a prestigious German university. He did teach short courses sponsored by Catholic groups at universities and other centers of education but he was also available for talks to schools and for retreats to small groups. His degrees were granted by Jesuit theologates; he did not found any school through doctoral students, although his inspiration and influence on young men and women seeking their futures in a new, culturally open Catholicism was considerable. Przywara found something of an academic vocation in the course he gave at Leipzig or the lectures delivered at a symposium in Ulm where Karl Adam and Guardini also spoke. The young Walter Dirks, soon to become an important Catholic writer on social issues, said that Przywara's dramatic liberation of the word "Catholicity" from ecclesiastical constraints to serve again as a word of synthesis was "the highpoint" of an assembly in Essen in 1925.[21] He helped map the contours of philosophy and theology by sketching typologies of great theologians and philosophers. Impressed by the phenomenology of Edmund Husserl and Max Scheler or by "that prophetic spirit" Søren Kierkegaard, he was a popular lecturer to a variety of groups ranging from ecumenical gatherings to assemblies of Catholic students. The audiences of Przywara's lectures—the short courses and lectures were often published—are astonishing: Kant societies, a Catholic group at a university, academic clubs, devotees of Thomas Aquinas, special international seminars for prestigious intellectuals at Neisse or Davos, Switzerland.[22] German Catholics interested in theology or the spiritual life sought his counsel. The 1920s also saw contacts with Protestants: lectures at the University of Tübingen, seminars at Göttingen and Heidelberg, and two lectures in 1929 and 1931 at Münster at the invitation of Karl Barth. He reviewed the directions and publications of contemporary Jewish life in *Stimmen der Zeit,* observations made personal through contacts with Leo Baeck and Martin Buber.

At a meeting of Catholic youth in Cologne in 1930 (at which Konrad Adenauer also spoke) he criticized the darkly prophetic powers of Nietzsche and the creative destructiveness of Bakunin and faced the challenge of Christian existence in the mystery of the cross. In January 1933 a last public confrontation with fascism in Germany took place as he announced to a large assembly that there must be a clear rejection of the Nazi Reich: it was a distortion of the Christian *imperium* of the past. The Third Reich was only a shallow vapor of pantheism, of deformed Christianity, a movement and leadership bestowed by bloodshed and intent upon total power.[23] The international congress of philosophers held in 1934 in Prague was also an endpoint. The Nazi regime formally permitted him to go, although he already stood on a list of proponents of a combative Catholicism. "Prague as city and historical jewel left a lasting impression on Przywara. At the reception of the delegates, meeting Tomás Masaryk, he saw standing at his side his daughter in the simple, dark uniform of the Red Cross. He saw in her an expression of a sense of human dignity surviving in that city rich with tradition."[24]

Bibliographical sources list over 800 of Przywara's publications, with about fifty books.[25] He authored in the 1920s several quasi-systematic theologies arranged around contemporary issues, Catholic philosophies of religion based upon Aquinas, Scheler, and Newman. There were books on the church year and on conversion, books of poems and hymns, and of meditations on the spiritual life, and translations of Newman. The first volume of *Analogia Entis* appeared in 1932. Somber years under Hitler are evident in titles like *Christliche Existenz* (1934), *Heroisch* (1936), and *Crucis Mysterium* (1939).

The Jesuit had many friendships (we will look at a few of them in chapter 4): not only Edith Stein and Karl Barth but also Gertrud von Le

Fort and the future Jesuit cardinal, Augustin Bea. Knowledge took on color and life from the symposia where he spoke, from friendships with a broad range of people, and from Munich's galleries and libraries.

Przywara's burden of work had undermined his health by the 1940s, although his productivity slowed only slightly. Up to that time his usual day began not with a leisurely approach to the work of a professional writer but with helping out in parishes by celebrating Mass, walking there on foot. He had no secretarial help, and only some slight assistance with proofreading when a generous retired member of the Jesuit community volunteered. Although Przywara wrote on the arts, his small monthly allowance would not permit him to visit an exhibition more than once, and on his trips to give prestigious lectures he brought his lunch with him.[26]

In the 1930s articles on theology and spirituality at times address obliquely the growing madness of Hitler. In January 1933, Hitler became chancelor, and in August 1934 *Reichsführer.* In September 1935, the Nuremberg laws on the Jews were issued; in March 1937, Pius XI issued his encyclical *Mit brennender Sorge,* while in March 1938 the Austrian *Anschluss* took place and in the following October the occupation of Sudetenland. World war began in Poland in September 1939. Eventually, as happened with all independent theologians, the Nazis ended Przywara's publishing and teaching. "Since he was a respected and greatly appreciated dialogue partner of so many significant philosophers and theologians of his age, the Nazis viewed him as the leading intellectual propagandist of Catholic action."[27] The Gestapo closed his Jesuit house, whose members began to live in small groups, but "Przywara stood alone, threatened by the first signs of his illness. Members of the Bavarian nobility in Munich or women who worked in areas of social service cared for him with a room, conversation, and books. After 1941, he entered a private clinic for the first time. This was the Carolinum, where the Dominican sisters of Speyer (Edith Stein had taught in their school), who had been directed by the Nazi regime to work as nurses, cared for him."[28] The priest who had appeared to possess energy without limits became anxious, incapable of work, erratic, a condition only heightened by the opinions of others that it was partly psychosomatic, exaggerated, or easily remedied. In 1941 Cardinal Faulhaber asked him to take on a ministry to intellectuals, to alumni and faculty of Munich's university and advanced schools: his strength returned and he began to give courses and sermons in Munich for which he chose the theme of the Old and New Testaments or the issue, "What Is

God?" In Munich he preached on creation, sin, and redemption in the Bürgersaal, and on the Gospel according to John in the Jesuit church of St. Michael; in other churches whose structures were now partly destroyed there were sermons or lectures on the sacraments. Wilhelmy records, "Those who, because of the increasing difficulties of the years of bombing raids, had to miss one or more of the sermons received the text written down by someone in the congregation, passed from hand to hand and sometimes mimeographed."[29] Small, private circles discussed the poems of Hölderlin or Paul Claudel. Reinhold Schneider wrote: "If Erich Przywara found in the years of collapse a word of direction for others—he labored at a remarkable level of intensity—and at the same time found the courage to say that word in the presence of the persecutors, this is not just an accident nor some miraculous event. His theology for that hour was the result of his life's work, a form of the relationship between creator and creature, but in the sense of a holy, abyss-like paradox realized in an increasing dissimilarity and complete difference which calls forth grace from on high."[30] At the end of 1943 and during 1944 Cardinal Faulhaber of Munich and Cardinal Innitzer in Vienna requested a series of lectures from Przywara (they were published after the war). When an age is misconstrued in a commitment to violence, it ends in nothingness: its appearance of liberation brings truth without concern, actions without limits, at a Nietzschean will to power. That decadent sophistication is only masked anxiety although the threatening social situation is all too unmasked. Courage is needed, courage to seek a fuller truth, courage to realize that belonging to God and damnation are present in our times, for the Christ and the Antichrist are face to face. The Catholic answer is a ceaseless surrender of the world, life, and self into the omnipotence of the one Creator of all out of nothing; and the commitment to be an instrument of the creator out of nothingness as his creation continues. Christianity is not measured by anxiety and withdrawal; its mission and work are "*a ceaseless giving of self in the objective service of God.*"[31]

His brief political observations sought a balance between individuals and social groups. As a goal of his thought Przywara mentioned "a differentiating universalism of a 'unity in tension between individual and community.'"[32] There are two kinds of reactionaries: the first idolizes the past; the second idolizes the present moment. The first group flees the present day in a "secession out of time"; the second group seems to be Modernist, because their religion and ideas exist solely by and for themselves.[33] In Berlin, Przywara debated Friedrich Hielscher, a Nazi apologist, on January 10, 1933, twenty days before Hitler's seizure of power, and a few months later at a convention of German Boy Scouts. Those ideas, about mediation and violence in European history, were the foundation of the essay on "Reich" in the book *Logos*.[34] The "Reich" essay, part of which was written after the war, has only the most general observations on the recent violence in Europe. One would suspect that in the enclosed Nazi world of 1940 the following few lines were meant as spiritual encouragement for those controlled and embattled: "All personal suffering within personal limitations is submerged through the services of offices and members to the patience of God, God who is himself isolated to an extreme degree. Service becomes the mystery of the deeper unity of distance and identity: service to God's patience happens as a representation of this patience."[35]

The sermons delivered in Munich and Vienna in 1943 and 1944 emphasized the centrality of the Jewish Scriptures for Christians and was a modest counter to the Nazi program. The evening lectures during the war "so disturbed Berlin that Himmler came in a command vehicle to investigate but saw them as 'far too lofty' to be 'dangerous.'"[36] Those sermons arranged for publication in 1956 were the interplay of the old and new covenants, *Alter und Neuer Bund*,[37] and were clothed in clouds of rhetoric (much of which perhaps today hides deeper messages and outrages from 1944); the argumentation was not so much that the Hebrew Scriptures are fulfilled in Jesus, but that the covenants complement each other. Prophecy and law, incarnation and ritual are found in both religious realms even if in a highly metaphysical dialectic. He complained about the suffering and tragedy of the war years but offered no particulars about the Nazi dictatorship.

Eva-Maria Faber observes: "How little Przywara worries about the collapse of 'Christian Europe' is shown in the numerous (unpublished) sermons from the years after the war where he uncovers the character of the Christianity of the recent past as a façade, and sometimes he notes that a flight into a church community is simply a way of resolving the longing for a homeland."[38] After the war there is little allusion to the roles of Germany or the German church during the Nazi period, and Przywara repeats the sad prejudice that both America and Russia are similar mass societies, without European Christian culture and bound to technology. The four sermons published in 1948 but delivered at the end of the war, focus on Europe, affirming Catholic fronts against

Russian communism and against Protestant theologies, while later radio lectures are skeptical about the new Germany and critical of the rest of the world. Europe, though in ashes, will arise for a new mission, but what that will be remains lost in metaphors like "destruction brings advent."[39] The destruction of Munich is "the hour of the twilight of idols and the hour of the rise of the true and real God."[40]

The end of World War II saw a return to his life of writing and lecturing centered in Munich. In the following years, up to 1960, there are almost a dozen books on the Bible, the church, and modern philosophers.[41] One has to ask whether the voluminous and disjointed *Humanitas. Der Mensch gestern und morgen* of 1952 cannot be interpreted as a reaction to the collapse of his world between the wars, for it assembled notes and reflections on dozens of areas which interested him in the past. A section on "abysses" looked at philosophers, theologians, and a number of contemporary poets; one on "symbol" traces the influence of Plato through Hegel and Goethe to Newman; another contrasts Asia with Europe; a section looks at philosophical dialectics like person and idea, origin and truth, dialectic and gnosis, while the concluding sections treat the human person in terms of transcendence, history, mystery, and as a saint for today. The publications after World War II become repetitive, often taking up past publications and old favorite themes.

In a sense Przywara never recovered from the war. From 1945 to 1951 he resided in eleven different places; he was often sick, and his illness was increased by a hasty return to work as soon as signs of improvement appeared. In the Bavarian countryside in 1950 a permanent refuge was found with people who would care for him and help him with his work. "After the war," Friedrich Wulf writes, "he sought for a long time some situation that would allow him, despite the limitations of his health, to continue his intellectual work, a place he finally found in a small house near Murnau."[42] "The second period in Przywara's work [after World War II] is marked by various obstacles, particularly illness," Wulf writes, "and this explains the rather aphoristic nature of some of the writings which, nonetheless, saw a greater maturity of the author's basic ideas. The *analogia entis* found a wider application in terms of human existence and its concrete problems, the view of the world from the perspective of the Christian spirit, and the discernment of what was Christian in the movements of the time."[43] After 1945, however, he published an estimated twenty books and two hundred contributions to journals.[44] The small book from 1947, *Was ist Gott? Eine Summula*, ponders the human journey to God through creation, Christ, and with fellow travelers as knowledge, faith, and experience grow. In the early 1950s, the collection *Humanitas* was reviewed by the media, resurrecting his presence (some had thought he had died in the war), and then the collected essays of *In und Gegen* with the subtitle of "positions on the issues of the age" showed how much he had to contribute. A new platform and voice were found in radio: the Südwestdeutsche Rundfunk presented between 1951 and 1969 sixty-nine of his lectures, and the Bavarian and Austrian radio networks transmitted some of these.[45]

The 1960s held many days of withdrawal and emptiness. "In a sense," Zechmeister writes, "the late Przywara was in the danger of becoming 'an aesthete of catastrophe' and his overladen, expressionistic language was a trap for that direction. An aesthetic radicalism without concrete implications would be generally the consequence of the collapse of a tense apocalyptic expection into a chiliastic present. Holy Saturday would be silenced as the experience of the path of the Christian community becomes an existential-private 'mysticism of contradiction.'"[46] Nonetheless, in 1962 he published *Kirche in Gegensätzen,* radio lectures full of advice for the coming council of Vatican II, and in 1967 *Katholische Krise* collected nineteen essays on the state of Catholicism before and after World War II, particularly on ecclesiology. In 1962 the sick author was presented with a new edition of his major works, for just prior to Vatican II Johannes Verlag of Einsiedeln, directed by Hans Urs von Balthasar, began to publish volumes of Przywara's *Schriften.* The first volume held the early publications, while volume 2 gave the four philosophies of religion, and volume 3 held the two parts of *Analogia Entis.*[47] The series did not continue, although a number of earlier and new books were republished by Glock and Lutz of Nuremberg and other publishers. In the early 1960s there were periods of relative health: the lifelong student of philosophy reviewed Hans-Georg Gadamer's *Wahrheit und Methode,* a work, he said, that went beyond both Dilthey and Heidegger to offer a new view of method that was more than a survey of positions.[48]

Karl Rahner wrote that Przywara lived "after the Second World War in a stricter aloneness and freedom, burdened but not repressed, through serious illness."[49] What exactly were his illnesses? Certainly psychological and physical debilitations interacted; there were periods of lucidity and productivity but long times of depressed inactivity. With the Nazi extinction of the house of *Stimmen der Zeit* Przywara had lost his moorings, lost his place and charismatic vocation. In the widest sense, his world was gone. He had written that Jesuits should be spiritually *heimatlos* in an ecclesial spirituality for the world, and eventually he was to suffer that condition deeply.[50] While illness and the weakness of aging were rarely absent, visits of friends were frequent. Stefan Nieborak observes that the relationship of work to illness and the uncertainty of the final editing of his later publications remain a difficult area for a future biography.[51] He died in Hagen bei Murnau, that picturesque artists' landscape with its majestic view of the Alps, on September 28, 1972, and was buried in the Jesuit cemetery at Pullach, the Jesuit philosophate outside of Munich, adjacent to the scholasticate where his confreres had worked to draw together modern philosophy and the thought of Thomas Aquinas. Twice, in 1959 and 1969, his peers commemorated his life and work. The first book held brief commemorative essays from several dozen figures, ranging from Heinrich Fries and Karl Barth to Gertrud von Le Fort; the second *Festgabe* offered information about his career rather than honorary essays.

THEMES AND PROJECTS

Erich Przywara? A philosopher who wrote on analogy? He is much more than a philosopher of epistemology. That designation, however, has unfortunately reduced his presence, his theological contribution as a Catholic engaged with the twentieth century. He was a theologian, and his thinking and career unfolded between the poles of modernity and Catholicism: for instance, in an essay on Thomas Aquinas, Ignatius Loyola, and Friedrich Nietzsche he showed how a comparison of the three could engage both the reality of their thought and their contemporary import.[52] His earliest writings, whether on parables or philosophers, sought to make Christianity attractive and intelligible to people.

Przywara wanted his interpretation of Christianity to be concrete, and in this to be different from Baroque theology and recent forms of neoscholasticism. The Bible treats what happened; the Greek theologians and Augustine saw their themes as moments in a history of salvation; Loyola's spirituality leads to service, joining prayer and theology and praxis.[53] Concrete reality stands behind Przywara's creaturely metaphysics and behind his religious sensitivity to the struggles of men and women in the world. James Zeitz concludes that "Przywara shows the factual reality of the crises [of his time] with their polar tensions, and more importantly he traces them back to their historical and spiritual roots. . . . The real problem is the problem of God and the dualism that reveals man's incapacity to answer this question on the basis of his own created being."[54]

Przywara's intellectual and religious style is personal and consistent. Separating either ontological or devotional aspects from the totality of his work does a disservice to him. It also presents a European Roman Catholicism that is static, neomedieval, and void of the ongoing incarnation so prized by the great theologians, East and West. Przywara justified his style as necessary for understanding the history of many forms of thought and for letting contemporary ideas illumine the phenomena of faith. Thus his analysis of the moment, providing an "entrance, as much as possible, into the stream [of thought] from its sources as they touch today,"[55] is counterpoised to typologies of theologies and philosophies from the past.

His genre is the essay; his books are sometimes collections of essays where each chapter is a unit with its own problematic, development, and climax. His written German style can be difficult because of neologisms and elliptical constructions like a passage such as the following: "In the age of the great generation of problem discerners, Georg Simmel stood as one whose opposing pair of life and content opened most deeply the abyss that lay philosophically in the tired proliferation of multiple stirred-up questions, questions running off into a forest without paths; and even more from the artistic point of view there appeared the dialectical figures of Kant and Goethe pointing into the reality of Rembrandt's depths."[56] He placed many words and phrases in italics and quotation marks, and unfortunately what were originally signs of emphasis can become barriers on the road to understanding. The style in fact is a Neoplatonic and pseudo-Dionysian circling ascent where sources, opponents, motifs, and personal themes hover around the topic, leading to a synthesis. There is also the literary motif of crescendo, a rhetorical crescendo. His style, bordering on poetry, can seem too refined or rhetorical, and his interpretations have been occasionally criticized, although the views of Scheler, Aquinas, or Kiekegaard are usually accepted as insightful.

Przywara's style combined circular contemplation with historical research and a dialectical resolution; it sought to find implications of Christianity in diverse figures, to see how every idea holds intimations of more, is polyvalent, has a certain analogous and dialectical quality. One characteristic of his intellectual life is the arrangement of thinkers into types and directions, a search for the relationships of philosophers and theologians over two thousand years to illumine contemporary directions in the life of faith and intellect. A contrasting, somewhat Hegelian but not conflictual, dialectic of complementary positions is offered. Thus the basic thought-form is a union of analogy and dialectic. Analogy, which for most is a traditional form of language and logical thinking, becomes in his perspective a bridge between the human and the divine, a primal view of reality as much as an enabling mental format. Analogy is a structure of being that leads to incarnation. Wilhelmy records that editors eventually came to question the difficulty of his style and material, and so in the mid-1930s he began to publish somewhat less in journals and to concentrate on books.[57]

He lets the directions of contemporary life — they are not necessarily religious, virtuous, or healthy but they are also not inevitably corrupt — influence not the content of revelation but the experience of Christian faith and Catholic intellectual life. Rarely beginning an essay with an idea drawn from a past piety or a line from the Bible, he usually mentioned first some aspect of contemporary life, a philosophical aspect in which he saw implications; he then surrounded a theme or a thinker with sources. His mind saw endless connections. In an essay on Edith Stein and Simone Weil he drew in Plato and Parmenides, Aquinas and Husserl, and then Hegel and Nicolai Hartmann—all in less than a dozen lines.[58] Friedrich Wulf found the interplay of theology, spirituality, and German philosophy introducing "a totally new dimension into the discussion of faith in the German-speaking area after the first world war." That made possible a breakthrough not only within Catholicism but in the secular discussion of religion among nontheologians, non-Christians. "This interplay of philosophy and theology, on the other hand, did not make his life easy in his own camp."[59]

Przywara examined faith as challenged by the culture around him and drew the apostolic spirit of the Jesuits into German intellectual life after World War I. Zeitz observes, "Any study of Przywara necessarily involves the history of thought, specifically the movements in Germany in the 1920s, and the history of one's own time."[60] Despite its variety, the Jesuit's work is consistent: the same theological structure underlies a philosophy of religion in 1923 or a book on spirituality in 1953. Looking at the succession of writings through challenging times, Stefan Nieborak concludes: "The publications of Przywara fall into two periods. The first includes the time between 1922 and 1941 with the highpoint in the years 1927 to 1934, and the second holds the years from 1946 to 1962. . . . Some of the large works of the second period are to a considerable extent collections of writings from before 1950 and stand in contrast to the detailed systematic conceptions from between the wars."[61] A certain uniformity of format and themes did not hinder engagement with a broad number of theologians, philosophers, and topics which, nonetheless, were considered within consistent perspectives. Nieborak continues: "The work of Erich Przywara is from its beginning up to the final writings a *closed philosophical-theological total plan* which in its individual components is already completed in the early Whylen lectures just as it is present in the [later] books like *Humanitas* and *Mensch*. The lecture series of the years 1923–1926 form in their carefully fashioned pattern a structure of relations upon which the structure and content of subsequent works of Przywara are based. At the center of this entire opus stand the creature's experience of reality manifest in oppositions and the consequent direction of the human person toward the knowledge of the primal ground of life."[62] A personality with perduring insights is at work through the years.

Julio Terán Dutari finds in the writings a personal religious dimension. Ideas and forces of the realms of being and of grace, despite the dense or agitated language, are not just ideas but realizations of life and freedom. "In this way Przywara grounds the primacy of praxis over theory."[63] If Przywara's style and method are a circular dialectic, his themes stand out: (1) a search for the religious dimension in idealism and phenomenology; (2) the nature of the Catholic approach to life and Christianity in terms of philosophy, theology, and spirituality; (3) perduring and important interpretations of the Christian reality from Origen, Augustine, Aquinas, J. H. Newman, and others; (4) the liturgy and church as flowing from the Body of Christ as wider applications of sacramentality; (5) the clear contrast between subjectivity and transcendent divinity in Protestantism, and the interplay of God and creation, grace and sacraments in Catholicism.

CURRENTS OF MODERNITY

When Przywara was ordained a priest, German Catholicism was seeking beyond the ruins of World War I a positive appreciation of the science, art, and philosophy around it. "Expressionism" was a word of that age, implying emotion and objectivity, modern abstraction but also a depth of feeling, even religious feeling. Gone was the purely rational or transcendental subject of philosophy from Immanuel Kant to Paul Natorp. Words, colors, events gave an experience of reality, a reality which the rational and bourgeois styles and systems of the later decades of the past century had oppressed.

The world of modernity in literature and art was prominent in Munich, and Munich was Przywara's residence for much of his life. By 1900 Munich was the artistic capital of Germany as more and more exhibitions were sponsored by wealthy and royal patrons and by associations of thousands of artists. That autumnal time marked a late Romanticism in art and a late idealism in philosophy. Ibsen and Lenin, the poets Stefan George and Rainer Maria Rilke, and Thomas Mann lived in Munich, and in 1912 Kandinsky, Franz Marc, and Schoenberg had produced an exhibition, *Der Blaue Reiter,* to call attention to the changes taking place in art through Picasso, Matisse, and Cézanne even as it featured votive pictures from Russian and Bavarian churches and peasant paintings. Thomas Mann wrote in his novella *Gladius Dei:* "Art blossomed; art dominated; art extended its scepter adorned with roses over the city and smiled. . . . Munich shone."[64]

Through and beyond the expressionism of Richard Strauss or Franz Marc a new objectivity was appearing: abstract art whose revelation lay within the symbol and chiffre, within the juxtaposition of colors and forms. The new music and the new art, resembling physics, developed a format of small forms and calculated patterns. One could see a similar structure in the biblical form-criticism of Rudolf Bultmann and the existential ontology of Martin Heidegger which in turn recalled the piano pieces of Arnold Schoenberg and the paintings of Wassily Kandinsky. One of Przywara's close friends was the artist and interpreter of expressionism Hermann Bahr, who brought together poetic meditations with paintings by Matisse, Chagall, and Picasso.[65]

How would the modernity of Kandinsky meet the anti–Modernism of Pius X? Could Catholicism in the twentieth century free itself from being an imitation of Gothic and from the inept measures of the Vatican condemning randomly anything new? To take the risk, as Erich Przywara did, was to enter a certain solitude and uncertainty, to accept an existence caught between reactionary church authority and the arrogance of modern academicians. After the First World War, shaken by events like the red flags of a Marxist regime hoisted above the towers of the Munich cathedral and then by demonstrations of the National Socialists' antireligious militancy, Catholics could hardly escape a defensive posture. Shouldn't the church occupy itself only with medieval or baroque devotions? Wasn't it best to seek whatever ecclesiastical guarantees and privileges a government might grant?[66]

Przywara, rejecting isolationism and pursuing dialogue with truth wherever it could be found, explained modern philosophy from Schelling to Nikolai Hartmann, from Kant to Georg Simmel. Philosophy was a master-manifestation of culture; often philosophy was a language or a grammar for Christian thinking. The ideas of Schelling, Husserl, Scheler, Buber, and Heidegger were not those of the Catholic religion or faith although they could express religious meaning. He agreed with Rudolf Otto that the proper question of transcendental philosophy "is now the question about the epistemological conditions among which the ordinary man and woman, apart from scientific proof, arrives at the insight of moral and religious truths."[67] Perhaps the aphorism of Hugo von Hofmannsthal throws light on the personality of Przywara: "Each subject-matter at each point leads to the Infinite."[68]

What was modernity? Not something corrupt and corrupting, not something always ugly and deformed. Modernity was the recent history of Western civilization. "Modernism" had multiple, slippery meanings, for it was initially just the expression of an open attitude to what was new and emerging. The Vatican had uncovered a "Modernism" in the political forms of democracy and freedom and in the theological application of development; it sought to extinguish any traces of it in the church. Roger Aubert wrote of its forms in Roman Catholicism: "The term 'Modernism' was in use since the sixteenth century to characterize the tendency to esteem the modern age more highly than antiquity. In the nineteenth century it was used by some Protestants in a religious sense to designate the anti-Christian tendencies of the modern world and also the radicalism of liberal theology. When at the end of the century there was a movement in the Catholic Church urging reform of the Church and its doctrine in the sense of adapting them to modern needs, the term Modernism was at once applied to it by opponents, first of all in Italy."[69]

Toward the end of the pontificate of Leo XIII, very different Catholic groups had espoused speculative or practical directions, ecclesiastical, political or social, which their opponents, eventually including Pius X, summed up at the turn of the century under the term

"modernist." A modernist might be a thinker who tried to interpret
Christianity and Catholic tradition in light of socialist politics or a philosophy of life, but the term remains ambiguous for it could mean
simply the necessary task of relating Christian revelation to new generations or to different cultures. Reactionary conservative theologians
and bishops used the term "Modernism" to mean anything involving a
suspected dilution and replacement of revelation by cultural and philosophical terms and conceptualities. The course of German Catholic
theology from the middle of the nineteenth century to the First World
War was constrained. Censures and an increasingly repressive atmosphere exercised an inhibiting influence on theologian and priest. Is theology to be only a rereading of past ecclesiastical documents, a repristination of medieval texts? Is Christianity no more than a catechism, one
for all the world, one written in Rome in a language and philosophy
antiquated and hostile? The conflict between Modernism and church
authority reached its climax with the documents issued by the Vatican between 1907 and 1910: the Syllabus of Errors, the encyclical
Pascendi Gregis, the anti-modernist oath, and the ill-fated encyclical
on St. Charles Borromeo.[70] In July of 1907 the Holy Office issued the
decree *Lamentabili sane exitu* which condemned sixty-five propositions,
while Pius X issued the encyclical *Pascendi Dominici gregis* in the following September. "Modernist" errors were largely two: (1) an agnosticism
of reason which questioned the philosophical argumentation for the
existence of God; (2) an immanentism of the mind which derived the
data and truths of revelation and faith from human consciousness.
Those errors, according to the pope, flowed from pride, illegitimate
curiosity, and ignorance of scholastic philosophy.

The Modernism condemned in Roman decrees was not recognized north of the Alps as applying to Germany. First, there had been
throughout the previous century speculative theologies constructed
along the lines of Romantic idealism with the thought-forms of subject and process, freedom and history. The consideration of Trinity and
church in light of the transcendental activity of the self and a historical-
critical approach to doctrine and Bible had occurred without harm
to the church. Second, a one-sided or subjectivist role for Kantianism
developed by French thinkers was not present in Germany where a
more sophisticated understanding of the entire idealist tradition existed.
Third, respectable German theologians had not fashioned a dogmatic
replacement of revelation by epistemology but had included with criti-

cism new directions, for instance, immanentist apologetics. If some theologians in Germany lived under a cloud of suspicion, most escaped any action from the Congregation of the Index or the Holy Office, while a small number like Herman Schell were censured without being singled out for precise heresies.

Pope Pius X took a further step: he demanded from all clergy in 1910 a particular public and verbal oath that came to be known as the "Oath against Modernism."[71] This was a kind of creed with articles countering modernist principles. The oath eventually was required of clerics both orally and in writing before key events such as ordination or the assumption of a theological teaching position. Its purpose was to unmask modernists. If in the church throughout the world the clergy submitted without much outward resistance, German Catholics with their tradition of freedom and *Wissenschaft* were horrified at this primitive measure. Would it not ensure that Catholics were excluded from their own research and from academic life? Typical of the academic protest throughout the Reich was an article by Karl Adam, then a young professor in Munich. The issue, he wrote, was not Catholic professors secretly propagating modernist errors or rejecting papal disciplinary action. "What makes the oath for professors a burning issue in the life of higher education is *the issue of the right of the historical-critical method in the area of Catholic theology.*" The public and the press viewed it "as the official death sentence over the totality of Catholic science." Adam feared the worst: "the complete exclusion of Catholic theological faculties from the organism of the universities."[72] Rome had to respond to a German request for an interpretation of the oath with modifications and exemptions. The oath was not enforced in Germany, although Catholic intellectuals at the time when Przywara was entering the Jesuits experienced considerable constraints.

From his seminary years on, Przywara saw world and faith differently. The world and its age are not necessarily opponents against which Catholics must defend a timeless philosophy, and the time after World War I is not like the previous century. "The nineteenth century at its beginning and at its end," he wrote, "sees an impassable opposition between autonomous science, culture, and religion; it was an opposition to the ideal emerging from a Catholic Romantic view of science and culture having their immanent ideal modes in religion, in Christianity."[73] If studying contemporary philosophies of religion includes rejecting Modernism as an ideology, nonetheless, Catholicism has a

messianic mission amid a cultural and spiritual life ravaged by the war
and burdened with political and economic chaos: it is "to replace the
primal illness of the modern 'God everything alone' with the primal health of the Thomistic God who is everything in everything. In
place of a God over us or in us . . . [there would step forth] the great,
life-liberating 'God above us and in us.'"[74] Gertz writes: "[With the
death of Pius X] the conflict between integralists and modernists in no
way ended, because the church did not succeed in overcoming Modernism with the weapons of integralism. Perhaps in later times Przywara will be viewed as an evaluater of Modernism precisely because
he was in no way an integralist. Because of encounters with Newman and Scheler his work fell under suspicion, but he did not want
to 'Jesuitize' the figures of hope of his age—the verb is a linguistic
monstrosity and shows the neuroses on various sides."[75]

In 1929 (the Vatican's condemnations lay only twenty years back)
for a new edition of an encyclopedia Przywara wrote the article "Modernism." Modernism, he began, is not simply the secular pole to which
is opposed Christian "integralism": Modernism is not what is new
nor is it an alternative to reactionary fundamentalisms attached to past
objects, to pseudo-medieval forms. While Modernism has undergone
ecclesiastical condemnations, reactionary integralism rigidly fixed on
forms has escaped the church's censure, although it too is a historical
ideology, one propagated by some as a monopoly, one unacceptable to
Catholicism.

Przywara set forth three meanings of Modernism. The first, posit-
ing a particular relationship between faith and knowing, is condemned
in ecclesiastical texts, because it advocates "a religious-theological agnostic irrationalism which in its inner consequence becomes pantheism or atheism."[76] A second meaning, inevitably feared and condemned by the advocates of ecclesiastical restoration as smacking of
the "spirit of Modernism," encompasses thinkers critical of popular
but imprecise expositions of dogma or groups calling for the reform
of the church. Artists, scientists, or politicians may be in the eyes of
some too open to the patterns of the world, but the many thinkers,
programs, and movements so labeled are not "modernist" at all. Thirdly,
Modernism can mean simply the desire for the Catholic church and
its theology to address the questions of the time, and here we have not
heresy but the direction taken by Origen, Augustine, Anselm, Thomas
Aquinas, and Robert Bellarmine.

Modernity is rooted in the self, Przywara continued in a positive vein, and a modern philosophy of religion exists in three types: the infinitude of feeling, the knowledge of the infinite, and the infinitude of striving. There are antecedents for each of these directions in past epochs of European culture and Christian theology. The church is a place where the interplay of the created and the uncreated, human activity and grace, occurs in different personal and experiential modes. The foci of the self or the infinite are not heterodox; after all, both mysticism and liturgy are personal and subject-centered and seek to be religious ways for the self to strive toward a knowing of transcendence. Catholic Christianity can be modern with its own depth and subjectivity. "In Catholic interiority there is a radicalism of an 'immediacy before God' which can be viewed in the highest level of mysticism as 'immediate vision.' In Catholic cult there is the radicalism of a 'divine, unchanging liturgy' which includes an authentically creative change in the cultic forms over the course of the centuries. In Catholic praxis there is the radicalism of the 'purely supernatural ethic and culture' which can grasp God as the formal ideal of sanctity."[77] Thus some aspirations and approaches of modernity can be found in Christian theologies illumined by analogy and incarnation, theologies both traditional and contemporary.

What of the modernity of the young twentieth century, modernity a century and a half after Herder and Kant, modernity plunging after 1910 further into subjectivity through abstract art and atonal music? Are not faith and religion more than the activity of consciousness? Although Christianity can be expressed in terms of a religious ethos which is more than an Aristotelian force or a Baroque miracle, still a Catholic would be critical of some aspects of modernity. For Przywara God is never a transcendental ground or a projection, nor a final rhythm of created reality. God is a distinct reality from which every meaning and all reality exists. Religion as life with God is the ultimate content-giving content of all contents. It is a mistake of the modern period to take one side, the finite side of the dialectic, and to derive the holy and the divine solely from finite spirit. While Przywara could dialogue with neo-Kantian philosophers, he found the effects of Kant (to which he joined the effects of Luther) to be injurious. Postwar movements of objectivity and liberation are reactions in the 1920s against the frightful slavery brought on by the Lutheran-Kantian image of man, "which in pre-war years had become the insatiable work-oriented Moloch, the enemy of all the delights of the human soul."[78] Kantians had fashioned subjectivity into an idol, while Lutherans had isolated the believer in a prison of feelings and commitment; the emphasis upon the will, upon a remote God, upon Calvary presented a Protestantism alien to Catholic fullness. Christianity is incarnational; it finds its expression in living cultures and at the same time avoids distortion and limitation in the new dictatorship of the secular.

Nevertheless, Przywara presumed that the array of modern philosophies from Hegel to Scheler could and should be examined positively, if critically, and not dismissed as "isms," although in 1923 at the end of a review of ten books on epistemology and the philosophy of religion, he wrote that a psychology of religion must hold more than surveys, experiments, and speculative schemata, must have room for what is called "grace."[79] His publications in a gentle but trenchant way criticized Catholic isolationism and the shallow projects of integralist and ultramontane clericalism.

Vatican initiatives were not disdained but were interpreted broadly in the context of what was needed for educated Catholics. Przywara subtly observed that the interventions of Rome—he did not deny their frequency and negativeness and occasional destructive effect— could be an impetus toward maturity. "Will the liturgical movement show the same breadth of spirit as, to employ an example close at hand, does the encyclical on Thomas Aquinas by the Holy Father from 1923, indicating as it does an exemplary way to pose philosophical and theological questions, although one must reject the narrowness of one-sided schools with the axiom, 'No one should demand from others more than what the teacher and mother of all, the church, asks from all.'"[80] Przywara was of the opinion that his church and faith must study modern thinkers and directions positively in order to employ some of their forms to express the Gospel anew. Rahner summarized that attitude of the 1920s, a balanced and pioneering direction: "One need not be modernist or anti-modernist but . . . simply modern; that is, one could learn from modern and contemporary philosophy and from Protestant theology and would not always have to be in a defensive posture."[81]

As we will see, Przywara thought that World War I had brought Catholicism to a new stage, distinct from the dominant German Protestantism of the recent past characterized by the separation of the religious from the secular, the inner from the external. Drawing on culture's return to objectivity and interest in religion (perhaps more prominent than an interest in the church), Catholicism was now free to articulate its own worldview and forms of life, and to set aside what it had unconsciously absorbed from Hegel and Bismarck when German idols had been served to prove that Catholics were good Germans. "One must see the figure of the Catholic individual, gain some distance from the ideal of job, obligation, and authority which dominates us Germans, Protestant as well as Catholics."[82] Beyond Bismarck and Pius X there could be a partnership between positive Roman initiatives and the examples in contemporary German society of a flourishing Catholicism.

A Theologian of Culture

The life of this Jesuit philosopher and theologian was many-sided. Karl Barth described their meeting in 1923: "That evening he talked for two hours with me, bubbling over with his view of God, bubbling over like grace bubbles over in people within the Catholic church. . . . Picture a small man with a large head, a little person who to every-thing, everything that is said to him, right away has an intelligent answer, an answer which is to the point in some way."[83] Lecturing to large crowds apparently brought him some anxiety, while the con-templative life of the writer was congenial to him. Sometimes he val-ued his poems and hymns more than the speculative systems he had written. From the German mystics or Alexandrine theologians, from Newman or Simmel,[84] he gathered thought-forms and motifs, although his works never appeared ecclectic or superficial, never just a chain of citations. Published lectures and articles are focused; their language is direct and moving. An encounter with the thought of another was thorough and insightful: his goal was to enter into the text and to draw out its deepest meaning. The historical context is important, as are the existential issues of the reader.

Przywara combined speculative theology with Ignatian spirituality, pedagogy with personal counseling. While he taught in high school for some years but not at all in a university, his demand as a lecturer points to a gifted communicator. Przywara found memorable phrases to mix the metaphysical and the poetic. The lecturer is present in the writer.

From the printed page a certain contagious optimism springs forth, an enjoyment of all aspects of the intellectual and artistic life. For some, however, Przywara's lectures and articles were difficult, and his conclusions were not as clear as the dialectical unfolding of many positions that had led to the conclusions; his critique of others could be oblique, sometimes motivated more by what he feared had been said than the actual text. Did the breadth of ideas and sources threaten to overwhelm the theme under consideration? Regardless, this sailing forth on the waves of the grandest themes and sources demanded courage. In 1923 he wrote that what was needed was balance in the realms of being, society, or grace to serve believers to find for others "a tending further into the infinite."[85] This is the Catholic answer to the question of the relationship of Creator and creature, of Savior and saved. "This is a philosophy of polarity but one far distant from philosophies which ceaselessly fragment and replace or from those which never move from a static middle; it is a philosophy of dynamic polarity, neither object nor subject, neither becoming nor being, neither person nor form."[86] Gertz, however, describes the difficulties with Przywara's method of "for and against": there is an empathy for many positions and yet a critique of each, while the knowledge and employment of the thought of others may include a neglect of the idea's real historical meaning.[87]

Only five years after his ordination, Przywara wrote: "There always exists a remarkable interplay between the practical face of an age, that is, its visible surface expressing itself in various political and social movements, and its metaphysical core, its invisible spirit. The practical face of a time can be read in the great controversies occupying it from day to day. The metaphysical core reveals itself in philosophies and theologies which emerge from it. The observers and interpreters of the age should neglect neither of these, for what is of decisive import for the knowledge of God in particular also has its proper meaning for the temporal flow of this age. The invisible is recognized in the visible."[88] That face of an age appeared in the varied areas of culture. The theologian must notice the dynamic forms of the world around and without judging superficially see where the quests and enthusiasms are headed. Does modern culture manifest a thirst for God? Przywara thought so: his theology, which is both metaphysics and spirituality, is a discourse on the always greater God who is both mystery and intimacy but who is also present in the world around us. Balancing the highly metaphysical theology is the descent of the incarnation into history.

Przywara was engaged in evangelization and ministry on a broad scale. It is almost as if his public was not individuals but an age in which millions lived. His choice of subjects is determined by the times, his writing by his obligatory articles and reviews for the Jesuit monthly *Stimmen der Zeit*. "When we listen to the passionate and moving rhythm of our present cultural life . . . the symbolist movements of German poetry and art, we can see a real storm of longing for God."[89] In no way can the Catholic response be a flight back to the textbooks of the nineteenth century or to the art of neo-Romanesque monasteries. The guiding theme of the analogy of being is an interactive dialectic of participation by God and creatures, ending not in pantheism but in mystery, a mystery which according to Ignatian spirituality is expanded by contact with the world. Ultimately Przywara sought balance: sin but not total fallenness, creaturely cooperation but not replacement of the divine, transcendence but also immanence, human quest but divinely initiated incarnation.

Przywara was a lover of the arts and a literary artist. As mentioned, space and time had brought a *kairos* of the arts as Przywara began to write in the 1920s. In 1904 Paul Klee and Franz Marc had exhibited their Expressionist paintings, while in 1905 Einstein published three revolutionary essays including one on special relativity. In 1905 Richard Strauss composed *Salomé* and in 1908 *Elektra*, the year Gustav Mahler finished his symphonic *Das Lied von der Erde*. In 1913 the new trends in European art included those exhibited by the "Blue Rider Group." In 1923 Rilke completed the *Duino Elegies;* in 1927 Heidegger issued *Being and Time* and Thomas Mann published *The Magic Mountain;* in 1928 the *Threepenny Opera* by Bertolt Brecht and Kurt Weill opened in Berlin as Alban Berg was at work on his opera *Lulu*. Przywara frequented the galleries and museums of Munich, although his taste in music tended less to Wagner and more to Bach and Mozart.

Przywara spoke of the early inspiration for his philosophical theology coming from music. His musical education led him to speak of a fugal or sonata structure in his own writings, of a musical form and rhythm in his thought. He saw in the Psalms "a revelation-music," a fugue drawn from the music of the ancient synagogues, Gregorian chant, and Bach's *Kunst der Fuge* ("the greatest work of music from humanity up to this point").[90] Music was the "begetting earth"[91] of analogy: God was balanced by the counterpoint of creation's dissimilarity with the divine, all resolved in the silence of God in heaven.

Zechmeister writes, "Music is for Przywara in a particular way the medium bringing to expression what is essential in all of reality and human existence. Music is only present in the moment, in the tension between the past which is gone and a future which lies ahead in its uncertainty. Precisely here is the power of music breaking through the illusions in which the person hides and opening her to self and to reality."[92]

Fiction also inspired him. After the war he wrote of a world over which the demonic and the mystical hovered, landscapes found in the novels of Julien Green, Georges Bernanos, and Graham Greene. In Julien Green there was a faith pouring out of despair alongside a religiosity excluding God, while the characters of Bernanos and Graham Greene lived in a world of dark anxiety where gangsters and suicides strangely found in the course of suffering (a background that seemed to Przywara to be Calvinist) a daring mysticism of the cross, a divine love which never withdrew.

Przywara joined theology to poetry just as he joined the thirteenth, the nineteenth, and the twentieth centuries: "This interlacing mind and being is, on the one hand, a Thomism under the form of Hegel's spiritualizing of being and being's infinity. On the other side, it is a Thomism in the form of the poet Rilke which sees spirit and mind concretely in the 'finitude of created human beings,' and as the 'reality of things on earth,' the 'finite real world of the human person and the thing.'"[93] Reviewing a book of poems, in the style of the 1920s and 1930s but with a Christian perspective, Przywara wrote: "In all this talk about 'Coming' it is still clear that this cultural viewpoint is at an end. It is not for nothing that the language of Nietzsche, Stefan George, and even Rilke appears in a beautiful twilight. There is something nostalgic in the gold paint touching our time in poems of formation and growth, because the real development is unstoppably headed in the opposite direction, toward an earth of undisguised finitude. There is an unnerving attempt to turn away from the true sign of the future, the uncovered cross. Therefore the cult of death awaits this direction. Still, the cross implies resurrection and its dying is eternal life. As the Apostle says, 'We are like dead people and yet we live.'"[94] In a review of Paul Claudel's *Ars poetica mundi* appearing in 1930 he contrasted the West's activism with an inner life opening to God. Claudel leads into an interior world, within the spaces of the cathedral or the meditating soul, while journalists speak only of science and secularity. A study of the human person in Balzac could be paired with human existence as abyss in Nietzsche or with Albert Schweitzer's study on Johann Sebastian Bach. The Catholic novels of Sigrid Undset were typically Catholic because they held a "radical eschatology"[95] different from the equally Nordic Kierkegaard. Przywara discussed not only *Kristin Lavransdatter* and *The Master of Hestviken* but a number of her novels set in modern times. In all of them desire rather than resignation aims at the patience and love of God, while life itself is an education, a movement away from independence and violence. "The human being before the abyss finds a greater abyss, one of love opening up."[96] The Index of Przywara's published lectures given at the University of Leipzig in 1925 indicates the breadth of knowledge in the arts of this onetime professor of music as page after page lists figures such as Frederic Chopin and Vincenzo Bellini.[97]

Poetry describes the concrete and bridges the gulf between the divine and the finite. He wrote books of poems (sometimes issued in beautiful editions) and also composed what he titled "hymns." *Karmel. Geistliche Lieder* (1932) collects poems that referred to John of the Cross but were clearly German, with traces of Rilke, while *Hymnen des Karmel* (1962) was a translation of texts by the Carmelite mystics. *Hymnus* (1936) offered longer poems followed by *Terzinen,* poems arranged in units composed of three groups of three lines, some of which were poetically formed translations of liturgical texts. He also composed a book of texts (translated from Hebrew, Greek, and Latin) that led the reader through the liturgical year, *Nuptiae Agni. Liturgie des Kirchenjahrs* (written in 1934 but published in 1948). The early *Vom Himmelreich der Seele. Christliche Lebensführung* (1923) holds seven meditations on the "I am" sayings of Jesus, meditations composed in the genre of parables, while *Gebete in die Zeit* (1946) brings together prayers written in difficult years. Neufeld observes: "His early education saw him taking his first steps as a poet. He loved the poetic nuances of language, the rhymed texts for church songs, enjoyed etymologies and forms of language. An aesthetic sensibility unfolded: it never left him during his life and must be taken into account when one evaluates his works in the philosophy of religion and of course his spiritual and theological efforts."[98]

In 1945 and 1948 Przywara wrote studies on the poems of Hölderlin. Heidegger had lectured on "Hölderlin and the Essence of Poetry" in 1936 in Rome, a text published in 1937 and issued in 1944 in a book with other lectures on the poet. Romano Guardini had published a book in 1939 on the German poet's world and spirituality.[99] Przywara's *Hölderlin* is a series of brief meditations on one or more poems by the poet, twenty-two chapters seeking the deep and organizing message of the poems. The early poem, "Die Bücher der Zeiten" along with "Patmos" and "Vatikan" draw from the Apocalypse of St. John, and express the conflict of Asian wildness with Greek order, of Roman discipline with Germanic power. "The ultimate interpretation of the basic vision of Hölderlin . . . [is] that the fullness of suffering is the fullness of the cross and the fullness of love is the fullness of God." He is the poet of the age when Enlightenment yields to Romanticism and when there is the quest of the Reformation to get beyond its European rationalism and meet again "the unnerving and beneficent fullness of Catholicism."[100] The book, published in 1949, only four years after the end of the war, faced the German reality which Hölderlin criticized in *Hyperion* but expressed in poems on nature. The poet of the Neckar river area is the hymnist of German rivers. The Danube and Rhine have a sacral character, links with Asia, manifestations of the mystery. "Hellas, Germany, Europe, Cosmos — this total breadth of Hölderlinian prophecy ultimately finds its meaning in the mystery of the divine." Contradictions, infinity, madness are not the causes of a final condition but a kind of "holy mania" in the sense of the Hebrew prophets or Greek seers. Asia and Germany are linked as two sources of peoples; medieval Germany had a unity which is now lost. Disgraced postwar Germany stands before "a consuming fire which is the sign of God, of Christ and the Holy Spirit present in the Old and New Testaments."[101] All the concrete aspects of the content of the hymns and poems flow into two final, simple phrases: 'What is God?' 'What is human life?' If God is unknown, still the human being is the image of the Godhead. The poems can seem to be empty, heedless of anything separate and transcendent, although the Romantic landscape with a stream flowing near the church tower with bells and liturgies, words like richness and infinity, even mental fantasy suggest something more. For the theologian that dialectic of enclosure and breakthrough, that descending night of suffering, point to Easter.[102]

Przywara described himself to Gertrud von Le Fort as primarily a poet.[103] This priest of words — "turn," "swing," "real," "becoming," "commerce" — used them to understand his age. Was it "a new age," "a turning point," "a final time"? Was it a time of progress or an apocalyptic final age? The "end-times situation" of the 1930s is an intensification of "the demonic power of original sin carried to its most extreme."[104]

Yet the Jesuit was primarily not a poet but a philosophical theologian. Bernhard Gertz saw a dual direction in Przywara's work, one thought-form of the descent of the divine Logos and a second from the oppositions of real life; there was a horizontal process of thinking-through-reality and a vertical one of revelation, an analogy of being, and an analogy of faith in the resurrection beyond the cross. His theology spoke of a believing existence and hope for people touched by moments in the history of the twentieth century.[105] Zechmeister, emphasizing his theme of finding God in all things, speaks of a sense of the real, a mysticism of open eyes, a life-long exercise in seeing. "Precisely before the inexhaustibility of independent reality the narrow limits of the self collapse."[106] Przywara's task was to avoid pantheism and to permit a contemporary understanding and sacramentality of revelation and grace; this metaphysics does not remain with a concept of God but pursues human existence open to revelation. Denis Biju-Duval describes how two streams flow from this primal structure. "The first is this: metaphysics faithful to its own identity finds itself realized actually only in relationship to Catholic theology, although it proceeds from the capabilities of natural reason. The second follows: the reception by men and women of a revelation from God presupposing in human history a structure of authority which makes alive the authority of God speaking."[107] Przywara's theological metaphysics encompasses and informs everything, originating in philosophical questions, emerging in Christian theology and spirituality, and continuing in the history of thought which is more than an academic field. Perhaps the relational rhythms of the Trinity are latent in the interplay of thinking and being, in the temporal oscillation of the great themes of human thought.

The problematic which challenged Przywara remains, the relationship of the Gospel to subjectivity, freedom, history, culture, and language. The postmodern, even in its clearest exemplification, in architecture, remains the modern or the late modern. Terán Dutari found three levels in the interplay between religion and culture. The first is, in the broadest sense, the inner and external facets of the act of freedom between God and the creature, for religion is the personal meeting of God and creature in culture and creation. This leads to a second, narrower interpretation between the actual forms of religion and those of profane culture in various ages. These concrete forms themselves lead to the third meaning for religion and culture, one which has to do with the moment, with praxis, with the endeavor of knowing and living in a religious way.[108]

Przywara's is a multifaceted personality with a grand and vast enterprise: the relationships of abstract speculation with contemporary ecclesial life, the confrontations of the theological metaphysics of Augustine and Aquinas with the positions of Karl Jaspers and Leo Baeck. He is someone who finds both Newman of Oxford and Heidegger in Freiburg to be worth consideration.

The next two chapters look at Przywara's major intellectual works, at his university courses, his philosophies of religion, and his systematic works; at the same time a few figures and major sources are presented. The fourth chapter describes Przywara's intellectual and personal engagement with important contemporaries. Finally the fifth chapter looks at his theology of the individual Christian, the liturgy, and the church.

Chapter 2

The Challenge
to Be a Catholic

How would Catholicism exist as the twentieth century pro-
gressed? Could it flourish amid the cultural changes occur-
ring as the century moved forward after World War I? Erich
Przywara pondered those issues throughout his life. His personal mission was to show how Catholicism could speak to a
world that had passed through a time in which the only pros-
pect was the decline of the West. The interplay of subjectivity
and objectivity in philosophy, religion, and art were not always
distortions and not always innovations but could express the
Christian message. "For classical Catholic philosophy (Augustine and Aquinas) as for classical modern philosophy (Kant and
Hegel), the starting-point is the reflection of the ego upon itself. This kind of introspection is only apparently a purely epistemological matter, that is, something preliminary to all metaphysics."[1] Catholic thought implies both types of philosophy,
explorations of the self and of the world of being. Both the
approaches of transcendental subjectivity and a metaphysics of
being have their insights. Przywara sought to combine both
perspectives in the expression of a Catholic view of God and
Jesus Christ.

In Karl Rahner's view, between the two world wars
"there was perhaps no major breakthrough toward a truly
new and modern theology but there was a very fundamental breakthrough to a more open Catholic, and thoroughly
Catholic, way of thinking which departed from traditional
neo-scholasticism but was still part of the church's patri-
mony. In the years before World War I we passed through a
period of what is called integralism and a somewhat rigid

33

neo-scholasticism, but if you look at the period after World War I during which Guardini, Przywara, and others like them were writing, then
you see already a completely different atmosphere in thought."[2] Przywara was Catholic in his universal interest, in his correlation of past and
present. Przywara placed himself among those "who from an inherited
and never-shaken Catholic standpoint understand themselves and their
entry into the world around them, precisely now when this 'modernity' begins to enter a new development, to be an initiation of something like a 'Catholic balance' to the modern world."[3] The advantage
of growing up in a pluralistic society in Kattowitz and of going to
school with children from a secular or Jewish background was that his
strong religious roots came from his family and parish community and
not from state support or from the idiosyncrasy of the overly devout.[4]
The Jesuit saw a world and church impaired but full of possibilities.

    Correlation (a term from Hermann Cohen that Przywara employed
but also a word associated with dialectical theology),[5] marked Przywara's thought and his dialectical spirit of participation enabled him
to see existence flourishing between philosophy and revelation, between culture and faith. The new trend is to evaluate God and the
human person in the midst of culture. "All philosophy emerges from
a given manifold variety and from the given contrast of things, and
its goal is unity."[6] His first writings contrast philosophies in order
to modify their diversity into complementarity. Religious perspectives of immanence and transcendence join with the basic themes of
analogy and nature and grace to fashion the perduring perspective
of Przywara. His typologies of patristic and medieval theologians or
of modern philosophers were not rigid arrangements but pedagogical, inspirational frameworks. Przywara's life and ministry sought to
advance the meaning, survival, and presence of German Catholicism.

AN EMBATTLED CHURCH AND A CATHOLIC RENEWAL

In the decades following the pontificate of Pius IX and the repression
by the *Kulturkampf,* some in German Catholicism sought to relate
Christian faith and tradition to the modern world. Because Catholics
after 1870 were increasingly deterred by Rome from pursuing philosophy and theology, they turned to practical areas of politics, social life,
and the arts. During the decades leading to 1914 Germany surpassed

almost every country in economic and technological power; networks of railroads, electricity, medical laboratories were a reality, and the creations of modernity spread through the panoply of culture. German national culture of the late nineteenth century was largely Protestant, and Catholics were viewed as provincial, rural, conservative, even as enemies of progress. Paradoxically, both the government's attacks and the Catholic engagement with needy social groups helped Catholics resist the pressures of secularism and religious liberalism. Caught between Berlin and Rome, Catholics sought in a proliferation of addresses, books, and journals a renewed, even a reformed, identity.

The Jesuits to which Przywara belonged were themselves divided in enterprise and image. Some saw them as reactionary, papal, neoscholastic, and rigid, while others saw the milieu of *Stimmen der Zeit* leading in the opposite direction.[7] German Catholics advocated different directions for the church. "Reform Catholicism" was a name given after 1890 to various movements and figures advocating change and renewal in the church; their interests ranged from an acceptance of developments in natural science to an advocacy of pastoral changes that were displeasing to the Vatican. They held, however, a traditional understanding of divine revelation and were loyal to the church even though they dealt publicly with the problems of the times.[8] Very few of the reformers left the church; they sustained their loyalty to Catholicism and, in contrast to the Vatican's description of modernists, intended to respect the basic teachings of Christianity. This Catholicism of renewal quickly found after 1900 and 1919 a new vitality as evidenced in bishops' conferences, national Catholic assemblies, popular associations, movements concerned with the working class, liturgical renewal, and Catholic gatherings on a large scale.

In the first years after World War I, Przywara began as philosopher and priest, journalist and theologian, his career of commenting on the church in the society around him and of observing how the war had brought a new situation for the church. He wrote articles about "radical Catholicism," "total Catholicism," "contemporary Catholicism." Catholicism is not first and foremost a collection of rituals or dogmas but a deeper ethos; the life of the church is the kingdom of God in historical forms; Catholicism is a reality too rich to identify with some canons of law or one Eucharistic prayer.[9] Dependent on God but present in created, free realizations where the divine transcendence is maintained within immanence, Catholic life, drawn to totality and sacrament, is different from the theological perspectives of the Protestant Reformers. There is indeed a vertical, dissimilar element in the cross where time cuts into history and where contrary to human idols Calvary stands amid a horizontal dynamic flowing from religion before Christ through the centuries to today.[10] Mainly, however, the Catholic inner form lies in the middle, an "interplay," an "oscillating rhythm."

Toward the end of 1925, after presenting his ideas in public lectures at the cathedral of Essen and the University of Munich, Przywara published two articles on the current state of Catholicism. "Catholicity" looks at the social conditions causing a new situation for Catholicism, while the second article on "Catholicism and the Contemporary Religious Crisis" looks at important themes in contemporary philosophy and theology.

"Catholicity" described how German Catholicism was in the midst of two forces. "On the one hand, the events of recent years have without doubt unleashed a creative and vital power in German Catholicism to an extent that could not have been expected in the years before the war. We need only think of the flourishing of Benedictine abbeys or of the Catholic youth movement. German Catholics now enjoy freedom in various professions. Catholics should not fear freedom, for Catholicism flourishes and unfolds in the air of freedom. Catholicism is the religion of freedom, of the creative freedom of life, and where there are narrow rules and narrow ideas in control Catholicism remains in a ghetto."[11] Some Catholics, however, looking only at the past and enamored of strict laws, still want a German church supportive of immovable class structures and empty of self-examination. Regardless, Catholicism has left the ghetto where it was enclosed by middle-class Protestantism, Bismarckian politics, late idealist philosophy, and scientific positivism: it has taken for its theme and task for the future unity-in-freedom.[12] That article looked too at the proliferating social issues of the 1920s, at the goal of harmonious living among different professions and vocations, at the interrelationships of men and women, and finally at tensions, tensions between adult life and the life of the young, tensions arising from the role of industry and technology, and from the mobility of life and work. The inner nature of Catholicism needs to summon up courage in changing times to make present in a changing society the power of God.

How does Catholicism influence society? Christianity has no single program for all social and political and economic questions. It lives and flourishes, to use two phrases from Pauline writings, where God is all in all and where Christ is active yesterday, today, and forever. Catholicism is not one form of politics or society, not a precise program for human society, but a gift of God. If, strictly speaking, there is no human or political Catholicism, there is, nonetheless, a Catholicism born of God's immanence, while God is "the inner life-principle of humanity." It celebrates immanence in persons: there is a charism for every person (1 Cor. 7:7), a Catholic presence in forms "for every age, for early Christianity and the Middle Ages as well as for modernity, for Roman Catholicism, for German Catholicism, for Slavic Catholicism, for Asian Catholicism."[13] Varying architectural styles bear witness to different forms of ecclesial life in history, ranging from the Roman basilica to modern churches. Incarnation and not some one past form of Christianity is both primal image and original soul. "Catholicism is the deep trust in the power of God in the midst of change, in the midst of the human, in the midst of the contradictions of human life."[14] Illustrative of ecclesial limitations in those years is the essay's weak conclusion: the concluding Latin line of the Mass, *Ite missa est,* would send believers out to serve society.

The second article, "Catholicism and the Contemporary Religious Crisis," spoke of a religious crisis. "The horrible experience of the years of war during which a world that deified itself flew apart into fragments, when humanity in which some sought to enclose and secularize God showed itself as a pack of predators, and all of creation appeared as a volcano."[15] The crisis of religion is a European and worldwide crisis. Catholicism has existed for several centuries in northern Europe in a defensive posture; Catholic books in philosophy and theology have stayed with proofs for God's existence and teleology, with Aristotelian philosophy, a too general morality, with apologetics. In 1930, Przywara, alluding to a church previously seen as "unproductive" and "negative and apologetic," lauded the appearance of a "living Catholicism of the present day," "an open Catholicism" flowing from the Benedictine contemplation of the liturgy and the Dominican accent on the free activity of created causes. The destruction of the war led Catholics to look for more than "the papacy, church law, veneration of the saints and the rosary," to look for new self-consciousness beyond apologetics, and to leave their "ghetto Catholicism." The world is not evil; the church is not the sacristy; a wider mission is marked by a religious ascendancy of the laity.[16] The *Kulturkampfkatholizismus* of a minority struggling for its rights against Bismarck had understandably lost the creativity of the earlier age when Johann Adam Möhler and Franz von Baader worked to present a Catholic modern theology and when Friedrich von Schlegel fashioned a Catholic literary criticism. Beyond the lifeless rules and the false spirituality of sacrifice there appeared from 1919 to 1926 a "transitional Catholicism" focused on life and community. Catholicism with its realism and objectivity about the world and revelation was fashionable for some: there were converts among intellectuals and aesthetes enjoying antiquity in church art and Gregorian chant. Now a further stage, a "New Catholicism," has appeared, coming from the youth movement, from the difficulties of workers and labor unions.

The 1920s witness momentous shifts: from subject to object, from the individual to community, from a pure and autonomous thinking to nature, from culture to religion, from interiority to church. Philosophy is leaving behind the rationalism of the Enlightenment and Kant and turning to what is human, to God as more than the giver of morality or the architect of the universe. Protestantism, whose original Reformation was the opposite of every state church, suffered the consequences of removing Trinity and grace out of history, for Calvinism identified grace with social forms while Lutheranism prepared the way for Schelling and Hegel and Schleiermacher to reduce the Trinity to inspiring inner-worldly forms. Now too the dialectical theology of Karl Barth and Paul Tillich offer a different God from that of state Protestantism, God experienced by the human being within disaster and failure, God facing the uncertainty and violence of contemporary times. Contemporary culture is fashioning movements tending toward an Absolute; political movements call up the power of the masses; the person experiences a cosmic totality which is both enormous and somewhat chaotic; the individual exists before what Tillich calls the demonic and Heidegger names care and nothingness. It is time for Catholicism to cease being afraid of time and culture, to show the supernatural realism of Catholicism as an alternative to both Protestantism and philosophy. Karl Neufeld writes: "Przywara sensed for his service to [the mystery of God] the new opportunities emerging in the religious ethos after the collapse of the First World War, after the collapse of the social order. With one stroke the prejudice, lying so deep in modernity, that religion and Christianity were relics of long transcended epochs of past human history, was eliminated."[17] What was new was a discrediting of subjectivity, of excessively abstract thinking:

the subject lives in a world; the thinker in a life, the theoretician exists. Both Kierkegaard and Husserl point to an inclusive person who does not *have* life and time and existence but *is* these. This is the true end and crisis of modernity of which so many were speaking.

What could Catholicism contribute? Przywara referred to the thought of Max Scheler where values and religion have an immediacy toward divine presence, and also to the ecclesiological development of a theology of the communal Body of Christ. If Protestant dialectical theology can assist in seeing the world as it is, the Catholic analogical perspective holds together the difference of God with the supernatural participation of the creature in this different life. "What is first and foundational is precisely this towering distinctiveness of God. There is also the self-communication of God reaching from creation to the human person where, . . . as Thomas Aquinas says, there is a 'movement of God' in that which here emerges from God but is essentially 'other than God.'"[18] Catholicism is incarnational and a sacramental presence, an interplay of immanence and transcendence. That ethos can lead to display and arrogance, but a mature Catholicism eschewing display exhibits the simple silence and patience of the servants of the reign of God. In the last analysis, what Catholicism is and contributes is *katholische Sachlichkeit,* realism, a religious objectivity, a faith ending not in words but in realities.[19]

The "new Catholicism" touched several times on the movements of the 1920s, seeking not power or glory but "active participation in the life of the church."[20] There could be, however, no attempt to produce a "Catholic culture," to fashion politics and economics out of ecclesiastical directives; second, theologians and bishops should not attempt to dictate what should happen in science and history. Clearly there are unresolved tensions between laity and clergy, between community and the individual soul. "The creative power of German Catholicism has not been broken through fights with the Vatican."[21] He referred positively to the ideas of Pope Pius XI and his encyclical approving Catholic Action, to Cardinal Michael Faulhaber of Munich, and to the nuncio to Bavaria and the Weimar Republic, Eugenio Pacelli, soon to be Pius XII (Pacelli is cited as describing present-day Catholicism as a "supernatural optimism"). Ultimately, Catholicism is not the workshop of the hierarchy; it is the presence of God.

Exhortations and programs for German Catholicism continued as new decades arrived. In 1930 Przywara wrote that a true *Führer* or

Prophet would understand the culture of his day positively, as an outstanding time, a time of freedom and radicalism, of gigantic and dynamic movements.[22] When the dynamic of the present age pursues a theory and commitment to violence, it ends in nothingness, and the freedom sought reaches truths without human concern, actions without limits, a Nietzschean will to power. The resulting decadent sophistication is only masked anxiety. Courage is needed, courage to seek a fuller truth, courage to realize that both belonging to God and dabbling with damnation lie within the present age. The Christ and the Antichrist are face to face. The Catholic answer is a surrender of life and self into the omnipotence of the one Creator of all *ex nihilo,* out of nothing; it is a commitment to be an instrument of that Creator out of nothingness as his creation continues. Christianity is not measured by anxiety and withdrawal, because its mission and work are "a ceaseless giving of self in the objective service of God."[23]

In 1941, well into Germany's campaign of world war, Przywara still offered that analysis, talking about Catholicism before and after World War I, the shift in philosophy to the objective, the liturgy, and the ecclesiology of the Body of Christ. The "official church" or a "church of law" cannot be identified with the immediacy of the divine, with the immediacy of Christ and his Spirit, for Christianity is neither a simple sect of love nor a church of organization. Like Christ, the church is incarnational, human and divine. Perhaps in later mentions of Catholic realism vis-à-vis the kingdom (*Reich*) of God there was intended a veiled counter to the Third Reich.[24]

When one speaks of Catholicity one speaks not first of the dogmas of creed and church but of thinkers of broad and encompassing thought-forms, religious and human perspectives which reach out to include all, the whole. "The 'Catholic totality,'" Martha Zechmeister observes, "always remains in his thinking mediated through an intimation of the brokenness of historically concrete nonidentity. And since he knows that each provisionally reached 'synthesis' holds its basic inconclusive character, he can never rest. His inability to find a definitive 'solution' remains the stimulus to his activity as much as his Augustinian restlessness toward God."[25] The personality drawn to study contemporary theologians and philosophers is a person for whom sectarian narrowness and personal exclusion are not natural. There are today no holy places outside of which pagans live; no thinkers who have nothing to contribute to the search for truth; no medieval golden age. Karl Rahner said that "what was proper, almost unique in the work of Przywara was precisely that he is 'Catholic' in a real, life-long dialogue with the past and the present, Catholic as open to the totality of European intellectual and cultural history."[26] Zechmeister finds in this Catholic mentality a bridge leading to theological and cultural existence, to what Przywara called "cooperative knowing in the community of knowing."[27]

Przywara did not become a university professor but remained a commentator and theologian, a critic active through journals and books, and a much-requested lecturer. The two courses outlined in the following section exemplify how, in the mid-1920s, he sought to make Christianity interesting and attractive to the cultural world around him.

A Philosopher-Theologian amid German Culture: The University Courses at Ulm and Leipzig

Karl Rahner wrote of "the numerous attentive hearers"[28] who attended Przywara's lectures at symposia and congresses. The Jesuit lectured in the university world not as a professor but as a guest. He was invited not by a department or by the faculty as a whole but by individuals or groups with some link to the university. Particularly important were the lectures given in Ulm in 1923 and at the University of Leipzig in 1924; when published, the title of the first collection was *God as the Mystery of the World,* and the second was simply called *God.* The first thematic of the age, however, was not Christ and church but God and the world. Is God over all or in all; in us or above us?

The Lectures at Ulm

The lectures at Ulm were held in 1923 at the August symposium of the *Verband der Vereine Katholischer Akademiker* (The Union of Catholic Academic Associations). Romano Guardini took part in that assembly of Catholic academicians, as did Ildefons Herwegen, abbot of the Benedictine monastery of Maria Laach from 1913 to his death in 1946. Well-known as a leader of the liturgical movement and the youth movement, Herwegen founded in 1931 a Benedictine academy for the study of liturgy through conferences and scholarly publications. He thought at first that the church might work with the Hitler State, but after being investigated and threatened by the Gestapo he discarded

that position. Herwegen emphasized the role of liturgical prayer in the
life of the church. At Ulm he spoke of how the goal of Christ's work
on earth is liturgical cult and the mode of cult is mystery: the liturgical movement is a community contemplating the divine through the
signs and symbols of sacramentality.[29] Guardini published in 1918 *The
Spirit of the Liturgy* and four years later, as he completed a second doctorate on St. Bonaventure, he published *The Church and the Catholic,*
lectures given in 1922 at the University of Bonn whose success gained
for him a professorship at the University of Berlin. At the time of the
Ulm lectures in 1923 he would have been beginning his teaching at
Berlin and increasing his work with the youth movement, Quickborn.
Przywara referred to Guardini as a presenter of a new Catholic spirit.
"Through the undiluted work of Romano Guardini and his circle we
are at a point in time of relative clarification and analysis of the individual spirit in the youth movement . . . of a will to the individual
value of the person in contrast to servanthood . . . of a free and inner
growth of love in contrast to obligation . . . and of a will for forms and
laws which are the external expression of the inner nature of life."[30]
Hanna-Barbara Gerl observes of Przywara, "It is striking that he used
various formulas which were very much those of Guardini, although
the Jesuit had developed them independently. The two quite different
thinkers with similar approaches indicate the common intellectual
atmosphere of the time."[31]

   At Ulm, Przywara gave three lectures. In his opening lines he spoke
of leaders and people, of *Führer* and *Volk*. Academics should not be a
condescending elite but should be part of German cultural life: the
streams of the times cannot help but touch Catholics and be influenced by Catholics. "Consequently, we stand in the midst of this crisis, and the outcome of this crisis depends upon us. On us!"[32] What
is the ultimate, all-encompassing resolution of the world's mystery of
God? A relationship with and in the life of God. What is the atmosphere joining the person and God? Is it a solution of either/or, or is it
the Catholic approach of both/and? "According to the old custom for
these days of prayer and intellectual struggle, I suggest and call upon
a patron saint. This patron can only be he who has furthered the
phenomenological movement in its first phase, who consciously or
unconsciously honors the liturgical movement with its primacy of the
Word and its ideal of the *vita contemplativa*, and whom the youth movement in its search [for person and love] seeks. It is he who in the inner

rhythm of his thinking bears that direction of Catholic balance, and toward whom our questions in a proliferating way seek: Thomas Aquinas."[33] The Jesuit alluded to the 650th anniversary of the death of Thomas Aquinas and the encyclical on him issued by Pius XI in 1923.

Three movements (we meet Przywara's preference for schemata and typologies) compose "the picture of the hour":[34] the phenomenological movement, the liturgical movement, the youth movement. Phenomenological philosophies receive the major treatment, for modern phenomenology is a helpful aperture, a way out of the mental prison fashioned by Descartes and Kant. Phenomenology is not so much a knowledge about something as an intending of something: an object, a nature, God. It pursues the immediacy of ideas, perhaps even the idea of God. Nonetheless, this Husserlian intention differs from the Catholic teaching on the mediacy of all our knowledge of God, and so "phenomenology is not an inner-Catholic movement."[35]

The second and third movements of the present hour do lie within Catholicism: the liturgical movement and the youth movement. In liturgy there is "the intention of form." Form, intellectual and not just emotional, stands for image and word, ritual and movement. The forms of liturgies and church architecture can be contemporary and not just Baroque or Romanesque. "Form is the expression of community and the will to form emerges along with the will to community. The liturgical movement furthers the unfolding of a religion of community, total and particular. That religion of community balances individual piety and counterbalances a piety of law."[36] Przywara mentioned the union of aristocratic priesthood and private mysticism in the poems and followers of the writer Stefan George. The liturgical movement differs from a sacral literature. "It is not a quiet island of sacred culture and lofty souls."[37] Liturgy, where forms meet community, is called to change and expand. "Could not liturgy, precisely because it is the garment of that high priest who is the incarnate God, could not liturgy be as broad and inclusive as God is? Could not liturgy perhaps bear an inexperienced depth out of its tension of opposites, and in its infinite breadth of life bear the most energetic will to form even within the remaining mysterious desire?"[38] Liturgy and church are form in life, but which renewing reforms they might assume were left unexpressed.

The youth movement (found also in secular, Protestant, and Jewish forms, in ecologically-minded groups, and in political parties) means for Catholics the affirmation of the individual person. In Germany the person is reduced by office and vocation, by government ministries and ecclesial abstractions. The value of the person—an individual is never a slave or a servant, not something disposable—has been reawakened; a desire has been enkindled for a free, inner awakening of love in a world long dominated by duty, and a search has begun for forms and laws expressing the inner nature of love. The personal, this mode of subjectivity, has a value for Catholics too. The journey to being a person is invisible, unconscious, not something to be compelled. A journey within society, it involves dedication and self-offering through the forms of life and work, of culture and devotion. Self-realization itself intends and moves toward only one—God. Is not that form of changing polarity called absolute also the Incarnate One? Incarnation gives the true absolute which church and dogma serve, proclaiming a polarity of the human and the divine in an active life transcending dualism. "We stand at the end. The philosophy of polarity which I have tried to sketch for you is a program, certainly a program on whose realization the one *philosophia perennis* has labored up until today, but . . . not a program of one individual or of a limited community. It is the philosophy of humanity, one for all the various kinds of human beings; all peoples will have their own contributions to bring forward as gift."[39]

At the end of the three lectures he summoned Thomas Aquinas forth again—now as the partner of John Henry Newman: they are both guides into the future of the church. Complementing the monumental gift for clarity of Aquinas, "Newman, the theoretician of knowledge, reached a theory of reality toward which critical realism today strives." The Englishman's motto of "perseverance in changing" furthers the German's themes of transformation and polarity. "Must we choose Thomas *or* Newman in this unhealthy epoch, struggling as it is between integralism and modernism? . . . No, the choice of this hour as we stand at the central point of the spiritual crisis of our time is not Thomas or Newman, but, true to the spirit of Catholic polarity, Thomas *and* Newman."[40] A few years later Przywara described the conclusion of another of those Catholic rallies, the final morning of the first assembly of the united Catholic youth groups of Germany. Architecture, liturgy, and faith moved him (the description puts Nazi rallies in a wider context of what excited the age). "Then the leader of the united 'new generation,' General President Wolker, announced the final hymn, '*Wenn wir ziehn Seit' an Seit'* ("When we move on side by side"). We sang the first verse and then a final verse added by Catholic youth groups. The old concluding line, 'With us a new age enters,' is replaced by 'Christ the Lord of the new age.' In that sign and gesture we entered with waving flags into the old cathedral for a final blessing."[41]

Przywara spotlighted the issues of the hour, the atmosphere in Germany, and the challenges Catholics faced. The substantive theological sections at Ulm are much the same as in the lectures in Leipzig given three years later, and the following summary of their content comes from the Leipzig addresses.

Lectures at Leipzig: Modernity Turns toward God

The series of lectures given in 1924 at the University of Leipzig was sponsored by the Catholic Academy there, although the audience held many Protestants, for Saxon Leipzig was a Protestant city. The published version was dedicated to Cardinal Andreas Cardinal Frühwirth, an Austrian Dominican and a former superior general of the Order of Preachers. Papal nuncio to Bavaria from 1907 to 1916, he was a moderating influence on the Vatican's propensity, occasionally mean-spirited, to attack indiscriminately theologians during the antimodernist years. A source of accurate information about the church in Germany and an advocate of exemptions from the Oath against Modernism, he was the subject of gossip in Rome, namely, that he was unfaithful to Pius X.[42] In the published version (a preface links these lectures to the earlier series given in Ulm) the five chapters correspond to five lectures, although the fifth chapter is twice as long as the others. Scholarly notes with references to literature and explanations fill a quarter of the book,[43] and page after page of its "Index" lists religious and cultural figures like Vermeil and Paul Verlaine, Giordano Bruno, Wilhelm Bousset, and Joseph Mausbach, indicating the breadth of the author's knowledge. Philosophers and artists were important for "entering into the stream at the point of its sources" and for following "men and women whose creations are gifts of mind and spirit."[44]

An overall motif of the lectures in Leipzig is "the turn" (Die Wende). That cultural reorientation, influencing contemporary philosophies, the arts, the history of ideas, and theories of religion, is also a turn to God. "When we drink in the passionate pulse and rhythm of contemporary intellectual life, the direction in which it is moving is undeniably a direction toward God."[45] A longing for a home, the experience of limitations, powerful feelings — these pass beyond the agnostic philosophies of 1890, beyond the arts as they existed before the war and colored by too symbolic a style. "The sometimes despairing, sometimes devoutly peaceful songs of Gustav Schüler, the delicate, emotionally fatigued but destiny-filled mysticism of Rainer Maria Rilke, the curious contemplations of Franz Werfel on the tragedy of life and the darkness of life . . . , the tragic struggle of Ernst Troeltsch . . . (just to name a few randomly selected figures) had all undeniably set out on the search for God in journeys sometimes strange and erring" (9).

Is God above us or in us? Or both? While the broad directions of modernity are continuing, what is new in the 1920s are philosophies leaving behind subjective systems, setting aside new and old schools of neo-Kantianism, leaving behind too neoscholasticism and even the old voluntarism (is Schopenhauer or even Ockham meant?). There are three new directions for thinking: the object, the idea of infinity, and the idea of mystery. Their subtle intimations of God can go further and serve to explain religion and Christian revelation; indeed for some they already point to Christ and the Christian community.

The Leipzig lectures are a kind of philosophy of religion and illustrate Przywara's preferred method in the 1920s: first, an extensive and direct knowledge of contemporary thinkers; second, an arrangement of them into directions; and third, an indication of how basic orientations of new philosophies are related to Greek and medieval philosophies in the past. That typological preamble will lead on to contrasts and similarities between contemporary thinking and Christian philosophies and theologies reaching back many centuries. Thereby a Catholic intellectual offers theologies, past and present.

The *first lecture* sets forth some prominent, distinct marks—he calls them "the stigmas"—of the new turn in philosophy. "The stigma of our age today is a turn to objective thought. . . . Husserl means the victory of recent philosophy over psychologism, naturalism, and historicism. Truth is not a formula for subjective processes; truth is recognized as something independent from knowing. . . . So it is not astonishing that almost the entire new philosophy of religion moves away from the old path of the needs and postulates fashioned by Schleiermacher's feeling of dependency" (12). The new direction taking the place of the old Kantian consciousness (too interior, sterile, and schematic) posits an intentional consciousness of something opening onto a life in the world of objects and recognizes a world of objective truth (13, 15). An objective reality implies an objective knowing which for each subjective knowing is inexhaustible. Brittle objectivity in rigid paradigms of science and solitary mental constructs is set aside, as progress and knowing are offered a new ground in Being. "The stigma of our age is ultimately the abandonment of *a priori* systems joined to a struggle to know the unique, the concrete, the individual, the real" (21). Now every objectivity illumines subjective thinking.

Through an interest in the object Husserl and other phenomenologists lead beyond their still somewhat subjectivist philosophies: surprisingly they point to ways similar to those of John Henry Newman's interplay of reason and faith. "Here is a small path to Him who is the reality-ground of each reality, who is the Infinity-Is in its 'becoming toward and into the infinite,' and thereby is *the reality*" (14–15). Attention to reality offers the opportunity to view God as intimately linked to humanity but also as existing above it. Later, in the final lecture, Przywara will explain how this philosophical objectivity spills over into a contemporary Christian interest in liturgy and community, into a renewal of sacrament and ministry.

Of course, such turns to reality say little about God: they are symptoms of a search for God. If the real and the concrete are leading to mystery, will philosophies absolutizing the world and dismissing the deity survive? Such approaches may well end in that monism of German philosophy running from Schelling to Hermann Cohen where an ultimate being is one with creation. God is not easily reached because "he is the mystery of mysteries, the primal mystery, the universal mystery" (23). Can God be described in human life or only apart from it? "When God is the one above conceptualization and is, too, the mystery plain and simple (a mystery we cannot just puzzle over), when we place everything good and beautiful in this world in an absolute mode, and even when we search in the most recent explosion of total suffering in the world for something primal . . . , then God is, one might say, the absolutized mysteriousness of human existence" (23). If this does not describe the true God, facets of culture analyzed through such a philosophy do, nonetheless, raise potential approaches to God.

The *second lecture* compares the God of modernity with the God of antiquity—not to place them in conflict (as much of Catholic neoscholasticism had done) but to see if they could address and complement each other. As a return of objective realism, Przywara saw two currents flowing into contemporary philosophy: one anthropocentric (Kant) and one cosmic (Spinoza). The first strain emphasizes God's transcendence and ends up with a God who is distant but who can relate directly to an individual; paradoxically, because human beings can tolerate only so much transcendence, a Kantian God ends up as humanity, even sinful humanity. The second strain has several developments: there is a positive branch (Hegel, Nietzsche, Bergson) and a negative one (Schopenhauer, Eduard von Hartmann) which in the spirit of Schelling develops its view of God from nature and the universe.[46]

But those approaches are all weak and passé. "Is not the turn in today's philosophy of religion perhaps a simple consequence of a general collapse, a failure of nerve in science?" (24) Przywara knew and appreciated Catholicism's encounters with Schelling in the first half of the nineteenth century,[47] and of that Romantic idealism inspired by Schelling and articulated theologically by figures like Franz von Baader. Greek patristic thought had developed a history, an economy of salvation, and that influenced Baader who, the colleague of Schelling and the spiritual advisor of Czar Alexander I, influenced Russian theosophy. Przywara saw the thought of Hegel, unlike that of Schelling, to be that of an abstract self and so a total idealism. "The realism traversing the Romanticism of Joseph Görres or a Baader is irreducibly opposed to idealism, for it finds in all things the ultimate dialectic of the relationship of man and woman,"[48] that is, a polarity which is objective. This dialectic of anthropological or cosmic theosophy influenced German philosophy from Jakob Böhme to Martin Heidegger. There were Protestant and Catholic mystics from the thirteenth to the eighteenth centuries concerned more with the mind than with the cosmos, and that direction continued in the transcendental self-hovering between an objective realm and a ground in divine reality. Romanticism was balanced by the study of Augustine and Aquinas on nature and grace, for Przywara employed a dialectic that is neither a Hegelian thought-form nor the irrational pulse of night but analogous degrees of the interplay of the divine and the human. The influence of Romantic idealism remained: "Baader, Möhler and Scheeben dominate today's Catholic thinking so much that the German Thomists read Thomas through these three. This is clear in the way in which the entire philosophical and theological creativity of a Guardini or Eschweiler comes out of the atmosphere of the youth movement (which emerged in German Romanticism) or in how Karl Adam and Josef Engert give a new form to the old Tübingen school. . . . Of the five thinkers we mentioned, Eschweiler,

Adam, and Engert aim at a new theological methodology; while Guardini and Peter Wust circle in a new way the problem between faith
and knowledge."[49] Regardless, history, a kind of metaphysically driven
dialectic, impels ideas and thought-forms forward. The central motif
of polarity seeks a union of faith and knowledge in theology, a mutuality of Trinitarian economy of creation and redemption.[50]

Philosophies of religion in antiquity also recorded a history of the
dialectic of being and consciousness; it was a last stage before Jesus
Christ, and after him it spawned devotees of mystery religions and various Gnostics. Antiquity was calling vigorously for an incarnation—
Przywara mentioned the line from the liturgy of Advent, *Rorate caeli
desuper* ("Rain down from heavens a savior")—and now the modern world again presents the human and the real as transparent to the
divine.

This theme of subjectivity and universe in philosophies past and
present leads to the next three lectures, unfolding in God, incarnation,
and church.

The *third lecture* treats God in light of the dialectic of immanence and
transcendence, the theme underlying all the lectures. God is not a creature, and the cosmos is not grace, while subjectivity is not inevitably
solitary and atheistic. The explorations of science and the experiences
of the soul do not account fully for the longing for the infinite.

Within Romantic idealism's dialectic between the active forms of
transcendental consciousness and organic nature, Przywara posited the
goal of cosmic nature to be the human person, and the goal of community to be mature men and women. Like the later Schelling, he
explored the image of God surfacing in religions of various peoples,
pausing for a critique of Eastern illusionism and Protestant individualism. Also, like Schelling and Hegel, he sought philosophical meaning in
the history of art; the arts, whether Greek sculpture or Dostoyevsky's
novels, draw on nature and a cultural moment to realize the ideal in the
concrete. All this points further to a God who is not just infinity and
mystery but a person close to us. "He is the one who illumines us when
we keep our distance and when we approach; the infinite light which
is always further the closer we come. Every finding is a commencement
of a new search. His inner being is the experience of his infinite above-
being. No mystical marital morning can be a definitive embrace of his
fullness, no mystical night of despair is separation from his intimacy. The
rhythm of ego and universe sounds from him" (59).

The *fourth lecture* is on idea and history. Humans have a propensity to be restless, to begin anew, to seek to live with others. Nearness and distance mark history; what emerges for us in God is a tension between immanence (within Being) and transcendence (above Being). That same tension manifest in idealist and phenomenological philosophies, calls for incarnation, the event summed up in an aphorism: "God is creature *as* the all-creating God; God is visible human being *as* the invisible God" (61).

Human reflection encountering the motif of idea-in-history unfolds in the same typology of philosophical systems sketched earlier. Too strong an Aristotelian direction leads to Pelagianism and rationalism, the forgetting of the divine; too strong a Platonism leads to mono-physitism or docetism where the divine overpowers the human. Since the Reformation and the Enlightenment there is a tension between pantheism (the cosmos as God) and theopanism (the self as God).[51] In Lutheranism and Barthianism theopanism dominates: it rejects the finite and the created and disdains forms mediating revelation. Paradoxically, the two come to resemble each other: "A pantheistic shell is fully theopanistic just as the theopanistic ground is in its essence totally pantheism. Both are the final ends of a line, a line which closes in a circle, as each form, pantheism and theopanism, falls into the other" (66f.).

People too much in love with culture or people too afraid of culture — those fugitives can be consoled by incarnation.

The inner reality of Jesus the Word, what Greek and Latin theologies call the hypostatic union, does not have to do with a choice for God over creation or a permission to select humanity over God. Incarnation understands God as the Divine One who, while remaining God, becomes a creature. The form of Christ is the great paradox: "Infinity itself enters into the tension of the world. God in Christ is himself the tension between God and creation" (69). Przywara's Christology stresses Christ's bodily humanity with its visible aspects.

The schools of Christian spirituality down through the centuries have selected varied perspectives; some emphasized community, some the individual; others chose sacrament or eschaton. What does the phrase in Colossians, "Christ our life" (3:4), mean in terms of the philosophical currents active in the twentieth century? In contemporary spirituality Jesus is not a replacement for my subjectivity nor is he just an inspiration for my personality. My life and the infinite God meet in an incarnational pattern, a pattern illustrated by philosophical theologies, past and present. Not an ideal person, Jesus Christ is a statement of God coming to me in the moments when I grow deeper and mature.

Occasionally Przywara pauses in his lectures to replace ontological analysis with lines of literary exaltation, a prose poem. At the opening of the last lecture there was an emotional picture of the individual's life amid the four seasons. "Out of the light breath of spring moving in leaves soft and delicate and suited only for child-like strokes by breezes, new, young life expands" (46). Pulsing nature opens to a God of silence beneath the world's conflicts, to a God of aloneness in autumn or of human aging in winter, to a God always changing and remaining, transcendent and yet present (48).

The *fifth lecture* draws the individual into community. God is present in me directly but also present indirectly in societies. Should religion be utterly interiorized so that there is no longer any religious group but only a "rhythm of existence"? On the other hand, should the community demean the individual by becoming a "God-community" that vaguely contains everything? Continuing the theme of immanence and transcendence, Platonic and Aristotelian metaphysics as well as Reformation theologies and subjectivist philosophies unfold their competing ecclesiologies in a severe contrast between intense individualism and state control. There have been political ideologies where Christianity is subject to government authority, whether in Constantinople or Vienna, and there have been small enthusiastic sects rejecting every ecclesial and liturgical form. Aristotelian realist politics joined to the theology of the Body of Christ in the Middle Ages only to bring its own exaggerations, while modern subjectivisms — the rigorist sectarian, the linguistic analyst, the academic theoretician, the ethician of duty — have their own dangers (90). There will always be tension between the individual and the community, between a church that is pure interior experience and a "cultic hierarchy" or "heavenly court." Every distortion should be set aside (96).

One cannot help but notice that Przywara's rejection of individualism is more eloquent and rich in illustrations than his critique of a too-domineering ecclesiastical directorate. Nonetheless, he did criticize a church of sin, a church of riches and power, "a scandal of an un-Christian Christian people, a scandal of an unpriestly priesthood, of unmonastic monasteries, of clerical envy, of ambition of the religious orders, of the scandal of the papacy itself" (126). If this is an age of returning to the object, where is the new objectivity of the church to be found? Drawing on the Pauline letters, he focused on the community's Eucharist and creed. A sacrament is a realization of grace, symbol and celebration, while a creed expresses the inexpressible in language. Both bear witness to the objective.

This fifth lecture on the church remained metaphysical and poetic, as the theologian of culture located the church amid philosophies of religion and typologies of theologians. There is the promise of new movements and new ideas in general, but life in the local church, even enhanced by them, remains much the same.

Sources from the Past: Augustine and Thomas Aquinas

A student of prominent philosophers and theologians, Erich Przywara sought a metaphysical perspective that was polar and realistic as he pursued a Christian theology which was synthetic and supernatural. Ultimately, as the lectures illustrate, the history of ideas and the historical epochs of thought-forms disclose the pair of transcendence and immanence. Every being exists between Creator and creation in analogy, and between faith and culture in grace. Experts list, as sources for Przywara, the Bible, Augustine but also Greek patristic thought, Thomas Aquinas and Ignatius Loyola, John Henry Newman, and German phenomenologists. Individual philosophers and artists, past and present, complemented each other. A conversation with Karl Barth or Paul Tillich was illumined by the study of Origen and Tertullian; Newman was not alien to Max Scheler. To compare, to learn, to think—these were ways of seeing. The insights of others were arranged in models and typologies that led on to synthesis. Thus the past illumined the present and showed that today's issues and ideas were not unprecedented.

This chapter now looks at the influence of two of these figures, two theologians from the past particularly seminal for Przywara's theology. The next chapter looks at three other sources from the century before 1920. Thus Przywara's understanding of five influential figures is sketched.

Augustine (354–430)

Not a few theologians open to dialogue with modern philosophy found Augustine's varied writings a sympathetic point of departure. A personal figure, a seeker, more neoplatonic than Aristotelian, he was a source for Aquinas, Newman, and Scheler, a spiritual intersection where Parmenides and Plato meet John the Evangelist. Przywara presented Augustine in the 1930s as "a European genius"; amid the quest of religious philosophies of late idealism he was a theologian of polarity, a searching existence, a person amid sin and grace.[52] Augustine's writings (but not an Augustinian type of theology) begins a line of religious thinking, personal as well as speculative, running from Duns Scotus in the late thirteenth century up to Franz von Baader in the early nineteenth.[53] Could not Augustine even serve as a mediator between Western Catholicism and Eastern Orthodoxy?

Like other French and German patristic theologians in the mid-twentieth century, Przywara offered Augustine's motifs of love and emotion, of sign and word to enable and justify a theology other than one of neoscholasticism. God is not first a supreme being but the sublime totality of all that is good and true and beautiful. Augustine's theology, unlike Greek patristic thought, however, is centered in personal development and not in monastic detachment. God is a source and ground of our expressions of life and reality. Grades of participation flow from and to the One intimately present in the rhythm of the universe.[54] "The theology of Platonic Augustinianism is the theology of the idea-bright God-Truth whose symbolic language of images is the world of pure essences posed as ideas."[55] The self-sharing of the Trinity flows out into faith, hope, and love, and then faith unfolds further into understanding and insight. Augustine understood the richness and complexity of the verb "is" and understood that vis-à-vis creatures God "is not." Divinization is central: a view of the North African theologian as only a struggling will or a private sinner is incomplete. Human nature is not purely passive or evil but has in its search, its morality, and in its detachment from the world and discernment about one's own life, a discernment that is simultaneously receptivity for grace.[56]

Augustine's life and writings certainly incorporated polarity, for Augustine followed good and evil to their deepest grounds and thought for a while that both were divine. Eventually a Manichaean radicalism was overcome by the unity and depth of love Augustine found in himself and in God. "The opposition between good and evil opens into a deeper opposition between mercy and justice, and this further into the real groundlessness of God."[57] Polarity opened onto a God whose love included not evil but a goodness so powerful as to overcome evil. The African theologian helped Przywara see that polarity was a form that had various temporary resolutions, and one ultimate divine resolution present and hidden. Participation in the divine, grace, must be held up as central, for this is Augustine's solution to the problematic of the independence of creatures and the transcendence of God.[58]

In 1934 Przywara offered a collection of texts from Augustine preceded by a long essay; sometimes this introduction (or parts of it) was not included in subsequent translations, and so he reissued it in the 1960s in his book on the Augustinian "Comportment of Spirit."[59] The quest for God is always a discovery of God, and that quest indicates that God's mystery cannot be so easily grasped by the human intellect. Augustine, as illustrated in the variety of his themes, is a thinker of movement and transition, a particular form of faith that is that of insight. While the early philosophical Augustine and the later anti-Pelagian theologian are important, Przywara focused on the incarnation in Augustine, on the realism of Christ where the Word has become flesh, as developed by Augustine's commentaries on the Psalms and the Gospel according to John; there is also some attention to Christ and grace in history, in *De Civitate Dei*. The incarnation is an exchange: the Logos is a human being so that men and women may be taught and empowered by God. The Risen Christ continues in his Body, the church: in a Christological and ecclesiological counterpart to analogy, the Jesuit theologian develops his "realism of a corporate 'Head and Body One Christ.'"[60] "In the mosaics of the early Christian period one sees the face of the Roman which in his strict form has penetrated into the Mystery of opposites, opposites which tear apart the old format."[61]

Despite the intricacy of his theology of finitude and sin in the human person and of the loving mystery of the deity, Augustine alone does not hold a complete "Catholic answer"; Aquinas on causality and participation is needed.[62] Augustine and Aquinas are the archetypes of theological thinking, two modes of the rhythm of analogy.[63] Przywara noted the limits of Augustine, who might inadvertently lead the individual into a sect or gnosis: God as the all-in-all of much patristic literature needs the balance of the medieval emphasis on the human person as the creator of culture. Martha Zechmeister, in her study of the relationship of Augustine to Aquinas in analogy, concludes that, while the balance and serenity of Aquinas had a prominence in the middle third of the century, after World War II Augustine takes on a new presence: perhaps the experience of human suffering and the

violent self-contradictions of civil society had rendered the metaphysical order of Aquinas less attractive and drew people to a more
human theology.[64] In the 1920s and 1930s Augustine led to Aquinas,
while after the war, the bishop of Hippo brought a needed tragic personalism of eschatological redemption.

Thomas Aquinas (1225–1274)

An Augustinian mystical affirmation of God spurred on by the fatigue
of the ancient world—Przywara found a balance for this in Thomas
Aquinas. The emotional enthusiasm, the convert searching through
various stages, the observer of the decline of social history should
be complemented by Aquinas' "cool penetration into reality where
Thomas distinguished between the all-reality and all-efficacy of God
and the true proper reality and proper efficacy of the creature."[65] Przywara observed insightfully at a congress of Thomist scholars in Prague
in 1932: "The supratemporal vitality of Aquinas came to life anew only
through living thinkers, even through non-Christian or even anti-
Christian thinkers."[66]

Before and after the First World War, the Roman Catholic Church
was officially dominated by a monopoly of neoscholasticism, a reexpression of the philosophical logic of medieval theology. The
terms "neoscholasticism" and "neo-Thomism" came into use in the late
1870s. The pioneering historian of medieval thought, Martin Grabmann, defined neoscholasticism in this way: "That direction which
has emerged since the mid-nineteenth century and is usually found in
Catholic theology and philosophy; it takes up again the traditional
links with (medieval and Baroque) ecclesiastical scholasticism which
were broken by the Enlightenment; it searches to make fruitful for
contemporary problems the thought-world of medieval scholasticism, particularly that of Thomas Aquinas."[67] Pope Leo XIII's encyclical *Aeterni Patris* (1879) singled out Aquinas as the outstanding teacher
for the church and indicated his method as normative; his works
were republished in several editions, particularly in a new critical text
begun under Leo. Papal sponsorship increased with the publication of
Doctoris Angelici (1914) of Pius X; the controversial twenty-four theses
from the Vatican in 1914; *Studiorum Ducem* (1923) of Pius XI; canon
1366 of the Code of Canon Law (1917/18); and *Humani Generis* (1950)
of Pius XII. What had brought back Aquinas as modernity was moving

through the nineteenth century? After 1850 it had become clear that the optimistic expectations of the previous decades of idealism— a universal science bringing the benefits of art, physics, and politics to all—had not been fulfilled. The Catholic church, along with other institutions in the late nineteenth century, moved from a time of optimism and creativity to one of reaction and positivism. It was time to counter idealist systems by a philosophy grounded in the realism found in Aristotle and Aquinas. Thus was born another revival of scholastic philosophy and theology, a further "neo-Thomism." That restoration, lasting over a century, up to the 1960s and Vatican II, was part of a larger neo-Gothic revival whose branches could be found in architecture, the restoration of medieval religious orders, and Gregorian chant.

In the writings of most neoscholastics the restoration was as much of Aristotle as it was of Thomas Aquinas. The Greek philosopher's conceptual clarity was prized along with proofs for the existence of God. One can detect three stages in the course of that neoscholasticism from 1860 to 1914. The first years, from 1850 to 1875, found scholars educated in earlier German historical and idealist ways of thinking studying the medieval thinkers but not fully replacing modern thought with neoscholasticism. At the same time, young enthusiasts assumed a rather ideological stance on behalf of Aristotelianism, proselytizing for scholasticism as the dominant, indeed the sole philosophical stance for Catholics. Those first neo-Thomists did not always grasp the theological depth of Aquinas. A second period, from 1875 to 1890, presumed that Thomism and scholasticism were known in content (numerous books on Aquinas had appeared) and worked on a philosophy and theology destined by church authority to give the intellectual format of Catholicism. A third stage, after 1890, held a variety of genres: (1) manuals and multivolume textbooks; (2) works explaining the meaning of Aquinas, mainly on philosophical issues; (3) applications of Aquinas and Aristotle to social and ethical issues; (4) histories of medieval thought.

After 1900 Aquinas was presented at times as a judge ruling against what was new or different and rejecting experience, change, development, and pluralism. Consequently, many in European intellectual life saw in the Catholic church only antiquarian and imperious stances supported by a Vatican politique that would last through the first half of the twentieth century. This third neo-Thomism, from the 1860s to

the 1960s, in its narrow scholastic form could identify truth and life
with immutability and rationality and opposed being to history, ignoring concreteness in human life and in the economy of salvation.
Its Aristotelianism was too conceptual, and religious education at all
levels consisted in little more than philosophical passages on God or
virtue. In a child's catechism or a priest's manual Christian revelation
appeared to be a blueprint of religious laws and the mechanics of
grace. Scriptural themes, different periods in the history of doctrine,
personal faith, and communal liturgy were neglected. Any other theology, not only modern but biblical, patristic, or medieval, could be
dangerous. Theology was to have the same narrow standards as dogma
and to avoid growth, originality, and pluralism. All of this found its
climax in the selection in 1914 by anonymous figures of twenty-four
theses (all concerning philosophy) which would perfectly present the
thought of Aquinas. While neo-Thomism, aided by Vatican authorities, aspired to become dominant in the classroom life of Catholicism
from 1860 to 1960, actually any superficial neoscholasticism seemed
to qualify. Viewed positively, however, scholastic thought warded off
the absorption of Christian revelation by philosophy and by the
liberal Protestant reduction of God's action in history, but biblical
faith ended up in a castle guarded by metaphysics and canon law; the
authority of the church replaced the intrinsic criteria of truth prized
by Albert and Aquinas.

Erich Przywara imagined and fashioned alternatives to the neoscholastic program. From the time of his first publications he had a
good understanding of Aquinas, seeing a relationship of Aristotelian
science and metaphysics to Trinitarian presence and avoiding the separation of nature and grace. He was able to gain "the necessary distance
from ordinary neoscholasticism" and to see Aquinas' work not as a collection of theses from a classroom but "perhaps the most vital field
of tension within philosophy and Christian thinking."[68] "The supratemporal vitality of Aquinas . . . in his own time grew not out of a
ghetto of 'Christian schools' but through looking face to face at pagans,
Jews, Arabs, and Manichaeanism (the deepest of all heresies with a
real kinship to Augustine). . . . He is not the shallowly praised master
of all overly systematized (and thus dead) 'schools' (from Thomism to
Molinism to neoscholasticism, and so on) but the uncrowned and
unnamed master in the real abyss of the vital questions of the contemporary age."[69]

Przywara was one of the European scholars to see the many differences between the theology of Aquinas and neoscholasticism and
to appreciate the historical context of the philosophy and theology of
Aquinas. His knowledge of medieval schools in the thirteenth and
fourteenth centuries moved through the Baroque to modern neoscholasticisms to the Kant-Aquinas enterprise. He continued the tradition of his Jesuit education in Holland of seeing how Thomism and
modern philosophy could illumine each other, and he also favored a
historical approach like that of Martin Grabmann, among others. Przywara does not identify himself as a Jesuit theologian vigorously advocating Molina and Suárez, although their theme of the independence
of the self is important to him. He sought to transcend the division
between Molinism and Bañezianism, and, when he came to treat
analogy, he wanted to stand above all parties. While the church wisely
includes various theologians, examination shows that they complement
and even contain each other. "Thomism underscores in the mystery of
the hypostatic union the one 'divine existence' of Christ and so stands
in the line of the school of Alexandria . . . , while Molinism takes what
is authentic in Antioch and emphasizes the true 'human existence' of
Christ. . . . It is not surprising that Thomism is the special advocate of
the invisible church of grace in the Corpus Christi mysticum, while
Molinism presents the visible constitutional church as the church of the
pope."[70] Sometimes, however, the Jesuit's description of the two types is
somewhat inaccurately idealized, as the Dominicans become too contemplative and sacral, and the differences are too easily transcended.

He distinguished too between different forms of contemporary
neo-Thomism without joining any one direction. "In the years after
the war a stronger movement to a 'speculative metaphysics enters'
whether it draws from French Thomism (Karl Eschweiler), from
the positive meeting with German Idealism (Theodor Steinbuechel),
or from the formation of motifs found in the philosophy of life of
Simmel and Troeltsch (Romano Guardini, Peter Wust). There was a
similar accent in German Catholic theology. While in the years before
the war there was a 'historical theology' with few exceptions, now
there is Karl Adam, reawakening the lines of Augustine, Karl Eschweiler drawing on the Thomism of Maritain and Garrigou-Lagrange
and on the tradition of the Catholic Tübingen school, Josef Engert
in dialogue with modern philosophy of religion in order to build
systematic theology in a new method. The position of this author is
to offer a critical reflection of a patristic and scholastic unity of the-

ology and philosophy."[71] The texts of Aquinas were an aid in going beyond the shallow logic and static metaphysics of manual neoscholasticism that flourished around 1900, as the structure and dynamics in the *Summa theologiae* were explored. Przywara had anticipated slightly a later time of interplay between study, spirituality, and pastoral change at the centers of Fourvière and Le Saulchoir, the end of fixed mechanics of freedom and actual grace, and the beginnings of a deeper theological ground of knowing and willing, of uncreated and created grace.

In 1928 Przywara wrote a magisterial overview of the modern neoscholastic movement with its variations and its deficiencies.[72] The neoscholastic movement promoted by Leo XIII to protect Catholic theology was destined to be more than a repristination of the axioms of Aquinas, and in a few decades historical research into the Middle Ages emerged with Franz Ehrle and Martin Grabmann. Is neo-Thomism a living philosophy, more than a simple transmission of a past product? Did Leo XIII want the entire potentiality of creative philosophy to pass away? Probably not. He certainly wanted thinking itself and the presentation of Christianity in language and thought-forms to contain a protest against "the spirit of modernity." The beginning of neoscholasticism in the nineteenth century does signify, if superficially, a dividing line between two periods of Catholic philosophy. The first, engaged with the philosophies of its age, is represented in Germany by the names of Baader and Görres, Schlegel and Deutinger, and in England by Newman and William George Ward; in France by Auguste Gratry and Félix Dupanloup; in Italy by Salvatore Tongiorgi and Domenico Palmieri. The second period, in the decades before World War I, is generally less creative and characterized by the handbooks and textbooks, mainly in Latin, appearing in every country, most containing philosophies "according to the doctrine of St. Thomas" or "in the spirit of St. Thomas."

Przywara observed four kinds of neoscholasticisms flourishing from 1870 to World War I. The first direction he called *critical:* this was exemplified in the literal and textual Dominican school at, for instance, the Angelicum in Rome or the philosophical and theological faculties in Fribourg, Switzerland. Not looking favorably on the Platonism of Augustinianism or on the critiques of Kant, it criticized all other philosophical and theological approaches by comparing them to its own lengthy and clearly delineated tradition: Aquinas understood in light of the Dominican commentators through the centuries. It eschewed historical context in favor of metaphysical structure, and its drawbacks were a one-sidedness, an absoluteness of interpretation. The second, *historical* direction was begun by Ehrle's and Heinrich Denifle's research into the diversity of medieval scholastic theologies and mystical schools. The third approach Przywara called a *productive* neoscholastic philosophy serving theology and dogma by stressing objectivity and external reality in the areas of logic and theodicy, and too it might incorporate new discoveries from psychology and natural science into a neoscholastic framework. The *fourth* stage was dialogical and pursued positive conversations with philosophers such as Henri Bergson, Husserl, and Scheler. All these forms, ranging from an independently active neoscholasticism to a Christian philosophical apologetics, oppose in different ways the positivism denying metaphysics.

Are the structures of contemporary Catholic philosophy a living philosophy at all, or are they simply using a past philosophy for theological goals? Forms of Scotism after Aquinas depreciated creation or reduced metaphysics and faith to a too-personal mysticism.[73] Przywara saw, as few did, that Baroque and nineteenth-century scholasticisms were not the same as the theology of Thomas Aquinas. Those frozen expressions of Aristotelian and Christian ideas were in fact shirking their responsibilities to the present age. Aquinas is best understood by looking at the schools of his own time and not just at the neo-Thomist schools after him. Nonetheless, "a school is certainly the continuation of the master, but only for 'the one master, Christ,' is a school really his living-on in history. All other schools are more or less the dying of the master, a dying that takes place within the modest collection of problems which the master made his own but are now altered by the proud limitations of the systems built by disciples who want to explain everything."[74]

What is Thomas Aquinas' thought? Przywara's essays in the 1920s presented Aquinas and his teaching on grace and human causality. Like the great figures of modernity, Aquinas sought to join opposing currents, Augustinian Platonism and Aristotelianism (the one representing an eternal world, the other a world becoming). Aquinas, living and working between those two different systems, placed a sober emphasis upon intellect, nature, and act. Form and goal hold together a high participation in divine life and the realization of the divine love and plan in the free actions of men and women. The Dominican accentuated both a living God and a living world; creatures have their relationship to God, but they also have their own identity, movement.

If the creature is its own agent fashioning its own forms, the measure, however, by which God communicates God's self to the creature is determined by God: "the supra-creational God is precisely what makes possible the developing stream of creatures."[75] He is a thinker of multiple polarities: not only between Creator and creature but between nature and existence, between body and spirit, between thinking and experience. At the same time, Aquinas, "the thinker of balance" in his "apersonal silence and balanced simplicity," is a master at preserving the dynamic leading beyond the tension between creation and Creator.[76] The fullness of God's being and the reality of creatures' activity, the omnipotent efficacy of God and the proper causality of the creatures, have a supernatural as well as natural sphere of realization.[77] Human nature holds a preparedness for God and has the capability to receive the special revelation of God, but the supernatural is not deduced from nature nor is it an object for an activity.

In 1925 Przywara wrote on Thomas Aquinas "as a problematic figure," meaning in German not someone questionable but stimulating. At the turn of the twentieth century everything, even religious truths and values have been reduced to symbols. Modern thinking has been constrained from two directions: by a rationalism for which thinking has no history, and by an irrationalism for which thinking proceeds fully from life. "The real Thomas, in distinction to Augustine, is not at all the systematician who explains and derives everything smoothly: rather his final word is nothing other than that primal Augustinian *invenire quaerendum:* to find everything is only a discovery by someone invited to seek further."[78] Thomas could contribute some aspects for a contemporary philosophy of religion: the individuality of the subject, an active and insightful intellect, an immanent and transcendent God, revelation that approaches the human intellect.[79] Other essays sketched similarities and differences with Kant and Hegel. The moderns and the medievals agree in the activity of self-reflection, in a unity of opposites, in an interplay of the dynamics of the human personality. Hegel, however, viewed the developing self as God, while Thomas in both being and grace sees the self deeply referred to God but infinitely distinct.[80] A dialogue with contemporary thinkers, like a study of all of his writings, will revitalize Aquinas, will permit him to rise in a new way. "Thomas must emerge in a new, vital way out of a wrestling over phenomenology: Husserl, Scheler, Heidegger."[81]

Przywara found the basic principle penetrating Aquinas' thought in real causality and its consequence in the activities of nature and grace.

If Platonic, Augustinian, and Protestant directions emphasize that God is all, the Aristotelian-Thomistic approach presents the creature as quasi-independent, active being before God. The Thomist perspective of proper and independent activities of the causalities of finite creatures unveils a "fabric of actions" where the Creator furthers creatures' proper, immediate (secondary) causality. Central to Catholicism, central to Aquinas' theology and to Ignatius' spirituality is secondary causality, the effective activity flowing from creatures through their natures into the world around them. "Thomas' basic law is that of the *causae secundae,* and it is the untouchable heritage of classical Catholicism."[82] That is "Catholic radicalism," the fullness of God's being not diminished by but displayed in creatures' active individuality, "the supra-creational God making the 'becoming streams' of creation possible."[83] Aquinas wrote: "The more free is a creature the closer it is to God, the more it rejoices in receiving the gift of directing itself."[84] God enjoys giving goodness and being to creatures and is capable of the most intimate presence, enabling but not producing the existence and act of a creature. The concrete form of a Catholic religious mentality emerges from the conviction that nature and humanity, body-self and spirit-self are the creature of God and not the enemy of God. The sovereign dignity of human action reaches a further realm in the reign of God where, according to Aquinas' theological axiom, "grace draws nature to fulfillment." This fundamental proposition of the intimacy of nature and grace has a dual form, for it implies harmony both in the order of grace and of belief. "Grace does not extinguish nature, faith does not extinguish reason; each offers a new vital form of nature, of reason. The creature appears not as perfect nature in itself but as something which one can designate in an unusual expression as an existing-being-of-grace. ... "[85] The goal is not to have either a rationalized faith or a nature adorned by some extrinsic force or covering quality called "grace." Aquinas is always a thinker of incarnation.

How is Aquinas' thinking Christian? First, it gives an example of a philosophy serving theology but rejecting the claim to be revelation or religion. Second, various drives and intimations—what the scholastics called an obediential potency—open out toward the mystery of the supernatural. Third, in revelation Jesus Christ is not an unusual God-man but the second Adam, the new and ultimate graced head of the human race loved and redeemed by the incarnate Logos. "For the supernaturalness of the new heaven and the new earth is precisely the goal of the mysteries of Christ."[86] Aquinas saw the mystery of Christian revelation not initially from the point of view of Jesus crucified but from God present in a cosmic and anthropological sense through what is called grace. Still, the graced individual does not enjoy a direct, problem-free life but passes through death to life. In a negative theology God remains even as the source of grace, apart in the abyss of the night of unknowing, although the crucifixion of Jesus points to the ultimate level of this generosity, and not to an irrational faith. Przywara understood what many do not: what is fundamental in Aquinas is the supernatural order grounded in the plan and missions of the Trinity; in human history this becomes concrete in Christ and the events of his life, so that the underlying history of grace finds its concrete source and climax in the person, cross, and resurrection of Jesus.

An allied issue is the controversy over the supernatural character of Christian virtues and life. Some Jesuit theologians held to a theology where grace or charity elevates essentially natural virtues. Przywara saw things differently: the rootedness of love, as supernatural love, in Trinitarian grace. Christian acts were supernatural in sources and reality, rooted in a grace which is free and supernatural. The neoscholastic moral and ecclesiastical machinery of virtues more or less elevated by passing actual grace led to a neglect of divine Spirit and human freedom.[87] Przywara did not hesitate to sketch Aquinas' spirituality, although he recognized that its extraction from theology was artificial. Thomism is centered on the essentially supernatural, and we see it in "the religious face of the Order whose doctrine is Thomism, the Dominicans. It is the form of *analogia entis* in the form of spirituality, living on in Eckhart, Tauler, and Suso."[88] The Dominicans venerate the objective and the mystical. Aquinas resembles his later brother in Fiesole, Fra Angelico. "Both in their white habits, standing transfigured out of the confusion of concrete life, give what is specific in the Dominican friars. . . . The church presents the great 'common doctor,' as the liturgy says, 'in the midst of the church'; he has his own identity distinct from other doctors of the church such as the volcanic Jerome or the burning seeker of God, Augustine."[89]

The Jesuit has marked out his own position, his Catholic position. Bernhard Gertz describes it: "The young Przywara emerges with a highly charged consciousness of his mission, entering the battle ground of directions and movements coming from various positions struggling with each other to announce a unity of the tensions glimpsed in Aquinas and Newman, 'the deepest fulfillments of the true messianic mission of Catholicism into the fragmented intellectual life.'"[90] We have seen Przywara's openness to study modern and contemporary philosophies, to find great insights and great impetuses toward God and revelation. What remains is to find a key, a synthetic principle for immanence and transcendence, for the polarity of Greek objectivity and modern subjectivity. That would be analogy, and analogy as the divine permission of human and divine exchange, an analogy fulfilled in the Incarnation.

Through his university lectures, Przywara engaged the intellectual world around him and urged Catholic thinkers to do the same. The next chapter looks at Przywara's philosophies of religion, Christian systems of intuition and incarnation, of interplay and analogy; while not neglecting past thinkers, these writings are also stimulated by John Henry Newman and by contemporary German philosophers.

Chapter 3

Philosophies of Religion in the Service of Theology

For his lectures at German universities in the 1920s Erich Przy-wara summoned forth diverse sources — patristic thinkers and German phenomenologists — to offer directions for Catholic theology. His first books worked at drawing these sources into a system, a philosophy of religion. Composing a philosophy of religion was a popular enterprise in the decades around World War I,[1] and the following pages look at two examples of his philosophy of religion. Then sources are explored, three modern thinkers inspiring his efforts in philosophy and theology are examined.

PHILOSOPHIES OF RELIGION

Przywara pondered for forty years the dialectic of religion and culture. Who was to be the model? Justin Martyr or Tertullian? Paul Tillich or Karl Barth? Was culture opposed to religion? Or was religion the theonomous power of culture, as Tillich put it? Theology in the Catholic church should address the questions of the time; if this is a kind of modernism, it is a legitimate stance toward modernity, for the journey to express religion anew is not a road to heresies but is the path of life and spirit as it has been pursued by so many, by the Alexandrians, Augustine, Anselm, Aquinas, and Robert Bellarmine.

Christian theologians have interpreted differently the relationship of Creator to creatures, ranging from Augustine (the desire for God in a hierarchical cosmos) to Aquinas (respectful and independent life and service before the mystery of God).

Because modernity implies the self, a modern philosophy of religion begins with the activity and limits of the human person, particularly with the form of consciousness. Hans Urs von Balthasar wrote:"Erich Przywara lived in a time which was, with all its powers, interested in the world and the human person, a time of philosophical speculation for which world and individual were the reality and the theme, while God was at best a 'horizon' of the world's being, a chiffre of existence."[2] To think as a philosophical theologian was to contemplate forms—the forms of being, historical thought-forms—able to re-express revelation. The forms of human reflection are many, but, above all, "the religious is the form of thinking."[3] The human subject with its powers to create science and art, with its freedom and history, ought not to replace God. God, however, is not an ultimate rhythm of created reality but a different kind of being, an infinite source of all reality. Life with God is religion as the ultimate content-giving content of all contents.

There was no confusion of philosophy and theology in Przywara's mind or in his writings because he found around him no confusion of God's creation and grace. A Jesuit education as well as the Roman Catholic mentality of distinguishing before uniting nature and grace kept those two varied horizons distinct, while the theme of participation in divine life, important to Augustine and Aquinas, drew them together. Philosophy as a reflection on being and society could be the language of the expression of faith but not its total source or judge. The mistake of the modern period had been to take one side, the side of subjectivity, to the exclusion of the objectivity of the realm of being—even to derive from self and process the realm of the real. Modern transcendental philosophies, some religious, some aesthetic, were partly influenced by prior Christian teachings, but modernity failed precisely by deriving what little remained of the holy and the divine solely from finite consciousness. One might be interested in religion but not in the church, in the sacral but not in revelation. In his philosophy of religion Przywara affirmed insight and intuition in faith but argued against the unity of the holy and the human and rejected theories of immediacy; he always defended the transcendent reality of God (Augustine's "If you grasp it, it is not God," and, from Exodus, "No one can see God and live," are often cited).

Przywara's important writings in the 1920s sought a philosophy of religion. The early *Weg zu Gott,* composed from 1922 to 1926, worked to present that area as an attractive project in the style of the times.[4] The way to God is not a few careful steps along the lines of a logic but a journey through personal life; an implicit learning about God comes, for instance, from experiencing the love of parents. There are two ways to God. One is the inner reality of being loved, for instance, in a family or a community; there the person sees with the eyes of another and the lover and loved reach a unity. In a second way — Przywara had in mind the philosophers of life ranging from Nietzsche and Dilthey to Heidegger and Nikolai Hartmann[5] — the individual sees, despite conflicts and storms, the power and potentiality of life, and sees life leading to God. The first way proceeds through love, and the second through truth. Interestingly, the two central chapters of *Weg zu Gott* discuss not philosophy but the variety of spiritualities and mysticisms. The spiritual life is not simply external ethics or monastic liturgy but a unity flowing from a personal interplay of nature and grace. The varieties of spiritualities from one century or another offer a spectrum of views on the relationships of knowing and believing, of conceiving the Infinite and the finite.[6]

A chapter in *Weg zu Gott* on religion and culture recalls that this problem for Christians today existed also for Christians in the second century. A man, a woman is a being fashioning culture: there is nothing to fear from the ongoing production of cultures, and a culture cannot be a priori wrong. The human being as the image of God, God as present in all things — these are principles behind a Catholic understanding of culture. Christianity, because Godhead and humanity are unmixed in one person, the Christ, watches the stormy upheavals of culture with reserve and criticism and also with expectation and sympathy. The church cannot remain within one frozen past tradition: indeed, Christian root-insights for each culture can be found in the writings of Paul and John.[7]

As we saw, the lectures in Ulm and Leipzig had described how culture after World War I was moving away from the mists of late idealism toward realism. In the 1920s, Przywara developed his own *Religionsphilosophie* and published two forms of it. The first, from 1923, serving as a doctoral dissertation, was a study of the foundation of religion in terms of ideas and culture drawn from two focal points: John Henry Newman and Max Scheler; the second, from 1927, was based not on individual thinkers but on past and present typologies of analogy and grace.

Two figures, Scheler and Newman, would lead his first book to lay the foundations for a study of religion. *Religionsbegründung: Max Scheler—J. H. Newman* also gives a history of the development of Catholic thinking on fundamental theology, for the Introduction is titled "Between Scholasticism and Modernity." The reader is offered general ideas on phenomenology and the philosophy of values along with a survey of dozens of books and studies by Catholic philosophers and theologians as well as a look at philosophers from the German intellectual world after 1900. Countless authors of neoscholastic articles and books or philosophies of religion, some little read and most long forgotten, help the author to find a new foundation enhancing the active subject: the Catholic understanding of Christian faith. The book is largely a dialogue with Scheler over "Method and Summary," "Phenomenology and Reality," "Values and Feeling and the Independence of Religion." This is followed by a sympathetic discussion of revelation going beyond this philosophy of religion. To conclude, a Postscript, not a summary of positions but a constructive fundamental theology, describes "the new Catholic school of intuition and its historical background" in Augustine, Pascal, and Newman.[8]

New Catholic thinking lay in a return to objectivity brought by phenomenology and by an approach to revelation and church which lay in intuition. Intuition had passed through many forms: from Bernard of Clairvaux and Bonaventure, Anselm and Malebranche, to Schelling and his contemporaries who selected it around 1800 to be the center and climax of transcendental consciousness, and then to late idealist philosophies of life and art and on to Newman. Newman did not reject intellect but enhanced intuition, proceeding not from traditional logical proofs but from inferential reasoning. An observer of life and a person of deep faith, he is not enclosed in the mental structures of phenomenology and is not a captive of neoscholastic logic: Newman illumines modern philosophies of life. "At the center of contemporary German Catholic intellectual life is the question: does the grounding of God's existence for the foundation of faith find the old way useful, or should it be replaced by a new way?" A new phenomenology of religion was not to be a vague religious personalism, however, but was to help Christian dogmatics express what was given in revelation.[9]

Who were the sources for "a new Catholic school of intuition"?[10] What did modern philosophies offer to contemporary Catholic fundamental theology? Przywara focused on the contemporary Catholic convert Max Scheler. How had he come to view God as "the mystery of the world"?[11] "In Max Scheler there is an openness to God through existence in the world of objects. Husserl shows the victory of the recent philosophy over psychologism, naturalism, and historicism. Truth is not a formula for subjective processes; truth is recognized as something independent from knowing.... So it is not astonishing that almost the entire new philosophy of religion moves away from the old path of need and postulates fashioned by Schleiermacher's feeling of dependency."[12] There is a new realism, a new attention to the individual; if Scheler is too optimistic about the contact of his philosophy with grace and the Trinity, nonetheless, he respects the realities.[13]

If some reviewers thought that in Przywara's book neo-Thomism played too central a role, others were shocked at his overture to contemporary philosophy. Most, however, recognized an accuracy and a creativity, "the remarkable delicacy and inward perception of a thinker grown up in the milieu of phenomenology"[14] who could present Scheler in a Catholic light without distorting him or scholasticism.

In 1927 Przywara published a further study of formal philosophy of religion which flowed from and to Catholic theology, "A Philosophy of Religion for Catholic Theology." *Religionsphilosophie katholischer Theologie*[15] was commissioned to be a Catholic counterpart to a similar book commissioned from Karl Barth (the work was eventually written by Emil Brunner)[16] and has three sections. Its opening part treats in a modern way phenomenological, transcendental, and psychological views of the self. What gives people an attraction to religion, faith, and God? The question concerns not so much the metaphysical possibility of human religious knowing as the inclination of a person in the twentieth century to embark upon life's journey toward the mystery of God. All religion lies in a tension between the gifts of God and the human being as the free and knowing image of God; God works in this tension but remains outside and above it. The second part describes a Catholic "grounding of religion," a presentation of the basic principle of the analogy of being, its ramifications, and its entry into Catholic theology. Next comes an understanding of types of religion, types of religious sensibility. There is a Catholic form of religion, a Catholic expression of transcendence and immanence in church and liturgy, a Catholic striving and liberation. A view of God as "concrete self-communication" leads to the pages where Przywara links the analogy of being with nature and grace, the primal forms of

the Catholic mind. The third part of this philosophy of religion is a
typology. The analogy of being has six types, ranging from the Greek
Fathers to Luis de Molina, the sixteenth-century Jesuit, to Aquinas
(not to neo-Thomism), and those six types interpret the areas raised in
the first two parts of the system: immanence and transcendence, the
consciousness of the concrete self, the Body of Christ, nature and
grace, and the Trinity. The result is a portrait of how Catholic religious
sensibility disdains two extremes: first, an immanentism where there is
a real self-disclosing God but one located fully and solely in humanity,
or in creation's unfolding; second, a transcendentalism that is a static
worship of a god in an eternal beyond, a deity for whom the self-
changing life of humanity has no meaning, or is at most a negative
self-offering. In contrast to these, Catholic religious sensibility sees
God in the mirror of the surge of living creation.

As we have seen, Przywara liked to show how the explorations of
modernity in religion had ancestors in the past, thinkers living between
Augustine (the desire for God in a hierarchical cosmos) and Aquinas (a
respectful service before the God whose world consists of levels of created beings always touched by and seeking the mystery of the divine
being who is not a particular being). While a Platonic-Augustinian type
emphasizes that God is all, an Aristotelian-Thomistic one focuses on the
creature's true nature and proper activity. The Incarnation flows from a
drive to participation. "The ultimate meaning of Incarnation lies not
so much in a spiritualization of the corporeal as in a corporealization
of the spiritual; it lies in a complete and thorough penetration by
God of the spiritual world of the senses beginning with the Incarnation and proceeding in and through the mystery of the sacramental
church, and completing itself in the resurrection of the dead."[17] In
these forms of incarnation "God appears as the 'super-spiritual,' just as
after an analysis of the modern self and community God appears as the
'super-personal',"[18]—but as distinct from both the Absolute of German
idealism and the absolutism of a contemporary aesthetics of the symbol.

Heinrich Fries, later professor of fundamental theology at Tübingen
and Munich and a pioneer of new directions in ecclesiology and ecumenism, published in 1948 a *Habilitationsschrift* (done under the direction of J. R. Geiselmann) whose goal was to survey Catholic philosophies of religion in the first decades of the twentieth century. Like
Przywara, he saw phenomenology, particularly that of Scheler, as the
enabler of Catholic philosophies of religion and revelation that went
beyond apologetics. "Scheler," Fries wrote, "is in fact the point of depar-

ture for the modern Catholic philosophies of religion. In his rich, although fragmentary, work we find a cluster of directions commonly
used by all the new sources of contemporary Catholic philosophy of
religion."[19] The dissertation ends with the philosophy of religion leading into a fundamental theology: "a Catholic philosophy of religion is
a philosophy of religion within a Catholic-Christian existence."[20]

Fries divided the various Catholic theologians into groups: some like
Karl Adam continued Scheler's phenomenological method while
others like Guardini espoused foundational perspectives coming from
a philosophy of life. Alois Dempf looked at the sociology of religion
while Karl Rahner pursued existential aspects for a religious anthropology. Przywara was placed within a group called "the attempt at mediation": they fashioned a philosophy of religion of both/and, of polarity
and tension-bestowing unity. The Jesuit's interpretation of Scheler is
"the most positive written from the Catholic side." If some similarities
between Scheler and Aquinas are evident, a difference between the two
is that "the intentional act-object in Scheler is directed towards the
object of what is known, while scholastic thought goes toward the real,
existential, extra-subjective reality of the thing existing."[21]

As we have just seen, Przywara fashions a philosophy of religion
linked to analogy—Heinrich Fries saw this in the 1940s and it is a
theme of Julio Terán Dutari in the 1970s—inasmuch as the interplay
of being becomes the interplay of the tension between God and the
human person. But to Fries, analogy is not, in fact, a helpful source of
religion (it suggested to him the word "mediation"): it is too metaphysical and remote, not a thought-form of tension and polarity but a presentation of the levels of being, solid and independent. Przywara's interpretation of Scheler and Husserl does not always reach metaphysics
and analogy. "It is no real philosophy of religion," Fries concluded,
"but a philosophy of religion in Catholic theology and so a faith-
philosophy. . . . Through his philosophy of mediation Przywara sees surprising connections, but his analyses drawn from the history of thought
weigh down or alter frequently the historical reality of the positions in
favor of a polarity. Despite breadth and openness, here polarity is the
foundation (not always expressed but always at work) of a system sometimes lacking an ultimate respect before being, before what is given,
before what reveals itself to careful and laborious thinking."[22]

Published articles mark Przywara's subsequent lectures on the philosophy of religion: a course in the international seminars at Davos,
Switzerland, in 1929; a lecture to the Kant-Gesellschaft in Munich in

1933; a series of lectures at the Katholische Hochschulwoche in Prague in the autumn of 1936. Reviews of writings by Husserl and Scheler and their followers in the years before 1930, however, did not keep him from seeing where the postidealist movement toward objectivity was leading: Husserl was being overshadowed by Heidegger's existential ontology, his solitary, tragic existentialism. Could this new existential thought ground a further philosophy of religion, a new theology?

Heidegger's philosophy of existence and tragedy, detachment and patience, proceeds from being and time emerging as existence and personal historicity. It is not difficult to oppose a philosophy of existence to one of essence—such a dialectic can be traced back to the early Greeks and to Descartes and Kant—and that tension is not new, inevitable, or total. Existential anthropologies, despite what their increasingly famous authors presume, are not completely original. "The historical emergence of an explicit *existence-philosophy* lies in the relationship of Hegel and Kierkegaard. Hegel grasps ideal being as a dialectical becoming that takes place in the sphere of essence; the unfolding of natures and being, although touched by act, remains the highest approximation of a philosophy of essence. . . . On the other hand, from Kierkegaard comes a proper philosophy of existence."[23] Nonetheless, Scheler's insights are not expanded by Heidegger, and existence would serve other questionable theologies. Moreover, there are different kinds of existentialism: an objective one coming from the philosophy of life; a subjective one coming from Heidegger; and a third form, present in Bergson and Jaspers, focused on the tension and distinction between the human and the secular.[24] Clearly phenomenological existentialism is not materialism or psychologism, and time does occur in a problematical way, swirling around the subject rather than moving resolutely and chronologically forward. The Jesuit did not find Heidegger's thought congenial: there is a timelessness and an isolation in that existentialist ontology. Was Heidegger's end of metaphysics a new beginning or the beginning of the end after Descartes?[25]

Creaturely existence is a kind of becoming, and Christianity too is concerned with becoming, with fulfillment, with existence. Philosophies of existence (Przywara recognized Heidegger's Christian sources) could stimulate anew human understanding of the interplay of nature and grace, something new for a world dominated by the tragic, by patience before service and suffering in a world where modernity *malgré lui* had indeed exalted the cross. Today's challenge is to find a way beyond an existence caught between "tragic distance and ideal identity."[26] In terms of salvation Christianity makes the invisible visible, makes it visible in the schema of the human person. Over against the world of original sin seeking to be like God, in Christianity total God appears as total human being, crucified and risen. While religion is a facet of transcendence, it also lives within experience. Doesn't a solitary and anxious existence in the new perspective show how the human always includes the cross? Theology should conclude not with being but with the church, a church where striving and tension between being and nonbeing, essence and existence is "redeemed in the patience of service."[27] Przywara remained a lifelong critic of Heidegger while the next generation in Karl Rahner and J. B. Lotz found seeds there for philosophy and theology.

To look at Przywara's philosophies of religion is to find the Catholic dialectic of nature and grace approached through contemporary phenomenologies of intuition, life, and existence. Through Przywara's language Newman and Scheler give something new to Aquinas. Still, a philosophy of religion is not just transcendental structures but a description of what lies beneath the religious act. Przywara thought that in the first third of the twentieth century the philosophy of religion had brought people not to the void but to the basic forms of the Catholic mind: analogy and the interplay of nature and grace.

The search for a Catholic philosophy of religion continued throughout his lifetime, and a book from 1963 (drawn from lectures given during and after World War II) is a postwar philosophy of religion: *Logos* consists of four chapters on Logos, Europe, Reich, and Commercium.[28] Some of the typologies of the 1920s are still there; the text, however, is less concerned with phenomenology than with history; it is less metaphysical and more biblical and patristic. Insightful but without originality, the book links too many ideas and aphorisms as it reaches from the Greek logos to Egyptian gods.

CATHOLIC SENSIBILITY: THE ANALOGY OF BEING AND THE PRESENCE OF GRACE

The goal of Przywara's tireless review of philosophers and theologians past and present was to prepare for and fashion a fundamental theology, that is, a philosophical approach for the Catholic self-expression of Christianity in the world around it. He did not choose biblical themes but philosophical-theological structures, not axioms

but forms of thought, not religious metaphors but dynamic orientations present in being and knowing. The two most important are the
analogy of being and the interplay between grace and nature.

Analogy of Being

Erich Przywara is usually known, if known at all, as someone who
wrote on the analogy of being. Analogy is traditionally understood to
be an aspect of logic and language, a compartment of Greek, medieval,
and neoscholastic philosophies. If he were a philosopher of analogy in
the literal and strict sense, he would be a theoretician of epistemology
and logic, a neoscholastic concerned with theories from other neoscholastics of the sixteenth or the twentieth centuries. Not a few fine
studies have been dedicated to Przywara on analogy, and most dissertations on his work have chosen it as their focus.[29] Certainly analogy
is central to his thinking—it grounds a realistic philosophy of religion
over against German idealism and Protestantism—but his theory of
analogy is somewhat idiosyncratic.

   The term "the analogy of being" appears in late scholasticism, perhaps first with Thomas de Vio (Cardinal Cajetan) and then with
Francisco Suárez. During the neo-Thomist revival of the first half of
the twentieth century, analogy was discussed to the point of exhaus-
tion, dissected in neo-Aristotelian treatments of logic or summoned
up from the passages in Aquinas' *summae* justifying human discourse
about God.[30] A look at the indexes of journals of neoscholastic philosophy and seminary textbooks indicate how prominent the topic
was. The following pages do not compare Przywara's writings with
neoscholastic divisions and definitions (often removed from a Christian theological context) or with the work of figures from universities
and religious orders such as Thomas de Vio (Cardinal Cajetan), John
of St. Thomas, Norberto del Prado, or Reginald Garrigou-Lagrange,
but they let his theory unfold in its own theological mode. For
such Catholic philosophers in the mid-twentieth century as Gustav
Söhngen and Lotz, men knowledgeable in scholastic and modern
philosophies, analogy of knowing means a relationship, a mode of
knowing by which one being points to another being according to a
relationship: "The being of a being is unlocked or at least given
meaning through a comparison with another," and in analogy there is
"imperfect similarity through comparison."[31] The fact that two differ-

ent ways of being are called by the same word indicates a relationship and discloses a slight mode of similarity even within a considerable difference. An analogy is not a univocal utterance in which two words mean the same thing, nor is it one word indicating two utterly different realities (an equivocation), nor is it only a metaphor. In Thomas Aquinas' brief treatment,[32] the ground of analogy is causality; creation brings the quality of "attribution" he mentions. While the proper being and life of God transcend all human ideas, the divine creativity has left in the structure of being and in each existent real traces; the metaphysical and physical universe is a product of a divine artist whose mind and power are present in it.

Not only philosophical knowledge of God but clearly all knowledge of revealed religion employs human language and so is, because of God's otherness, intelligible and believable only within the framework of analogy. Language is drawn from the human experience of creation. Faith too can draw language for its message and examples only from this same contact. Thus the structure of being permits us to receive revelation, to know what the teaching about the triune forces of the divine Trinity would communicate. Thus human nature is prepared by its intellectual receptivity to understand structures of being and beings, to make conclusions about a Creator, and to understand the special message of a Revealer.

Julio Terán Dutari offered on the occasion of Przywara's eightieth birthday in 1969 a discussion of the personal background to his study of analogy.[33] At Valkenburg the young Jesuit would have had in his philosophical education classes on logic and epistemology typical of the seminaries of the larger religious orders. He received a metaphysical formation which was Thomist and Suarezian, a form of neoscholasticism which attaches an importance to concepts. Because of the influence of Suárez, so important in the history of Jesuit intellectual life, Przywara's education tended toward an analogy of attribution; this analogy of words reflecting different manners of existence and different natures is particularly grounded in that faint similarity of some reality posited in the creature by the act of the Creator.[34] This is in contrast to an analogy of proportionality where the proportion of common words used of Creator and creature persists in a verbal, but less directly metaphysical, realm, an analogy of terms. Some would say that the Suarezian *analogia entis* furthered the direction of similarity, identity, and even univocity, and that, on the other hand, some strict

disciples of the Dominican Cajetan remained within an abstract proportion of words disconnected from their ground in God's causality.
Regardless, Terán Dutari is correct that Przywara avoids the limitations of scholastic logic treating analogy and represents an attempt to
stand above all parties. Przywara went further: led by a passage in
Aristotle speaking of the "analogous as the mediating,"[35] he developed analogy not only as logic but as theo-logic, not as a philosophy
of ambiguity but as a theology of incarnation.

Przywara was drawn to analogy in the early 1920s because of the
difficulty in holding together subjectivity and objectivity in religion.
Contributing to the Catholic undertakings around him were Newman's analysis of the mind ascending to God, Max Scheler's phenomenology of nature and revelation, Joseph Maréchal's transcendental
Thomism, and Karl Adam's analysis of faith.[36] Where should Catholic theology go? He saw Rudolf Otto's numinosity and Scheler's values as attempts to revitalize Schleiermacher's subjectivity of religion,
while Karl Barth's theology, preferring an analogy of faith to an analogy
of being, had too little reality outside of the believing subject and
the biblical words. On the other side, Guardini's theology of tension
at the personal level might push the supernatural to the side, while
Heidegger's *Being and Time* had no place for considering anything
beyond finitude. Analogy offered a Catholic position in the contemporary milieu and a response to excessive subjectivity: Przywara's own
interpretation of transcendental thinking would be the best ground
for religion and faith. In 1922 he wrote: "God is not an ultimate, final
rhythm of created reality; God is the content and the reality from
which all content and all reality exist. Life with God is religion as the
ultimate content-giving content of all contents.... But God is equally
the content and the reality in created contents and forms and realities."[37] If this kind of analogy is obviously not what is meant in the
neoscholastic *analogia entis*,[38] Przywara thought he had found an "ultimate formula" of analogy in the Fourth Lateran Council which speaks
of similitude and greater dissimilitude between God and creatures;
this formula moved analogy from the logical to the ontic and then to
the theological, to disclose "the mystery of the one for and in the
triune God (as the highest and deepest mystery of supernature and
redemption) as, at the same time, the place where the most formal distance between the God-Creator and creation appears."[39] In short,
Przywara's approach is not an exegesis of neoscholastic texts, not a

logic, not a tenuous application of the same words to infinitely different spheres of being, but a metamorphosis of logical analogy into religious incarnation.

Courses given in the mid-1920s like those at Wylen in Baden developed *analogia entis* as the resolution of metaphysics and religion, the ground of mysticism and culture.[40] In 1926 Przywara interpreted analogy as human-divine commerce, as incarnation, as an interplay of the human and the divine in being, in Christ, in graced life. The "Catholic primal principle" is the analogy of being.[41] The philosophy of religion of 1927 presented analogy not as a theory of logic but as a principle of metaphysics with a variety of implications, not as a logic of propositions but as a way of looking at reality, a "thought-form," a "primal structure," a "philosophical principle not a theological form."[42] Analogy expresses God in and above creation's relationship to God, and all Catholic schools of theology and spirituality flow from this form of philosophy and theology, as does revelation in both Testaments. Przywara never tires of sketching how analogy appears in various Christian thinkers.[43] In the twentieth century, far from being a facet of language it replaces modernity's "explosive unity of contradictions" with "a unity in a tension of opposites," offering a total structure for the issues of philosophy of religion and of theology. "In place of the explosive unity of the absolute identity of the self and God or the absolute contradiction between the self and God a unity of tension enters, one of a relative similarity and a relative dissimilarity between God and self."[44]

The book *Analogia Entis* was published in 1932. Opening lines announce how Max Scheler re-presents Augustine's "God in us and God above us," while Pseudo-Dionysius, the dark night of Carmelite spirituality, and Kierkegaard speak of the divine in us as both difference and presence.[45] The original book has two sections: metaphysics in general and analogy (for a new edition in 1963 the first edition was enlarged by the inclusion of thirteen sections drawn from essays published subsequently, elaborations of what the book presents or theological explorations of related themes, essays not integrated into the text). Letting the worlds of Greek and medieval thought meet that of modernity, the author's "logic of analogy" examines both *meta-noetik* and *meta-ontik;* next comes a dialectic of "philosophical and theological metaphysics." The religious dimension is first drawn from creature and Creator—for Przywara creation would seem to be a central teaching of Christian revelation—and then moves further to consider areas of faith: namely, the axiom of faith (grace) not destroying but supposing and heightening reason (nature), the statement on analogy by Vatican I, and particularly the phrase of the Fourth Lateran Council about the dissimilarity in the similarity between creatures and creator (*quia inter creatorem et creaturam non potest similitudo notari, quin inter eos maior sit dissimilitudo notanda*).[46]

The section on analogy proper looks at analogy in a modern way: as dialectic and as levels of being. Przywara's dialectic, influenced by Newman and Kierkegaard, is not the stolid structure of Hegel where opposites eternally oppose each other, nor is it the dialectic of Schelling where all is resolved aesthetically; it is instead a polar tension of independent realities. In contrast to the pantheism of idealism and the theopanism of Protestantism, the relationship between philosophy and theology is seen differently by Catholicism: belief is grounded and expressed in a metaphysics of degrees. Analogy, defending all modes of causality over against the monism of idealism, centers on the interplay of divine activity in creation and revelation. This sets Western Catholicism apart. "It affirms a critical position over against the Alone and Exclusive of the theologies of the Greeks and of Augustine. This Alone and Exclusive leads to an identity with God, as in the Joachitism of the Middle Ages. The Greek version is the theology of the Greek Orthodox church as a supranaturalistic theopanism of *Logos* and *Pneuma* in *Gnosis*. Przywara is concerned with the version of Augustine employed by the Reformation and by Jansenism; ultimately it placed the paradox of the cross in the immanent theology of German idealism, modifying thereby the supranaturalistic theopanism of a divine dialectic with divine tragedy.[47] The exclusivity of reason led through the Enlightenment into pantheism, monism, or theopanism where there is no distinct God.

After that history of the problematic of analogy from Plato to Aquinas, the book reaches its theme—as its subtitle says, "a primal structure and a total rhythm." This is not an analogous logic of terms but a dynamic transcendental self meeting a dynamic Trinitarian Creator in knowing, speaking, and living amid reality. In Przywara's thought, deeper than analogy, linking the poles of his project, is the presumption of the creature's participation in what God gives. There are two moments in the underlying analogy of being. First, the human being is not God, although he is something before God (God is all in all but the Creator does not repress the creature). Second, analogy is dialectic, "an oscillation without end between two extremes,"[48] extremes not based simply on being (scholasticism) or biblical faith (Protestantism) but upon love and participation. With this, Przywara's thinking moves from logic to theology as he concludes: "*Analogia entis* is not a principle in which the created can be conceptualized for linguistic usage but one in which the created swings in its restless potentiality without being constrained."[49]

An oscillating tension between consciousness and being, "a structural principle of a possible reality-theology"[50] is the beginning of religious reflection, because it explains and emerges from the interplay of faith and reason, grace and nature. While philosophy explains how being is present in creation and affirmed of God, revelation says that we participate in the divine nature and are one with God. Both lead to degrees of participation. The metaphysician cannot neglect the Pauline exclamation that God is all in all. Thereby analogy becomes exchange, commerce, incarnation. *Commercium* is interchange, and incarnation is commerce par excellence. "This *commercium* is then the actual concrete reality of *analogia* . . . , the primal law of that order between God and creation; thus the essence of '*analogia entis*' is in general: 'Being as Analogy.'"[51] This structural principle is not about the distance and relationship in words between the divine and the created but about God enabling a realistic life in one order of salvation, a life moving through created nature, supernatural participation, supernatural redemption.[52]

Przywara did stress the divine transcendence. The human person is situated infinitely distant from God but in such a way as to pass beyond this severe antinomy, to resolve it in some way. The realm of knowing is also the realm of being and of life. Analogy's first purpose was to safeguard God's transcendence, and now its purpose is also to guarantee the creature before God. "The naturalness of the relationship between Creator and creation appears only 'in' the 'so great' supernaturality (of one historical order of supernatural participation and redemption), and it occurs within the relationship between Creator and creation where the always greater dissimilarity appears 'in' the 'so great similarity.'"[53] The analogical aspect of "greater dissimilarity" does not stand in a hostile, naked negation over against the finitude characteristic of German philosophy and culture in the 1920s. Non-similarity is part of the mystery of God, of God and us. The "greater dissimilitude" flows into the great similitude of incarnation and grace and Christian service.[54] In short, Przywara pursued analogy not as a way of thinking or a form of logic but "ontically and noetically," and both kinds of analogy, attribution and proportionality, point to something deeper,[55] an exposition of the structure of created being as diverse but also as participative in God. "Catholicism is a surrender to the mystery of the ungroundable God. *Analogia entis,* not a logic, but living relationship, implies a basic tension between love ('God in us') and reverence ('God above us')....Theology is then *reductio in mysterium.*"[56]

Tension and oscillation fashion the mediating role of analogy. "Nature, supernatural participation in God, and supernatural redemption depend in their true relationship to each other in the forward and backward of 'analogy.'"[57] Polarity and swing (*Schwebe*) fashion a theology of pairs: noetics and ontology, subject and object, essence and existence, transcendence and immanence, uncreated and created, nature and grace.[58] This enables a dialogue between Greek and modern thinking and opens Przywara's thought to the various forms of dialectic and ambiguity released by modernity.[59] "*Analogia entis* is in no way a principle that is fundamentally static from which everything else would be deduced or to which it would be reduced. It is essentially the basic dynamism in which the intracreated oscillates, as well as that which is between God and creature and which as intradivine is explained in theological language as the inter-Trinitarian relation of Father, Son and Spirit....Analogy exists as a primal dynamic rhythm."[60] Analogy is a metaphysics of dialectic, oscillation, and interplay between the human and the divine.

Analogy can include the mystery of the cross, for the finite and natural and created include suffering. Human freedom is the place of suffering and sin, just as it is the place of grace and glory. Certainly this approach comes not from Aquinas, Augustine, or Newman but from Luther and Barth. The cross is not destruction but creativity and revelation.[61] Thus the historical context of wars, the politics of aggression, violence and poverty, and the suffering existentialism of so many philosophies from Kierkegaard to Heidegger enter into that sober and abstract axiom of the *analogia entis.* The metaphysical nonidentity includes suffering, although the human abyss of suffering calls to the abyss of divine transformation. What should we make of Przywara's important principle? Karl Rahner wrote: "Przywara succeeded in transforming *analogia entis* from a narrow scholastic term into being a basic structure of what was 'Catholic.'"[62] Nonetheless, the originality of his description of analogy exposed him in the 1930s to criticisms from both Catholic ontologists and Protestant theologians. Neoscholastics did not find there the traditional logic of analogy, while Reformed theologians objected to an approach that would draw God and creature too close.[63] Richard Schenk has analyzed Przywara's theology of grace in the person by comparing it to the scholastic terms of the basic axiom of grace not destroying but supposing and perfecting human nature. He finds a hermeneutic that saves the employment of philosophy in theology, a mode of emphasizing limitation, and dependence on a philosophical theology of the cross, but also a one-sided, positive view of grace. Ultimately, he believes Przywara tries to do too much, to draw too many themes from his own formulations out of medieval theology; his understanding of grace in salvation history may neglect the de facto presence of sin and suffering and his understanding of human nature may remain on the surface.[64]

Since the 1960s there has been no lack of studies on Przywara on analogy in German and French, and those experts by and large accept analogy as a middle ground between Infinite and finite, between metaphysics and theology, between being and grace: their critiques are informative. For Bernhard Gertz, analogy—"no aspect is so frequently and so basically misunderstood"—is not logic or epistemology but theology, "an instrument of the Catholicity of thinking for encounters with the age,"[65] an effect of the divine Logos which bestows the plans and worlds of being and grace grounded in Christ. The primal structure does not remain a metaphysics or an abstract basis but is the horizon and point of encounter between God and the human climaxing in Jesus Christ. Przywara seemingly is not talking about the traditional logic of analogous terms but about a structure of being, diverse but shared, metaphysical but related; the mediating wing of the dynamic dialectic differs from traditional metaphysics and metaphysical theologies. Eva-Maria Faber sees his verbal formulas as moving from theory into an expression of dynamic and vital relationships.[66] Analogy is neither the "primal law between being as identity and as contradiction" nor "the proportion of mutual being-different in the swing of a circle," as in Aristotelian analogy;[67] it is a primal structure enabling the interplay of the divine and the human, an immanent synthesis which includes philosophy and theology, creatures and Creator. In this sense Przywara's theory is original and also carries the traditional area of analogy further.

Friedrich Wulf describes it as "the interplay of the infinite, inconceivable God who *is* Being with the finite human being subject to the process of becoming in a striving for God."[68] Analogy becomes participation and then commerce; degrees of being become incarnation, as Greek philosophy serves Christianity. Analogy was the name of a philosophy of the balance of polarities; employing and yet holding at a distance the movement and dialectic of modern philosophies, it sought to root them in the structure of being and to show their openness to and fulfillment in God's special presence to humanity. Julio Terán Dutari sees the sources of analogy in the dialectic of metaphysics and religion and in the complementarity of theory and praxis. Analogy is a kind of religious existentialism where freedom and personal relationship let the created subject act and know the realities and worlds that an analogy links. Analogical knowledge happens when the subject enters the event of freedom, and that primal event permits a metaphysical experience of various levels ranging from science through kinds of philosophies to theology that is a journey to the ground.[69] How this access occurs is explained by the transparency of finitude and its openness to being. Analogy is both a philosophical principle and a theological form, a description not first of nature and grace but of the total causality of God and the limited causality of the creature that has various forms. Ultimately metaphysics is human self-expression and theology is life; Christianity and metaphysics, through a dialectical swing where finite beings are transparent to the depth of being, do not lose their identity.[70] L. B. Puntel, however, thinks that Przywara confused form with content, ontic and graced realities with logic. What should be a modest, formal thread for all of being and thought expresses too much content. Finite and created being is not well related to the divine creative act that is the traditional foundation of theological analogy. Moreover, the negative side of creation is stressed perhaps too much, and the sufferings of two world wars stand apart from the system.[71] Recently Stefan Nieborak, offering a new look at this basic principle, emphasizes how Przywara explained analogy in terms of such transcendentals as truth and beauty, and in terms of the human person. He connected many aspects of Catholic theology with this theme: a philosophical teaching about God, revelation's view of God, secondary causality in creatures, the desire and potentiality of the human for revelation, the incarnation and a kenotic and eschatological unfolding of salvation, and ethics in terms of the future of humanity. "The special characteristic of his language as well as of his entire philosophico-theological project consists in the 'dynamic of analogy.'"[72] Martha Zechmeister observes that Przywara's thought and his book on analogy emerge from the vital personal and theological efforts preceding the book, and this thought continues in the difficult times and complex works of later years. In the years of oppression and war, and afterwards, does Przywara draw what is negative into the fields of grace and being? In his typical style does he then make sin, catastrophes of history, the cross, necessary to history, instruments of God, to be normal? In the postwar years he speaks globally of momentous historical disasters but not of personal failures and evil choices with vast ramifications. A later resignation in sickness over the course of the years after 1940 need not imply that he was critical of the past or found all change and progress fragmentary and ambivalent.[73]

What Przywara called analogy is a metaphysical principle of divine and human relationship enabling and describing Catholic-Christian faith. It begins with metaphysics and logic but moves to participation, then through the climax of the Incarnation, Cross, and Resurrection, flows into spirituality and ministry. The human person enters grace as an existential being whose knowing and desiring life has multiple analogical dimensions. This exchange of the human and divine culminating in Incarnation leads to a second basic Catholic principle of Przywara's thought, the graced person.

Grace within Life

In 1924 in the opening issue of a new journal from the theological faculty of Bonn, Karl Eschweiler, whose widely read book of the same year had described the two directions of German theology, the neo-scholastic and the modern, wrote on the "crisis" in scholastic thinking. Przywara, he asserts, is a true disciple of Aquinas, extending the medieval theologian's emphasis upon individuality into existence and bringing order into tensions, although he too is "an agitator of Catholic thinking, an agitator suited to the times and widely influential, dragging the concepts of the classroom out to meet reality."[74] He presents a synthesis of revelation and faith, a concrete form of Catholic religiosity where nature and humanity, body-self and spirit-self are the creation of God, not the enemy of God. This is "the untouchable heritage of classical Catholicism."[75]

Aquinas wanted to grasp the mystery of the world of grace through the categories of being and nature, and questions developed from philosophical categories are asked of the world of revelation. As we have seen in previous chapters, Przywara's essays present Aquinas as the advocate of the reality of creatures' being and action, individuality and interplay. "The human being is not simply openness into infinity, a split between body and spirit . . . but is a formal unity, a formal coherence of body and soul: a kind of infinite which is 'somehow all things' according to both sense knowledge and understanding."[76] The creature is its own agent and lives effectively out of its proper forms. "It is not out of God's incompleteness or weakness that he gives to creatures causal power but out of the full perfection which is sufficient for sharing with all."[77] The measure, however, by which God communicates God's self to the creature is determined by God. Human nature is prepared by God for God. Each person has a capability to receive the special revelation of God, but the supernatural is not deduced from nature nor is it an object to be acquired. While it is true that grace might seem to exist in order to remedy the inadequacies of nature, this is not true in terms of the totality of nature, of matter and atoms, for grace brings more than healing. Creation and redemption are processions *ad extra* enabling human action. Thus Aquinas' theological axiom, "grace brings nature to completion," has a dual format—it bespeaks being and consciousness, and grace—and implies harmony both in the order of grace and of faith. The goal is not to have either a rationalized faith or a nature merely adorned by something called grace. "Grace does not extinguish nature, faith does not extinguish reason but each becomes a new, vital form of nature or reason. This emerges not as perfect nature in itself but as something which one can designate, in an unusual expression, as an existing being of grace."[78]

Is this theology of grace also a theology of Christ? Przywara's answer presents Christ not as an unusual God-man but as the second Adam, the new and ultimately graced head of the graced human race. "The supernatural reality of the new heaven and the new earth is precisely the goal of the mysteries of Christ."[79] Aquinas viewed the mystery of Christian revelation not from the point of view of the Christ crucified but from that of God present in a cosmic and anthropological sense through what is called grace. The meaning of the Incarnation leads to the revelation of the generosity of God, the meaning of the crucifixion of Christ to the revealed ultimacy of this generosity. Similarly, Przywara's Christology is based upon that dialectic of God and creation, transcendence and immanence, where the salvific causality and life of the God-man are presented in spirituality and liturgy.

Przywara sketches the similarities and differences between Aquinas and modern philosophers such as Kant, Hegel, and Schelling. The idealists and the scholastics agree upon the activity of self-reflection in a unity of opposites. Hegel, however, views the developing self as God, while for Thomas, in both the realms of being and grace, the self is deeply referred to God and is created and enabled by God.[80] Clearly Przywara entered deeply into the theology of Aquinas and fashioned early on the dialogue between Thomas and modernity.

How is the motif of analogy joined to the theme of grace and nature? According to Bernhard Gertz, Przywara refused to choose between analogy as philosophy and analogy as theology. "It is simultaneously theological form and philosophical principle. The foundation for this 'simultaneously' came from the teaching of St. Thomas on secondary causality. On the one hand, the secondary cause is the proper reality and efficacy of the creature . . . and, on the other hand, *Deus semper major* precisely in its supernatural self-communication shows its towering greatness in that it leads and enables its creatures to their own proper efficacy and reality."[81] A Catholic active harmony of nature and grace is an alternative to the divine transcendence of the theologies of the Reformers and the pantheism of the idealists. Grace and secondary causality, however, are drawn not from analogy but from the ground of analogy, namely, from degrees of participated and absolute being.

Przywara was part of the movement of the first half of this century countering too sharp a distinction between nature and grace and replacing a two-story world of nature–supernature with divine life. He and others were seeking to overcome the separation of a static person and transient actual graces, to offer an interplay of the longing, active human being moving toward grace without compromising the divine gift of self in grace. Neoscholasticisms reaching from the sixteenth to the twentieth century separated the human person and grace. While Catholic theologians did not then teach that existence stood apart from grace, analyses, too logical and metaphysical, gave that impression, and textbooks asked about the degree of positive or negative orientation to grace existing in human nature. Przywara belonged to that growing group of European scholars whose historical and theological studies formed a background to the speculative and pastoral and ecclesial rebirth of Catholicism after the Great War. Ulrich Kuhn surveyed some of the theologians contemporary with the Jesuit, pointing out general similarities with Guardini, Rahner, Karl Eschweiler, and Gustav Söhngen. The liturgical and biblical movements and research into the Greek theologians of the early church supported a deeper understanding of Aquinas and led to the inevitable decline of the Baroque theologies of grace as actual grace and of sin as only personal sin. Steven Duffy describes the result of that time of insight into grace. "A revivified theology of nature and grace, one that would emerge stronger from the fires of debate [provided for] the needed theoretical justification of Catholicism emerging from its ghetto at mid-century and of its new openness to the world."[82] Grace in people affirmed anew its origin in uncreated grace; sins flowed from an unhealthy personality or society; nature lived not apart from these but amid them.

Przywara did not derive grace from existence: he was quite traditional in affirming that the personality, with its religious orientation of human knowing and willing, is the active, searching place for grace, but it is not grace.[83] Not a crypto-Protestant or a modern monist, he gives those positions clearly. Precisely his expression of the interplay of incarnational Christianity and modernity makes him interesting. Reason is not purely passive before revelation, nor does human nature exist from grace. A Catholic thinks analogously, that is, incarnationally and personally, that is, existentially, as a subject which is a graced man or woman. "A Catholic is someone who is not rigid but is thoroughly relaxed, someone of happy ordinariness."[84]

SOURCES FROM MODERNITY: NEWMAN, HUSSERL, SCHELER

John Henry Newman (1801–1890)

During his first years in Jesuit formation Przywara came across writings by John Henry Newman and began to study them. Recent apologetics and German transcendental phenomenologies led him to appreciate Newman. The Oxford preacher was a modern Augustine, an alternative to Descartes, Pascal, or Kierkegaard. In the Englishman's view of faith and personality, of subjectivity and life, there is something of the vision of such German Romantics as Schelling and Joseph Görres,[85] and there was something too of Aquinas' intellectual faith and affirmation of creation. Newman offered a faith of experience, a Christian life of belief, directions different from intellectual neoscholasticism. In his early book on "the grounding of religion," Newman appeared in the final pages to complement Max Scheler, for the task facing Catholic philosophers of religion was to fashion a philosophy including modern transcendental and psychological directions. "Newman grew up during the crises of cognitive theory, and they disturbed him profoundly, but his greatness consisted in struggling through epistemological problems to his theory of reality, and constructing the wonderful, probative system of 'converging probabilities.'"[86]

In 1931 Henry Tristram of the Oratory wrote that the German Jesuit "occupies the foremost position, and stands without a rival, having pursued an exhaustive study of Newman's works . . . to a degree little short of marvelous."[87] He singled out Przywara for separating the English theologian from the French immanentist school. Thirty years later, H. Francis Davis thought that Przywara "was one of the earliest scholars of our century to realize Newman's present contemporariness."[88] Through shorter and longer writings (Przywara sometimes cited passages in English like "Fear and love must go together" and "Not only do we see him at best only in shadows but we cannot bring even those shadows together")[89] and by setting in motion a project of translation directed by Otto Karrer, one of his Jesuit confreres during their studies,[90] he had an important role in introducing Newman into German cultural life.

A Newman Synthesis presented striking texts of the English theologian in a systematic arrangement with a preface by the editor: the book is not an anthology but a system, "the most recent example of my method of 'an immanent synthesis' (which I tested earlier with Augustine, the German mystics, the Romantics, Nietzsche, and Scheler)."[91] "The growth of the human person to full spiritual maturity is seen in three stages: *first,* the fallen person's path to Christianity, the apprehension by the conscience of God as giver of the moral law, and the perception of one's own situation as that of sin, misery, and profound need of God's help; *second,* a conviction of Christ as God's divinely willed and commissioned Messiah and Savior through the fact of Christ in his historical life on earth, fulfilling the Old Testament, radiating miracle, and living on in the church, head and body, one Christ: *finally,* a redeemed path, the way of faith which leads to the beatific vision of the one God in three Persons, the way of complete surrender to God's guidance and of brotherly love as a member of Christ's one body, a life lived from and in God."[92] The writings and addresses and sermons of Newman brought this program to life.

Only two years after Przywara's ordination this collection of texts appeared, and in the next year, 1923, the book comparing the Oxford preacher with Scheler was published. Soon the translations of Newman's writings into German were ready for publication.[93] Julio Terán Dutari's essay on Przywara and Newman lists the German's writings on the English convert: two books which are a collection of translations, the comparison of Scheler and Newman, and twenty-five articles and reviews. Przywara wrote not only on the area that interested him the most, the philosophical theology of the believer, but on textual and hermeneutical issues, on Newman's spiritual life, and on his similarities to other great thinkers. "The efforts of Przywara to understand Newman's position had a very clear opponent: the quite different presentation of him by 'Modernist' directions in France, Italy, and Germany."[94] The cause of those incorrect interpretations, he thought, lay in an ignorance of Newman's historical context; he was neither a simple priest nor a liberal detached from issues in the church.

Newman's situation was modern, having a certain similarity to that of Immanuel Kant, for Newman did not accept a division of religion into rationalism and empiricism, into a clouded mind and faith versus a powerful emotion and will. In his first writings Przywara sought a psychology of religion within the concrete, personal embrace of faith. Newman offers not transcendental forms or scholastic proofs and definitions but a process, a process of "how in real life one comes to receive the existence of God, comes to faith, and how faith in God and in revelation works itself out in personal life: the psychology of religion in the total breadth of its object as something to be pondered and probed."[95] No severe dialectic, no thought-form of opposition will do justice to Newman, for he thinks out of the both/and of Catholicism as he unites belief with empirical reflection. That philosophy of religion leads away from the frozen mask of empirical psychology which describes religion as one facet of the personality. "What Newman develops in his writings concerning the form of personal faith is not conceived in opposition to the objective and scientific grounding of faith but as the concrete and personal form of the content of this objective grounding in a personal life."[96] Content as well as form, revelation along with faith, remain.

The proliferation of phenomenologies of religion and moral values—had not Newman already pursued successfully the same direction? Polarity, interplay, intuition, an apologetics of experience, courageous openness and deep respect for tradition—these mark the British Oratorian. Newman must be saved from those who would make him into a liberal Protestant philosopher or a Catholic reactionary; he is a catalyst for renewing theologies old and new. Przywara saw Newman's thought as thoroughly expressive of the polarity between theological positions filled with creative tension, and as a leader out of the ecclesiastical ghetto. For "a new Christianity" Newman is "the holy church father."[97]

As we have seen, Przywara's first exploration into contemporary philosophy of religion compared Max Scheler with Newman: both have "a remarkable similarity with the basic characteristics of the thinking of Augustine"[98] and offer an access to religion different from that in Aquinas and Descartes, in scholastic textbooks or transcendental systems. "The system of Newman is the fulfillment of that to which Scheler's system aims."[99] The experience of God, proofs for God, the grasp of values, the nature of person and love—those issues Przywara developed with skill in the light of Newman. The English theologian offered two important steps, two anticipations of the "turn" on the Continent in art and philosophy after 1919: the first was thinking as a grasp of reality, and the second was the idea of development in history, that is, tradition and doctrine.[100] Both aspects lead to seeing nature and grace not as cause and effect but as intimate union.

Not a few sympathetic to Przywara have observed that at times he ascribed too much of his own perspective to Newman. Occasionally he offered the English convert's thought in the language and conceptuality of late modern German idealism—the British nuances and differences faded away—while at other times he let Newman appear in terms of language and conceptuality too decisively as a Thomist. I. T. Ker sees the German followers of Newman, from Przywara to Heinrich Fries, as sometimes undermining the Englishman's originality, harmonizing his thought too closely with phenomenological or neoscholastic approaches.[101] German scholars respond that Przywara had to introduce Newman as a Catholic but nonscholastic thinker, as a modern but not Modernist theologian.[102] Regardless, through gifted expressions Przywara found inspiration for a contemporary philosophy of religion. Newman is not just a practical thinker or a preacher gifted in human psychology or a literary stylist but a true

philosophical theologian, one of originality.[103] Newman experts point
out that Przywara's broad selection of theological writings was a correction to the view of Matthias Laros in Germany in 1922 that the
great unifying force in Newman's life was the priesthood: in fact priest,
thinker, writer, and preacher were different aspects of a Christian intellectual ministry.[104]

For several decades Newman was Przywara's stimulus and guide, a
point where the medieval and the modern met in contemplative dialogue. As we saw, at the end of the three lectures in Ulm, in Przywara's
debut as a cultural and universal thinker, he summoned forth Newman
and Aquinas as patrons for the mid-twentieth century. Complementing
"the monumental gift for clarity of Aquinas, Newman, the theoretician
of knowledge, reached to a theory of reality toward which today critical realism strives." The motto of "perseverance in change" furthers
Przywara's themes of transformation and polarity. "Must we choose
Thomas *or* Newman in this unhealthy epoch of the struggle between
integralism and Modernism?. . . No, the decision of this hour when we
stand at the high point of the spiritual crisis of our time is not Thomas
or Newman, but, true to the spirit of Catholic polarity, Thomas *and*
Newman."[105] Zechmeister shows how Newman's thought not only
drew Catholic intellectuals out of the ghetto but showed them a way
through the empty nothingness of some of modern theory and art.
After World War II Przywara still saw Newman as the church teacher
for a new Christianity.[106]

Edmund Husserl (1859–1938)

Edmund Husserl and Max Scheler were thinkers contemporary with
the younger Przywara, and of all modern philosophers they influenced
him the most.

From his vantage point at *Stimmen der Zeit* in the 1920s he reviewed
many philosophical directions, whether in a new edition of Schelling
or the latest book of Heidegger. Surveys of Kantian and neo-Kantian
literature led to his own book in 1930 on Immanuel Kant. *Kant Heute.
Eine Sichtung* stands between the pioneering work of Maréchal and the
Jesuit generation after Przywara of Lotz and Rahner, Otto Muck and
Emerich Coreth. Not infrequently Przywara disagreed with the interpretations of some Jesuit theoreticians concerning the best way to draw
together Aquinas and Kant, although he agreed with their project and

was enthusiastic about drawing modern philosophers into conversation with scholasticism and Catholicism. His "Kant-book," appearing five years after that of Martin Heidegger, reveals itself in its title, "Kant sighted today." "This [book] is not concerned," Przywara wrote, "with an individual presentation of Kant but with an encounter with his vital presence today. 'Today' is understood personally and means the today of particular philosophical directions. . . . The 'sighting' in the title concerns not precise research but a mediation of views, of sightings from living philosophical discussion."[107] Aquinas, a creative innovator of the thirteenth century, was not unlike the revolutionary Kant. "The *Summa theologiae* replaces the Augustinian concept of 'participation' with the idea of 'causality' where the Aristotelian argument from motion lets God appear not as the unmoved mover of movement but as the grounding—a primal ground above the movement."[108] Kant's Copernican turn to the subject actually sought a unity between reason and will, the empirical and the intuitive. In terms of religion, Kant presents an unreconciled opposition of two forms: the "God alone" of the Reformation and the Enlightenment pietism of "God in us." Aquinas is different: he places the subject in the hands of a God who does not exist mainly to be a religious object or inspiration for men and women, but lives as a God whose praise is the reality and meaning of the world.[109] Two chapters are long essays, one on Maréchal and one on Heidegger. Ultimately Przywara found in the pioneering development of Maréchal too much of a Platonism presented as a neo-Thomism, a philosophy too conceptual, too mental (too Kantian?) and Platonic. The link between eternal essences and the concrete individual world is weak, and so Maréchal's movement from intellect to reality, from finite beings to God, is incomplete and too solid in his employment of "is." He needs a dynamic suppleness, a further opening brought about by the analogy of being as Przywara understood it.[110]

Modernity has in fact chosen not the answers of Kant but has moved on to philosophies of Romanticism in the nineteenth century and philosophies of life in the twentieth. "John Henry Newman's entire problematic is first of all born from the question for which Kant could give no other solution but a tragic opposition, . . . rationalism versus life."[111] Not Kant or neo-Kantians but a further stage in modern philosophy had appeared: Husserl and Scheler.

Edmund Husserl was born in 1859 and at seventeen was baptized a Lutheran, a faith he did not practice. He studied in Vienna under

Franz von Brentano: former priest, student of Schelling, and teacher of Sigmund Freud.[112] Husserl published the two parts of *Logical Investigations* in 1900/01: it was a critique of psychologism and a presentation of logic and mathematics as a priori fields. By 1907 he was lecturing on "phenomenology," and in 1913 the "ideas," the orientations for phenomenology and the phenomenological method were published. After 1904 he was meeting periodically in Munich with a circle of those interested in his philosophy, and as professor after 1910 at Göttingen he saw the flourishing of the young phenomenological moment in promising students, among whom were Alexandre Koyré from Odessa; the Catholic convert from Judaism, Dietrich von Hildebrand; the Protestant Hedwig Conrad-Martius from Munich; Roman Ingarden from Poland; and eventually Fritz Kaufmann and Edith Stein. In 1916 Husserl moved to Freiburg where Stein gained her doctorate under his direction and where she and Heidegger served as his postdoctoral assistants. Stein worked with limited success on editing and arranging Husserl's voluminous unpublished manuscripts, although the years around 1930 did see the publication of studies on transcendental logic, the *Cartesian Meditations,* and essays on the crisis in European thought. Husserl pursued a genetic subjectivity of the self realized in layers of activities around the becoming person; a radical interiority but something more was manifest in a reduction of all phenomena, all real appearances grasped by the senses to a basic law of the spirit. A new kind of logic where things express themselves in a consideration of knowing and the known was a further stage in idealism, a turn to the object but within a transcendental philosophy. The collection of characteristics of an object implied an active subject and real objectivity; at the same time there was the quest for the essence or central form of that collectivity. These questions might be asked of religion.

Husserl's life and writings were concerned with *Wissenschaft* and its significance for human culture (his writings on mathematics, astronomy, and phenomenology had their implications for European culture). While phenomenology remained largely an analysis of mental structures and activities, Przywara found its pursuit of noetic images and essences to be more than Platonism.[113] What ended a century of transcendental philosophy was the quest for a movement of knowing and intending toward objects and realities. Knowing and truth come through experience — through an experience of something over against us. "Husserl means the victory of the recent philosophy over psychologism, naturalism, and historicism. Truth is not a formula for subjective processes; truth recognizes something independent from knowing.... So it is not astonishing that almost the entire new philosophy of religion moves away from the old path of need and postulates fashioned by Schleiermacher's feeling of dependency."[114]

As we have seen, Przywara's writings inevitably stressed the new direction coming from Husserl's phenomenology, the *Wende* toward objectivity; at Leipzig it was one of the movements composing "the picture of the hour."[115] Zechmeister concludes: "Przywara's encounter with phenomenology is certainly a productive and not merely apologetic meeting of Catholic theology with contemporary philosophy; it is the courageous achievement of a pioneer."[116] Phenomenology was a positive movement, because it moved away from the neo-Kantians such as Paul Natorp and Hermann Cohen dominant around 1900, away from Kantian formalism manifest in mathematics, some natural sciences, and logic, and away from the epigonic philosophies of the nineteenth century that were revivals of Fichte, Schelling, and Hegel. Husserl's phenomenology, Przywara wrote, "is thoroughly dominated by the *problem of truth*."[117] It is also a philosophy of reality, a reality of the world that is no longer absorbed into or neglected by late transcendental systems. Realism—he spoke of a "realogy"[118]—is hard and physical like the assertive opposition of a mountain or like the cross as the real end of sin or prophecy.

Husserl, Scheler (recommended by his temporary conversion to Catholicism) and Heidegger composed for Przywara in 1928 the "three directions of phenomenology,"[119] ways opening back to philosophies from the past but also serving as ways out of the mental prison fashioned by Kant and Descartes. Phenomenology is not so much a knowledge about something as an intending of something; it pursues the immediacy of ideas, pursues even the idea of God. Presenting the real more subtly than do historicism and physics, phenomenology has a positive relationship with and a contribution to religion. Its analysis seeks not so much a description of doctrines and rites as intentions toward, intimations of, those spheres. Although "phenomenology is not an inner-Catholic movement,"[120] still it brings a new positive contact with the question of God, God as an ideal, accessible to intuition, God not as a marginal question but as the term of a "religious comportment which humbly bows to a self-communication of God, something not a few disciples of Husserl, following the indication of their teacher,

have pursued."[121] If Husserl is the victory over psychologism, naturalism, and historicism, nonetheless the thought and intuition of the
self is still too caught up in the old idealist identity of absolute and
the thinking subject, too reluctant to give up the idea that transcendental subjectivity is God and to seek the highest transcendence in its
objectivity.

Husserl himself watched the religious development of Edith Stein
and other students with sympathy. He wrote in 1933 to the Benedictine
Daniel Feuling that he saw phenomenology as the opening to the
theory of the problem of God, the highest issue, but that he as yet had
no theology.[122] Ultimately Przywara found Husserl to be vacillating: he
was open to God as the term of the ultimate intuition but that realm
was never described, and consciousness remained the absolute.

In 1955, when the benign cover-up of Heidegger's political and personal fascism in the 1930s was widely accepted, Przywara was critical of
Heidegger's relationship to Husserl as a person and as a thinker; he was
the selfish disciple, quite opposite to the master, Husserl. He wrote of
conversations with Husserl in Freiburg in the 1930s after one of Przywara's lectures there. At the first meeting Husserl avoided the topic of
Heidegger as successor and heir, but "at the second visit, he sat opposite
me like a judging patriarch of the Old Testament and no longer discussed the one who had not stayed faithful, saying only that future
works would be critiques of 'him.' Heidegger responded to this judgment by refusing in the Nazi period to help Husserl's son, who as a
half-Jew had lost his professorship. This was the opposite behavior to
that of Edith Stein, Husserl's most faithful follower. And the Catholic
city [Louvain] received from the greatest master of a radical idealism
exiled by the 'enemy-heir,' Heidegger, the totality of his inheritance."[123]
The passing of the admired Husserl in 1938 Przywara saw as a kind
of Catholic procession to Louvain attended in spirit by the Carmelite
Edith Stein and in person by the Franciscan priest H. L. von Breda who
preserved Husserl's manuscripts by smuggling them into Belgium.

Max Scheler (1874–1928)

Max Scheler went beyond the somewhat epistemological approach of
Husserl and, drawing some inspiration from Nietzsche, Bergson, and
Max Weber, shifted the focus of living consciousness from ideas to val-
ues, from the true to the good. Born in Munich in 1874, he died in

1928. He taught in Munich and Cologne. Husserl's thought freed him from the rigidity of later transcendental systems, while the war—he viewed it in a highly nationalistic way—led him to seek philosophy in social life. As a young man he entered the Catholic church, and in the words of Helmut Kuhn, "contributed like no other to the emergence of Catholic thought in Germany from its isolation into becoming an effective force in cultural life."[124] He left within a few years of his conversion for what Przywara called a gnosticism. "Pzywara followed and identified with the wrestling of Max Scheler through all its heights and depth, 'in und gegen,' defended and criticized him, even beyond the grave—which Scheler reached through 'a happy misunderstanding' of a Catholic burial service in Cologne, a service that was a messenger from the kingdom of love and that found him to be in his 'torn conflict' a representative of a 'torn' age."[125]

Could there be a phenomenology, religious in an Augustinian mode, which would give exhausted humanity a foundation for existence? Opposing formalism and rationalism, Scheler emphasized concrete values with their content, values that went beyond conditions of what ought to be done, to individual and social values. That empirical realism is, in Przywara's words, an alternative to "the dead desert of Kantian regions and . . . to the proofs of a scholasticism poor in experience."[126] The modern issue now is: what is the relationship of feeling to norm, of value to life? "The particular inner problematic . . . lies methodologically in the accent on the correlation between 'value-feeling' (as an act or axiological noesis) and 'value' (as the content or axiological noema)."[127] So Scheler found the interplay of the ideal and the real as forces within society and history. The weakness of this project, however, lay in a fundamental imprecision. Did the subject have a ground for its values? Was the subject related to the concrete areas of existence and being? The decisive point or orientation in the dialogue with neoscholasticism or late-idealist philosophies, Przywara concluded after studying Scheler, was not immediacy or mediacy in knowledge but empathy with values over against the knowledge of being.[128]

As we have seen, Przywara's first serious philosophical and theological work was a book on phenomenology as stimulating a new Catholic approach to the possibility and theology of faith and knowing. A sign of a broad interest by Catholics in Scheler, it sought out what was valuable in the phenomenologist, contrasted the views of Scheler and the Jesuit author with countless writers on the philosophy of religion since 1890, and then developed a Catholic way of thinking about revelation similar to that of Newman and central to a new school of Catholic theology based upon experience and intuition.

Turning aside from the austerity of Nietzsche (and, later, Heidegger), Scheler found resources in motifs from the Hebrew Scriptures and in the New Testament's love, while his view of the holy owes much to a Johannine and Augustinian theology of God as love.[129] He spoke of losing oneself in order to find life and God, of humanity leaving mathematical reason to find intuition. He praised the transnational Catholic church and saw in it the ethos and means of the transcendent and immanent God. His thought held more of the atmosphere of religion and faith-morality than did Husserl's. In terms of a philosophy of religion, his phenomenology of values posited the certitude that there is a God, and he concluded in 1923 that "God and the divine are not a subject-dependent objectification but an object independent of the subject."[130] "Scheler," Przywara wrote, "inspired my lectures given in Halle and Leipzig during 1924, where I sought to move from the problem of God to the problem of Christ and then on to the church. This actual primal-Catholic aspect of Scheler, however, entered into a crisis in his work of 1921, *On the Eternal in Man*. He intended a philosophy of religion which would ground the relationship between a natural knowledge of God and a supernatural revelation in the religious act."[131] From that point on, in the Jesuit's view, Scheler could not find a firm metaphysics for love and ended up in "a gnosticism where the Body of Christ became 'the world-process' and where God became 'the ground of the becoming of human destiny.'" Nonetheless, Scheler's values held some objectivity and they, drawing all religion into their wake, culminated in love. Przywara drew Scheler's principles further into Christian theology: "It is precisely love as the essence of God himself which is the highest good and as such is the source of all values, and so all the values are grasped in their objective nature as love participating in God."[132] A central idea for Scheler (as with many patristic and scholastic theologians too) is "participation." This both draws his philosophy to the divine unity and is the source of its errors, its lack of distinction between nature and grace, and its vague location of values and feelings in person and actions.[133] Of course Scheler's thinking raises the issue of "the holy," and a detailed study (Scheler was preferable to both Ernst Troeltsch and Rudolf Otto) came to the result that God is not a mysterious realm of culture but a person of love. Ultimately, "moral and religious knowledge for Scheler is the ultimate element in the grasp of values out of love . . . , the decisive center of his thought of a person-love-system. It is a religious philosophy of life, of person, of polarity, and of some objectivity."[134]

Does his thought, however, begin with a loving God and end with a tragic God? This philosophy, Przywara eventually concluded, remains at more of a distance from God than does Husserl's; it risks enhancing the responsibility of men and women at the expense of the presence of God. Nonetheless, contributions to an understanding of the other, prayer and self-transcendence, and the transcendentally divine remain.[135]

How does Scheler involve Newman? Both flow from an Augustinian source and represent neither a purely idealist philosophy of religion nor a neoscholastic mechanics of apologetic arguments. Newman like Scheler "has a living process in contrast to a trans-subjective object of a process, but he differs from phenomenology's Platonic and a priori path by having an inductive and empirical way."[136] Christianity has a practical source and a practical result: it is not about ideas but a life. Thus the tragic, solitary vagaries of Scheler are a kind of opposite to the Incarnation and the Body of Christ. There knowing is balanced by its objects, faith by the affirmation of revelation and grace; and bearing and enabling the personal moments of faith is the God of love. God exists as both subject and object in each of us, present but infinitely transcendent, incarnate mystery. The new Catholic school of intuition is both a theology of faith meeting objective revelation, and a modern form of what has been called apologetics.

In the thought of Erich Przywara, the exposition of philosophical axioms and Christian doctrines is not as important as the reexpression of them through different styles of thinking. People and motifs attract his interest because they hold perduring ways of thinking. Theology comes to us through thousands of years in different forms: there is a theology which is philosophical and scientific, and one which flows from insight, engagement, description, all in the light of truth. He remains the transcendental philosopher inasmuch as he sees broad thought-forms expressing realms of being and ways of seeing reality. Przywara was intructive for the history of Catholic theology in the twentieth century because he was transcendental in approach but not

Kantian, existential but not Kierkegaardian or Heideggerian, historical but not Hegelian. Modern Catholic theology opened itself to
modern stances more or less at the end of those developments. In the
1920s biblical theology was emerging not as literary forms but as mystery and mysticism borne forward on the past waves of Romanticism.
There was a resurgence of history and philosophy but in a new sense
where both are intent not in competing with revelation but seeking
to unveil it. "In the twilight of European theology its primal form
appears immediately as the eidetic form of revelation."[137]

We have seen the influence of Augustine and Aquinas, of Newman,
and of Husserl and Scheler, all teachers and mentors for Przywara.
Now we turn to his contemporaries, partial students, friends, colleagues, in order to see the theologian in his particular world.

Chapter 4

A Theologian's Contemporaries

The time after World War I was philosophically rich, culturally innovative, and politically unstable. Erich Przywara lived amid those worlds: far from being a withdrawn cleric or a confrontative Catholic apologete, he sought out not only in books but in people ideas in philosophy and theology, directions in art, and the renewal of Protestantism and Judaism. He drew not only from venerable figures like Augustine and Aquinas but from personalities around him, from a theologian on the way to great fame like Karl Barth or from a woman seeking advice for an uncertain destiny like Edith Stein. This chapter looks at seven men and women from the twentieth century: partners in discussion like Paul Tillich, philosophers whose books he reviewed like Martin Heidegger, and younger Jesuits like Karl Rahner. The sketch of mutual contacts is limited to explicit mention and writings and letters, for the precise influence upon the thinking of such diverse figures is difficult to discern.

KARL BARTH (1886–1968)

Przywara in the 1920s, as he was studying the writings of Harry Graf Kesselring, Max Scheler, or Martin Heidegger, was also learning about the history and forms of German Protestantism. In some ways he was a pioneer in ecumenism.[1] A sign of his stature is the request by the prestigious encyclopedia *Religion in Geschichte und Gegenwart* to write for its new edition in 1928 an article on "Protestantism. An Evaluation from the Standpoint of Catholicism." Przywara was always clear about the differences between other religious traditions and Roman Catholicism: his approach was to understand, to survey, and then to abstract from theologians and theological schools what was distinctinctive. For his encyclopedia article he designated as contrasting areas between Catholicism and Protestantism faith, grace, doctrinal content, Christ, and the church. He selected Martin Luther for Protestant origins, and Albrecht Ritschl for the religious ethos of modern Protestantism. That mix of religion, culture, and national entity, he observed, was being modified by dialectical theology, by Karl Barth. Catholicism, on the other hand, emphasizes the content of faith and not just the existential act; its grace is more the indwelling of the Trinity and less a religious ethos; subjective concerns about saving faith versus objective actions of service in the church also unfold that basic difference. "In conclusion, the Catholic can only judge that contemporary [liberal] Protestantism is where the original core of a religious individualism has reached reflex consciousness, where the Reformation with its strict concept of revelation and supernature has been weakened by theologies of a natural religious life."[2] He pursued one of his favorite themes: human secondary causality over against the sole and omni-active God. The private nature of faith and the hiddenness of God further the Protestant principle that God is the only effective and important agent in salvation history and in Christian life. "Through a clear self-reflection on the forgetfulness of self in an objective service of God the Catholic sees the decisive difference over against Protestant religious individualism with its concern for the certainty of salvation."[3]

The succinctness of the encyclopedia article should not obscure the sympathy with which Przywara in those first years of ecumenism approached Protestantism after Bismarck and World War I. The sociology of Troeltsch and the historical system of Harnack, the academic life of modern philosophy, and a cultural Protestantism which had begun in the Enlightenment are being confronted by the contemporary crisis, as all those Protestant systematic theologies and philosophies of religion, histories of dogma, and refined exegetical works fade amid the smoke of World War I.[4] Troeltsch and Ritschl have focused on the idea of religion—its high form is Christianity—as the product and expression of personal experience.[5] Religious experience and state church, however, are no longer strong enough to resist being dissolved into philosophy. Nevertheless, the Protestant struggle remains: ultimately it is one over belief in the individual.

Two forces were vivifying German Protestantism after 1920, and the Jesuit was aware of both: Martin Luther and Karl Barth. The celebration in 1917 of the anniversary of Luther's call to reform provided a stimulus for early ecumenical dialogue in terms of a rediscovery of Protestant origins and identity. A Catholic reconsideration, a milder, irenic appreciation of the course of history leading to the Reformation had begun.[6] In lectures and articles Przywara's mentality differed dramatically from that of his Jesuit colleague of a generation earlier, Hartmann Grisar, in whose view Luther was neurotic, and even more from the earlier interpretation of the Dominican Heinrich Denifle, in whose view Luther was immoral.[7] Bernhard Gertz writes: "Encounters during the year of the Reformation anniversary, 1917, were mainly of a literary kind [reviews of the pertinent literature], although for Przywara's understanding of pantheism and theopanism and the consequences of the Reformation for German intellectual life [the event] was of enormous significance.... Later, the time spent at Schloss Stolberg gave opportunities for extensive conversations with the director of the German Evangelical Church as well as a deeper study of Luther, the influence of which is shown in essays on Lutheran justification and the *theologia crucis* and later in the chapter on Luther in *Humanitas*."[8] Gertz thinks that Przywara's understanding of Luther contained original ideas then not fully appreciated by others or pursued by the Jesuit himself, while Martha Zechmeister sees Lutheran themes modified by the study of Barth and Kierkegaard. Regardless, Przywara was able to recognize from his study of Luther that the Reformation was a corrective, not an independent faith and religion; to neglect the origins of Protestantism turned it into a faith rejecting creation or a subjectivism of the Spirit.[9]

Przywara was drawn sympathetically to dialectical theology in Karl Barth, Friedrich Gogarten, Emil Brunner, and Paul Tillich: he wrote about it in 1926 and took part in courses with Karl Barth in Münster. Was not the "new theology" of Protestantism in the 1920s a struggle over theology itself? Emil Brunner wanted to offer a true Lutheran theology, an interpretation of faith which has an objectivity that is not rationalism and that accepts a Bible and God beyond sectarianism. Barth and Gogarten may be effecting a deep religious renewal with faint echoes of the dialectic of Hegel and the Greek etymology of "dialogue." Kierkegaard and other existential thinkers inspire a theology where one is personally addressed by God. Offering Calvin's majesty of God and Luther's pathos of personal sin, it stands against the

experiential theology of Schleiermacher and against the barren historical theologies of Harnack and Troeltsch. If the appearance of his
ideas in Swiss and German Protestantism brings a critique of state
churches and of bourgeois moralism replacing revelation, Barth is not
simply a biblical prophet but a German thinker in the line of the neo-
Kantian Hermann Cohen. Dialectical theologians in varying degrees
oppose an identification of culture with religion and are disillusioned
over a cult of progress; they offer the pure reception of the pure word.[10]
For Protestantism this dialectical theology brings a deep religious renewal, as young theologians describe a personal God and as churchgoers understand that religion is more than middle-class morality. Critics of society, frequently sympathetic to religious socialism, recognize
that everything social and human stands under the sign of sin. The
age, too, manifests "a radical eschatologism,"[11] something breaking in
or approaching from ahead and meeting people who are on a journey,
on a journey surrounded by unrest and anxiety.

There needs to be a Catholic response to the times, Przywara wrote,
something like dialectical theology, something more than neoscholasticism. What Protestants view as particularly Catholic—a Catholicism
of holy business and simple obedience—is not an expression of the
times but a scandal, an enemy of the times. Nonetheless, there are
Catholic reservations toward dialectical theology even if it affirms
the majesty of God and a new openness to traditional dogmas.[12] Can
this restoration of Protestantism's proper religious stance overcome the
basic tendency to remove to one side where the believing self exists
apart from the world? Dialectical theology, because it is weak on an
objectified church, could lead to a radical critique of the present times
or look away from the present to the kingdom yet to come.[13] In
another article, Przywara wrote of Barth's prophetic religiosity and
of the Swiss theologian's agreement with Luther's principle of God
alone active in grace, "the sharpest expression of today's philosophy of
polarity and tragedy."[14] A stage of decisive clarification has appeared,
a reentry in Protestantism of Christian teaching touching doctrine,
church, and preaching, a reassumption of basic Christian teachings
which for centuries had been seen as exclusively Catholic, such as the
Trinity, the *Theotokos,* Scripture, and the authority of the church.

Przywara became friends with Karl Barth while the Protestant theologian was teaching at the universities of Münster and Bonn from
1925 to 1935. Born in Switzerland in 1886, Barth studied at Bern and

Berlin, Tübingen and Marburg, and published his commentary on
Romans in 1919 with important revisions touching upon dialectical
theology added in 1922. He taught in Göttingen, Münster, and Bonn
before returning to Switzerland and the University of Basel in 1935 (he
had been expelled from Germany for anti-Nazi activities). In Münster,
the young member of the Protestant faculty met Catholicism for the
first time: the city and the university were imbued with it, and he welcomed the chance to learn about a new world from members of the
Catholic theological faculty such as the author of a widely used three-
volume dogmatics, Franz Diekamp, and the prominent moral theologian Joseph Mausbach. There was a circle of Catholics and Protestants,
not all academics, who met regularly in 1928 and 1929, discussing
appropriation in the Trinity or the nature of evil and grace (Barth observed that Catholics never fully grasped free grace).[15] In Münster
theologians of the Catholic Romantic restoration like Johann Adam
Möhler and Matthias Scheeben were being rediscovered.

Barth invited Przywara to the Westphalian University to take part in
a "solemn seminar" where he could present everything he had to say
about the analogy of being. Shortly before the Jesuit's visit, Paul Tillich
had lectured there, also "a remarkable visitor." "Tillich's presentation I
found really rather light," Barth wrote to Eduard Thurneysen. "Behind
his framework of Protestant form, formed protest, and yet other forms
which protested against themselves — and similar exercises on the high
trapeze — there was not anything visible except his father-complex
and his experience of revolution. Still, he himself is a completely 'attractive' person, as the North-Germans put it."[16]

In February of 1929, Przywara arrived in Münster to give a lecture
on the Catholic principle of church and to take part in Barth's seminar, enjoying the conversations which continued outside of class. He
called those days a first dialogue between the churches, a meeting of
two "objective dogmatic theologies."[17]

How had Erich Przywara come to be invited by Karl Barth? In
1923 Barth learned from Eduard Thurneysen that Przywara in *Stimmen der Zeit* had reviewed Barth's essay, "Not und Verheissung der
christlichen Verkündigung." "A remarkably keen and extensive essay
on us from the side of the Catholic partner. It is interesting because
he makes the Catholic standpoint quite clear; there are essential and
insightful observations on Augustine. The writer knows what he's talking about. We appear in a good light even if our most proper concern

is not seen."[18] A dialogue had begun. In 1924 the Preface to the fourth edition of the commentary on Romans observed that in contrast to some Protestant theologians Catholic reviewers—he mentioned Przywara by name—"have, for the most part, displayed a genuine understanding of the point at issue. . . . What is the meaning of this fundamental, and to me quite unexpected, understanding?"[19]

Przywara's lecture at Münster in 1929 spoke of three components in the Catholic theology of church—Christ, church, and the Christian—and its final words praised the grace beneath the *gratia increata* of the invisible God, a grace of the church in time and of the Christian in whom Christ lives.[20] A Protestantism, too, defended the transcendence of God, the divinity of Christ, and the priesthood of all believers (could not this priestly vocation refer to the Catholic teaching of sanctifying grace?). Barth described the lecture as a work of art, a masterpiece (his public response to the lecture noted an inadequate defense of the transcendence of God, and a failure to grasp that participative grace and the analogy of being were paradoxes). After being shown corridors with pictures of former superior generals of the Society of Jesus (the university had originally been a Jesuit school) Przywara answered questions in the seminar clearly and without compromise. Both men proceeded from the dialectic of God's work and human work, but disagreed over its intensity of realization in liturgy and life. Barth described Przywara as "a little man with a large head . . . who immediately had something intelligent and to the point to say about everything that was addressed to him and about every subject discussed."[21] Barth called their exchanges "the first coming together of theologians of both confessions since the Reformation,"[22] and later in 1932 he had to defend himself against the charge that he was absorbing Catholic tendencies.[23] Przywara's praise of dialectical theology stirred up critics, too, some for his appreciation of Barth, others for his too liberal interpretation of Aquinas' anthropology.

Barth complained that Przywara spoke incessantly of the church and tried to explain even annoying aspects of Rome, and bemoaned how the Jesuit bubbled over with descriptions of the many presences of God's grace—"Munich's Oktoberfest might be in a sense the main church festival of the year."[24] Barth, on the other hand, led Przywara to explore the relationship between the positive anthropology of Catholicism (devotions and sacramentals had their place) and the cross of Christ, and also to see how ecumenical differences were grounded not so much in church dogma but in the theological mentality of analogy, an ontic analogy sustaining interplays of nature and grace. Zechmeister observes a deeper impact: "an essential relationship with the Barthian pathos of the 'Totally Other' related to the ever greater dissimilarity of the '*Deus semper maior*' over against all that is created."[25]

Only a few years later in 1932, however, in his *Church Dogmatics*, Barth wrote, "I regard the *analogia entis* as the invention of the anti-Christ, and think that because of it one cannot become Catholic."[26] Przywara found Barth's *Dogmatics* to be Catholic in its genres of history and objectivity, in its use of patristics, but sharply opposed in its theology to the analogical interplays of Catholicism.[27] Ecumenical differences should not be covered over: they were to be pondered and resolved if possible, and one principle that led to quite varied differences was the Catholic axiom that grace did not destroy but led nature to its destiny. Catholicism lives through concrete interplays of nature and grace and so stands over against the attribution of all activity in the realm of faith to God. Curiously the "theopanism" of Barth resembles an extreme eschatology or a mysticism of the East carried to an extreme. Eberhard Mechels concludes, "The point of view of Przywara in the conversations of the 1920s, and evident in a series of essays, changed, but the tenor of his critique of Barth's theology from the Catholic middle position remained the same: every movement away from this incarnational middle point ends in a humanization of God or a divinization of the human person."[28]

Did the Jesuit's perspective on what it meant to believe as a Protestant or as a Catholic in a dialectic of subject and object do justice to Barth's attempt to recover objective service to the objectively grasped Word? The Reformed theologian observed that the Catholic church was in several ways quite subjective, and that the ecclesiology of dialectical theology was in many ways objective.[29] In the Münster lecture Barth found the real opposition of the Reformation to the Roman church in the rights of the institutional church. "Only after many detours does Przywara discuss the basic question, namely, the question of the right kind of obedience which makes the church to be the true church."[30] Catholic self-dedication stands opposite Protestant self-assertion.

Przywara too spoke of an *analogia fidei,* one continuing the *analogia entis.* The analogy of faith is a method of understanding the different books of the Bible in relationship to each other, but it should not become a "pseudo-analogy of faith" which rejects all philosophical understanding or replaces the analogy of being.[31] The mystery of God can be explored by both analyses, although there is no question of substituting (as Barth does) a faith commitment and an arrangement of biblical terms, supposedly without any relationship to ordinary life, for revelation and the structure of being.

In the late 1920s Barthian theology was for a while attractive to a few educated Catholics: it was biblical and Christocentric, an alternative to liberal Protestantism and neoscholasticism. Przywara's critique of Barth is a critique of a God totally above human beings and creation. In the early 1920s he had written insightfully: "I should not view myself so forcefully as nothingness vis-à-vis God that I then make God the 'all alone' of my knowing, and thereby through a devotion to extreme distance create, in fact, an identity between us. The ultimate, albeit unconscious, impetus of extreme distance is precisely a desire for identification. The human person makes itself before God so intense a nothingness in order to suck God into himself and so be 'like God.'"[32] Did Barthian theological control lead to what it abhorred, to having finite subjectivity and finite texts control God? While it is true that God is free and above all that is created, God is also free to dispose of his own activity and so can create other beings and establish their ways of being.[33] For Przywara the issue is not the activity of God in grace alone but the freedom of that divine activity. Natural theology or theodicy should not be pitted against theology, for a third sphere of reflection governs them both: an understanding beyond the Reformation and modern idealism of how God is transcendent and immanent. "Metaphysics goes behind *physis* toward a real ground, finality, and meaning . . . , leading to theology and fulfilled in God."[34] Then pantheism and theopanism are avoided: both God and creatures exist. This ecumenical conversation was ultimately an argument over the legitimacy of philosophy, over the relationship of theology and the Bible, over Christ and the indwelling Spirit within the human person. "Barth proceeds," Mechels observes, "not like Przywara from a basic openness of the dialectical field of faith and thinking in its unity and differentiation but from a strictly one-sided relationship of faith and thinking in which faith has the priority and thinking follows behind."[35] For Barth there is no neutral thinking, only the reflections of either fallen Adam or Jesus Christ.

For a *Festschrift* offered to Przywara in 1959 Barth sent a greeting: "My meetings with him in Münster and Bonn, the impression of his astonishing gift and art for being true to the world and his church, not only to understand everything but to integrate it into his own ceaselessly penetrating and encompassing thinking and still to remain in an exemplary way Catholic—this remains, confirmed by so many exchanges, unforgettable."[36] Przywara's theology certainly showed the influence of Reformation themes.

PAUL TILLICH (1886–1965)

A second example of the conversation with modern Protestant theologians is the exchange during the 1920s with Paul Tillich. Tillich began his teaching career in Berlin in 1919 after completing two doctorates on Schelling and serving at the front during World War I. A student at that time, Adolf Müller, described how the hearers of Tillich's first lectures, former soldiers still wearing their uniforms out of need or protest, were won over to Tillich's vision of religion understood objectively and existentially. Tillich and his ideas were not the product of the university but of the war. The young teacher "stood firmly in the present moment with its overwhelming problems and was full of the consciousness that a *kairos* had appeared, that something new was coming."[37] He moved on to become professor of *Religionswissenschaft* at the Hochschule in Dresden and in 1926 published his Berlin lectures which had made him known in the academic world. *Die religiöse Lage der Gegenwart* was a kind of philosophy of religion not unlike that of Przywara, one focused not just on philosophy and theology but much concerned with the contours of German culture in the 1920s. It is interesting to contrast this work with Przywara's lectures in Leipzig and his books on the philosophy of religion. Both men appreciated contemporary philosophers, the turn of Husserl, and the differing reality and stance of the Christian churches at that time in German society. Przywara was more concerned with philosophy, medieval and modern, while Tillich's work had long sections on art and literature; Przywara offered a typology of philosophical theology through the centuries, while Tillich considered the contemporary presence in Germany of Protestantism, Catholicism, and Judaism.

Tillich's dissertations on Schelling, one in philosophy and one in theology, had been part of the renaissance of German idealism taking place in the years around 1900. "The philosophy of German idealism," Tillich began, "which was mocked by the nineteenth century and

almost became forgotten was newly discovered and attained growing influence: Fichte, Hegel, Schelling, Fries have followers. There are
various reasons for this movement: the impressive power of Fichte's
personality . . . , the greatness and openness of Hegelian thought, the
depth and aesthetic magic of Schelling's romantic philosophy."[38] Like
Przywara, Tillich found a philosophical key in Husserl. "The decisive
meaning for philosophy in the twentieth century came from phenomenology. . . . Instead of dissolving every object in criticism or posing the
question of existence and its conditions, the essence of things itself
is looked at intuitively, quite independent of the question of their existence. With the phenomenological movement a mystical element
has penetrated into modern philosophy.[39]

Tillich became famous for relating religion to culture as substance to
form, and in the 1920s he spoke of paths from culture to religion and
then from religion to culture.[40] Religion is challenged by and formed
by natural science, psychology, art, and philosophy. Religion has not dis-
appeared: it lies beyond the optimism of a Hegelian system shattered by
war and beyond the evangelical fidelity of the church compromised by
the Kaiser's Lutheranism. The monism of German idealism with its aes-
theticism and pantheism is gone. All areas of intellectual life and culture
are being touched by the relationship of eternity and time, and by
forces in the cultural sphere opposed to the bourgeois spirit. "Today's
religious sphere is characterized by its shifts to time, to symbol."[41] Religion is again attracting people through cult and sacrament (and, too,
through forms of occultism), while movements like socialism as an eschatology of future change have their numerous followers.

In a modern society, Tillich continued, theory and tradition rather
than church affiliation express a person's identity and independence.
Protestantism had joined forces with bourgeois society—Lutheranism
with a state church and Calvinism with economic forces—but
Catholicism is different. Catholicism, since the Counter-Reformation,
has existed in a defensive posture against Protestantism and culture;
with Thomas Aquinas as an ideal, its forms and symbols are oriented to
the eternal. "The Catholic Church perdured in a measured opposition
but this compelled it to be marginalized as long as it refused any union
with the opposing social forces."[42] Nonetheless, Tillich saw connections between culture and Catholicism. "There is a clear line back from
Husserl through Brentano and Bolzano, back to medieval philosophy,
linking contemporary philosophy with the refined spirit of Catholic

tradition. It is no accident that phenomenology exercises a strong impact in areas influenced by Catholicism."[43] Catholic Christianity does not succumb to monist philosophy or to bourgeois culture, although its basic inclination is still "to apply a medieval ideal to the contemporary situation."[44] Moreover, Protestantism, despite its independence and cultural context, is not in a good condition. Jews, like Catholics, are an unavoidable religious factor and group in German society; they would appear to be much closer to bourgeois society than to Catholicism or to church Protestantism.[45]

In 1930 Przywara reviewed Tillich's recent publications: *Kairos* (1929), *Protestantismus als Kritik und Gestaltung* (1929), and *Religiöse Verwirklichung* (1929). In those books the Protestant theologian had drawn on a variety of sources, ancient and medieval, while the vocabulary and dynamic reexpression of selected themes were contemporary. Tillich espoused "a 'prophetic critique,' i.e., a critique exercised on all that presents itself as an absolute representation of God on earth," on the church and the sacraments. Still, this dynamic theology, including its "religious socialism," displays a certain harmony between personality and grace; a secular harmony, a psychology or a philosophy of secular religiosity. All reality has a religious direction because God by nature is "directed toward" reality. This is ultimately "a religiosity of reality based on a secularization of God."[46] In Przywara's book on Kierkegaard, Tillich's interpretation of anxiety was underscored: more than a vague insecurity, it is an objective but drastic mode of knowing how one is threatened and can be for some a positive dynamic toward the true God. He contrasted Barth with Tillich: the former's negative transcendence over against the positive, fulfilling transcendence of Tillich's "*kairos.*" "Paul Tillich sees himself to be one with Karl Barth in what can be called the consequent radicalism of the Protestant teaching of mono-causality.... But over against Barth, however, Tillich emphasized something that one might be inclined to call 'Catholic,' 'the transcendent being as present ... as the being of grace.'"[47] Barth's faith is drawn from radical nothingness and incipient faith, from being seized by something more, while Tillich leads beyond protest and anxiety to the disclosure of the divine in history and life: this theology of grace in nature is not excluded by Tillich's thought but drawn toward it.[48]

Several times Tillich and Przywara shared a podium; for instance, from the twenty-sixth to the thirty-first of March in 1928 at one of the important cultural seminars at Davos, Switzerland. Davos (where

Thomas Mann found the inspiration for *The Magic Mountain*) was the site of gatherings of intellectuals centered around discussions between prominent figures. A presentation by Albert Einstein had begun the courses, the *Davos Internationale Hochschulkurse* in March and April 1921: the famous discussion between Ernst Cassirer and Martin Heidegger took place in March 1929 before twenty-four professors and two hundred and forty-two students from twenty countries.[49] At Davos, Tillich's advocacy of a theology of grace as more than the transcendental being of the late idealist philosophies of religion and his motif of theonomy resembling Catholic sacramentality drew Przywara's sympathy.

To some Protestants, however, such as the theologian Gerhardt Kuhlmann, prominent for his wide ranging criticism, the Davos dialogue showed that Tillich's positive view of the knowing subject finding access to the holy was not Protestant. "Paul Tillich and Erich Przywara were present to clarify the religious problem of the modern person. . . . Tillich breaks with all traditional, objective, dogmatic formulas and wants an ontological level which in its origins is also religious. . . . Przywara goes the same way. He did not begin with Catholic dogmas but with the analysis of a specific problematic in the human being."[50] Kuhlmann found Tillich uninterested in defending the Protestant view of divine grace and Przywara too quick to employ contemporary philosophy. "Przywara presented the essence of Protestantism, the sole efficacy of grace, and thought that this robbed human existence of grace. . . . [Tillich] admitted that in his philosophy of religion he presumed grace, and that the unconditioned threat of human existence is for him at the same time grace. In this way he in fact confessed Catholicism, confessed the teaching of the all-powerfulness of grace. The immanent consequentialism of Tillich's system here emerged in a surprising way . . . , grace presumed for the totality of being. . . . Tillich found himself faced with the strange fact that the Catholic Przywara had reached a full correspondence with the challenge of a theonomous philosophy."[51] Tillich in response to Kuhlmann said that he did not agree with Catholic theology when it offers an easy knowledge of God and neglects the demonic and profane in religion, but this position does not imply a denial of all human knowledge of God or of religious forms. There must be a knowledge of God "through grace" and "beyond religion." "Radical Protestantism, however . . . destroyed for the sake of grace the being of the one who is to receive grace — that kind of grace is demonic."[52] In a subsequent issue of *Theologische Blätter,* Przywara was invited to respond to both Tillich and Kuhlmann. He began provocatively with the statement that "the only Absolute is 'God in the church,'" a statement which does not mean at once papal infallibility but all that is visible in the church, all that gives voice to revelation, all that makes formulas and faith vital. Christians should move beyond systems and schools to seek the essence of Christianity. "I see in the writings of Paul Tillich . . . the polarity of ground and primal ground, a translation of the character of tension brought by the created toward God . . . a new emphasis upon a real revelation of God in time."[53]

In 1958 Walter Leibrecht, an American Lutheran theologian, gathered writers to compose a volume for Tillich's seventieth birthday and Przywara was contacted in Germany. He wrote an imaginative essay, contrasting Tillich's theological position on culture and religion (one of Tillich's lasting themes) with those of Origen and Luther and noted its sources in theosophy, Lutheran orthodoxy, and dialectical theology. Was not Tillich, Przywara asked (as he had at Davos in 1928), fashioning his theology from the line of Jakob Boehme, Franz von Baader, and the late Schelling? All three agreed that the transcendental self and the processes of nature flowed forth from one primal ground. In Baader and Schelling, God becomes truly divine out of the tensions of creation, out of the polarity of ground and primal ground, and out of the potencies of the godhead effecting a theogony. Idealist philosophy, theosophy, and Russian mysticism, drawn together by Schelling after 1827, influence Tillich's conviction that "the Holy must be understood as an intrusion into the realm of meaning whose abyss and ground it is,"[54] unfolding the godly God and inspiring God's logos and prophet, Jesus. A cosmic incarnationalism, an intense divine presence active in creation, history, and revelation gives Tillich's thought at first reading a rather "Catholic" accent: although Tillich has lived in America where too often "everything of dogma can be reduced to a 'natural religiosity,'" still the source of his thought substantially is "France and Germany, the France of Pascal and the Germany of Böhme."[55] There is a danger of gnosticism; even worse, of permitting both theism and atheism to be rooted in the divine ground and abyss.[56]

Przywara saw Tillich building upon a "Christian grammar" whose root terms are *kerygma, mysterium, kairos,* and *oikonomia.* In the New Testament and the Fathers, Tillich finds a Protestant dualism of ages and times: the time of Jesus and the time of the Devil, the time of *kairos* and the time of *chronos.* Tillich, in contrast to the early Barth, affirms an acceptance by the Word of historical and cultural forms. The fourth term of Tillich, *oikonomia,* particularly draws out Catholic responses. Emphasis is given to the activities of the Trinity on earth which enable and freely direct the history of graced humanity. In this eschatology God is not caught in a Manichaean struggle nor in liberal Protestantism's monist, secular history; nor is God's logos and prophet, Jesus, trapped in struggle and ambiguity. "For this reason Catholicism holds this Christian root-term *oikonomia* to be its most fundamental term . . . and sees the dialectical character and double significance of *kairos* as rooted in the ultimate Christian root-term *oikonomia* and [even] represented in the ordering of the Church through ecclesiastical office-holders."[57] Incarnation in time is the response to modern idealism—is this sufficiently present in Tillich?

Przywara did not object to a Tillichian theology of the cross depicted in Christ crucified, in Michelangelo's *Last Judgment,* or in Paul confronting Peter—they were all historical realizations of God's presence. "Here in fact is the ultimate root of the unsolvable controversy, the presupposition of this entire theology: the experience of salvation does not mean in the Reformation, as it does in the Catholic faith and authority, a prayerful giving over to God as God for the sake of God but means an all-decisive binding of God to the salvation of people. Thus all later development is set according to a strict destiny. . . . Because of the way in which the human person stands in the midst of Protestant piety, all apparent objectivism of Protestant theology ultimately appears as subjectivism . . . [and] as a general tragedy."[58] The dissolution of being in nothingness weakens the quest for an ultimate ground for culture. Przywara continued: "Dynamism knows only the racing, temporary transition, the primitiveness of an existence before the face of nothingness. Paul Tillich's philosophy of religion with its theme of being threatened in an unconditioned way is therefore the right expression of the situation: everything fixed is threatened through what is dynamic." After a brief reference to Heidegger's philosophy of the destruction of metaphysics and of nothingness the Jesuit concluded: "The ultimate and most persistent aspect of the Renaissance and the Enlightenment has collapsed—the ideology of progress in a straight line."[59] Tillich's theology was new and parallel to some more traditional theologies. In its appreciation of cultural forms theonomy recalls incarnation and revelation. But the forms of religion encountering the collapse of being into nothingness were, if a liberation, only a prelude to the response of incarnation.

Leo Baeck (1873–1956)

Erich Przywara became intensely interested in Judaism. He reviewed new publications and attended meetings with such prominent Jewish intellectuals as Martin Buber, Hermann Cohen, and Leo Baeck. Rather remarkably for the time, in 1923 he saw "ecumenism" having a wider form, the encounter of Judaism and Christianity.[60] Since the end of World War I Jewish scholars had been particularly engaged with the religious dimensions of Judaism: Buber furthered "a Western Hasidism," while Franz Rosenzweig expressed what was distinctly Jewish in reaction to Hegelian categories. There were important developments in Judaism (Zionism) and important thinkers such as Cohen, "the last great Kantian and the head of the last Kantian school, the Marburg school," whose move to Berlin at the beginning of World War I to be a professor in a Jewish institute was a sign of the new magnetism of Berlin. Furthermore, there were widely influential German-born Jewish intellectuals whose thought was independent of religious issues, such as Georg Simmel, Edmund Husserl, and Max Scheler.[61] In an essay published in 1961 Przywara recalled his encounter with Judaism; it began at a lecture he gave in Essen when two rabbis suggested he study recent Jewish philosophies of religion. His published surveys led to an invitation by Professors Gottfried Salomon and Franz Oppenheimer to a discussion in Frankfurt with such Jewish scholars as Martin Buber and Siegfried Kracauer. The conclusion of the discussion was that the Jew cannot speak of God without speaking of the human being. Przywara asked, should not the reverse be true? Moreover, did not the Incarnation make such an approach sympathetic to the Catholic mind and resemble Buber's theme of the realization of God in people?[62]

Przywara's survey of literature on Judaism never criticized Jewish practices or faith but, just the opposite, feared the specter of secularity weakening them. An essay of 1925, "Judentum und Christentum. Zwischen Orient und Okzident," pointed out a similar marginalization of Jews and Catholics in German society, although both remained unavoidable religious groups and forces. The Jews appeared to be closer to bourgeois society than the Catholic or Protestant churches were to civil life, and in some ways contemporary Judaism in Germany could be evaluated partly as a secular social entity. Eastern European Judaism, however, was a reservoir of strong religious traditions, and Zionism inevitably contained religious elements.[63] Przywara found the turn to the object, often mentioned in philosophies after Husserl and in Barth's theology of the Word, also present in recent Jewish thinking.

Przywara's writings drew from his appreciation of tensions within contemporary German Judaism, the issue of Zionism, the conflict between older ethical thinkers and the younger mystical ones, and the role of Jews in German society. Amid his surveys of the views of a dozen or more Jewish scholars from Max Brod to Buber, he reserved a special admiration for Leo Baeck, "the classic figure of the science of the essence of Judaism in whom the opposition between Hermann Cohen and Martin Buber is resolved."[64] Baeck was born in 1873 and died in 1956; a German rabbi and a leader of progressive Judaism, he studied under Wilhelm Dilthey. After serving as a chaplain in World War I he lectured on midrashic literature and homiletics at the Hochschule für die Wissenschaft des Judentums in Berlin until its closing in 1939. After 1933 he vigorously defended the rights of Jews and was sent to the Jewish concentration camp of Theresienstadt in 1943; after the war he spent some years in America and eventually settled in London.

In line with the many studies from that time on the essence of church or religion Baeck published in 1905 *Wesen des Judentums*. Against the presentation of Judaism by Adolf von Harnack and going beyond Cohen's presentation of Judaism as ethical monotheism he offered a transnational Judaism that was a polar reality between mystery and command, a product of life as much as reason. Piety is achieved by the fulfillment of the duties between individuals, while ritual observances are directed toward an ethical goal. Jews need to stand apart from philosophical or religious assimilation, for ethics must be supported by faith in God. Pondering Christianity throughout his life, his critique of it was clear and total. Judaism, a "classic" religion, is positive, activist and outgoing, social and ethical, rational and masculine, while Christianity, a "romantic religion," is passive, feminine, individualistic, self-centered, inward, full of feelings and centered on grace. Wanting to offer an objective contrast through a phenomenology of religious types, "Baeck speaks of Judaism in liberalistic terms as an ethical, rational faith. He contrasts this modern, German reinterpretation of

Judaism with tradition-bound Protestantism and Catholicism."[65] He kept his distance from Zionism, pointing out that the Jewish communal people did not need a restored Israel, for Israel existed wherever there were Jews.

In 1925 Przywara called the second edition of Baeck's *Wesen des Judentums* the best of the recent Jewish philosophy of religion studies: "the apologetic character that dominated the first edition was considerably modified in the second and the extreme rationalism was eliminated."[66] Sprung from "a classical maturity,"[67] it had similarities with Przywara's method: an interest in typology, a phenomenological disclosure of religion, a perspective beyond rationalism and Kantianism, and an interest in dialectic and history. Przywara saw his prized motif of polarity in Baeck's writings. "Judaism bears as its inner essence the polarity between being created and creation, mystery and law. Thus it stands on one side of religion as a revolution, an enormous change of dying and rebirth, and on the other side it holds firmly a religion of eternal unity. There is an opposition to all religious types which exist between a pure God of distance and a pure God of nearness, between the pure passivity of mysticism and the pure activity of work. . . . 'Salvation' is not a marvelous treasure which divine grace gives to people to be saved and happy but is a task posited by God which the person should fulfill and thereby be vitalized."[68] The polarity which Baeck calls the primal element of Judaism—"it is a religious reality and not a postulate of philosophy, not a sentence of a faith alone but the life of the human person"[69]—is also the basic polarity within Christianity.[70]

Some years later, in 1934 (in September 1935 the Nuremberg laws on the Jews would be issued), he reviewed at length Baeck's collection of essays and addresses, *Wege im Judentum,* describing the emergence of Berlin as a center of Jewish culture and of Prussia as the patron of Jewish spirit. "The new astronomy and mathematics and the rediscovered world of the Old Testament shook an epoch."[71] And yet, Przywara asked, did not Baeck have a tranquil nostalgia for the older world of the Ghetto with its visible identity? Regardless, Judaism is for Baeck the great reality that contrasts with Hellenic antiquity. Jesus was a Jewish ethical teacher, but through Christianity Jesus before Pilate and Jesus on the cross were transformed into figures of Greek art with ideal forms pointing to the infinite. Paul is a convert to Hellenism and Plato is the parent of the church fathers. Judaism, however, offers an alternative and resolution: unity-in-tension. Incarnation and grace are not necessary, because "the Jew has the power of conversion, can always make life new, can always restore the direction of life."[72] If Baeck gave a creative interpretation of Judaism as a fulfillment or alternative to the dogmas and sacraments of Christianity, Przywara's response is to say that this is too much a humanism, too isolated in what is earthbound. The Gospel is not simply and originally Judaism, and the Enlightenment unfortunately, too, often turned a passive Judaism into a humanism. For Baeck, Paul divides Jews from Christians, while for Przywara the Enlightenment absorbs salvation-history into the unreality of reason and humanity. Albert Friedlander writes that Przywara saw polarity at the center of the Old Testament and as an invitation to Christian polarity. "In some ways, Przywara, like Baeck, goes back to the early centuries and links the Jews together with the first Christians through a mutual experience of the polarity. When he comes back to modern times and the confrontation with Baeck, he finds the Jew divorced from this Biblical experience in which the polarity was truly felt as the transcendent entering into the immanent."[73]

Judaism clearly has a religious identity and a supranational identity for earth's peoples. Przywara is caught between arguing for the religious identity of Judaism against both secularity and Zionist particularity and foreseeing its mysterious future fulfillment in Christianity. Judaism can be transcended and drawn in by Christianity only through an unconditional giving of faith to the God above creation. "All other weapons will and must rebound off of Judaism. Everything else, like the old politics of the Ghetto, leads only to the 'forcing' of Judaism into peripheral areas."[74] Przywara wants Jews to reject what he described as Eastern and Marxist Judaism and Western and American-capitalist Judaism. Those who are on a quest for some kind of secular "Jerusalem" are deluded—Judaism is a religion. If its fulfillment lies in Christianity, such a Christianity would be a polarity, a bridge, a "Palestinian" reality.

In 1932 Przywara published an article in a volume of *Europäische Revue* devoted to the theme of Judaism. Among the contributors were Baeck, Jakob Wasserman, and Hans Kohn. "Jew, Pagan, and Christian"[75] presents themes from a Catholic fundamental theology affirming that earth holds no purely natural world, holds no nations or races untouched by sin and grace. One history of salvation unfolds, moving from the call of Abraham toward the birth of Christ. Abraham began a chosen people: they do not become an imperial power but remain a minor nation with times of glory and times of defeat. What does it mean to be elected? Israel at times deformed its mission of priest, prophet, and universal herald by pursuing sacral superstition and religious hypocrisy, but its religious mission continues. In the aftermath of Pentecost, according to Paul, Israel, because it failed to recognize the Messiah, resembles the pagan world in an existential way — not by being condemned but by being anew the object of God's mercy. In this article Przywara was apparently arguing against several interpretations of the identity of contemporary Judaism. First, he argued against the view, whether held by Jews or gentiles, that Jews were a secular group special in race or state. Second, he attacked the view that their identity as a chosen people with a Messianic destiny had been transformed into a secular, national or universal entity mainly linked to the land of Israel. Christ, in his temptations in the desert, is a witness to the end of sacral nationhood, priestly superiority, and national messianism. Every claim of superiority or of isolation is confronted by the metaphor of the Body of Christ.

Przywara's introduction of this New Testament theme is curious because the Pauline image applies not to the human race or to the Jewish people but to the local church. Regardless, Przywara expands the metaphor so that all human beings make up one body; all races and peoples, all individuals and periods are one. "The Catholic, as one who believes in the entire breadth of the Christian revelation, believes neither in a 'sacral nationalism' nor in a 'sacral internationalism' but in one God in one Christ in one church who as the Infinite One announces his infinite love in the undulating fullness of differences and oppositions — but here precisely in the mystery of the cross."[76] A Zionist state or a ghetto is not the essential or inevitable realization of Israel as the people chosen by God.[77] Przywara is not sympathetic to modern Jewish thought when it leaves behind Jewish religious reality, when it is too assimilated and too secular. The modern Jew can end up as a hybrid between the Wandering Jew and a Titan or Prometheus, endlessly striving, active without rest.[78] At the same time, the Jew who is the gift of a religious covenant leads to Christianity; in a general and remote way all religious and Jewish teleologies lead ultimately to the church, albeit a church of the future.

Anti-Semitism is something vulgar and destructive. Judaism should not summon up fears of its own particularity but banish them. Przywara ridiculed "all the ordinary anti-Semitisms with all their grotesque

deformations....They are in fact admissions of apostasies and deform-
ing losses in Christianity."[79] He observes frequently that sectarian hos-
tility to Judaism is paradoxically strange: In reality the Jewish people
are the enemy of every race-particularity and the friend of all reduc-
tions of the barriers between peoples. Baeck referred to the Jew as the
great nonconformist in history, the great dissenter.[80] "Because the goal
which it has to offer humanity is always, more or less, simply proper
Jewish humanity, so every people must sense Judaism in the long run
to be something like an invading disruption of its peoplehood. Thus
Judaism is the antithesis of every *Volk*."[81] Hatred of Jews in the history
of the world is basically the inevitable destiny of "Ahasver," the wandering Jew, a hatred that has placed itself in the place of the transcre-
ational God."[82] Christianity fails before Judaism when it forgets its
vocation of human unity, but without "fulfilling itself" in Christianity
Judaism will remain the Ahasver of world history. Moreover, for
Przywara, inner Christian divisions flow from "the primal tearing separation between Judaism and Christianity which can be resolved only
through a movement toward unity in history which leads to the ground
of all ultimate grounds, God himself . . . where God becomes all in
all."[83] In short the history and Scripture of the Jews contains the primal polarity of God and humanity, but that people run the risk of forgetting one side, false directions countered by the Incarnation. The
Jesuit's language is dialectical and symbolic, wanting to preserve Jewish
identity in history but within a Christianity that also strives toward the
Jewish reality. The message of the Letter to the Romans of the lasting
redemption and vocation of Israel has the last word. Friedlander, in
his study of Leo Baeck, concludes perceptively: "The facts of German history in the two decades that follow this statement cast a dark
shadow over some aspects of it; they need not blind us to Przywara's
very real attempt to come to terms with a Judaism that did, indeed,
stand in ultimate opposition to what he believed and taught. It was not
only Baeck whom he opposed.... Przywara gives his full assent to the
description of polarity as the essence of religious life. But in his assessment of the religious enterprise, the stress must ultimately be upon the
mystery, to the point of surrendering to it in order to break out of the
immanent and its limitations. In Baeck he finds the exposition of a polarity that ultimately places its emphasis upon the commandment, upon
the enlargement of the possibilities contained in the immanent so that
it can open itself to the transcendent as the place of the messianic
age....The deeper the understanding, the deeper the opposition; in a

way, the sharpness of Przywara's attack is a testimony to the strength of Baeck's position."[84]

The many sermons delivered by Przywara in Munich and Vienna in 1943 and 1944, when published in 1956, were given the theme and title of the old and new covenants, *Alter und Neuer Bund*.[85] The sermons emphasize the lasting import of the Jewish scriptures, a modest counter to the Nazi policies. His argumentation is not one of supersession but of complementarity, not of one salvation-history flowing into the other, but of biblical themes expressed philosophically, historically, and psychologically for men and women living through a disaster. The two covenants are similar and complement each other. Prophecy and law and incarnation and ritual are found in both religious realms and one contemplates their deep religious meaning. The Hebrew scriptures offer questions, prophecies, and antitypes that make the revelation of the New Covenant intelligible. Underneath is the theme of God's attracting love for human beings. After World War II did Przywara see the Jewish catastrophe in its true prominence or was the Holocaust part of the multiple collapse of past culture, of Christian Europe? Wilhelmy reports that "Przywara worked again extensively with Jewish theology as he prepared the books *Mensch* and *Logos* for which he worked through all the volumes of the Talmud and studied all of classical Jewish philosophy and theology."[86]

EDITH STEIN (1891–1942)

A striking example of how Erich Przywara influenced a variety of people, young and old, struggling believers or recognized scholars, is Edith Stein. Stein was the eleventh child in her family (four were already dead when she was born two years after Przywara in 1891), and her father died when she was two. While she was studying at the University of Breslau, a professor of psychology enthusiastically recommended to her the works of Husserl: "Forget that other stuff and read this [the *Logische Untersuchungen*]." Attracted by the new approach of Husserl, she left Breslau for the University of Göttingen ("dear old Göttingen," she later wrote "springtime of the phenomenological school"), and then in 1916 moved on with Husserl to Freiburg im Breisgau.[87]

Husserl's phenomenology remained aloof from church and doctrine and yet influenced theories of religion in a general way through the widely celebrated turn to "the things themselves." Stein wrote of a turn away from the style in modern philosophy of thinking as criticism, a turn to the great traditions of the *philosophia perennis*. Skepticism in its psychological and historical forms was found wanting and philosophers were again sketching a formal ontology.[88] Phenomenological circles played an important role in the religious renewal of the early twentieth century, leading not directly to religious things but to an experienced horizon or realm of the sacred. Faith and mysticism, like the aesthetic gaze and the liturgical symbol, engage intuition. There were converts to Protestantism from Judaism (Adolf Reinach), Jewish converts to Catholicism (Edith Stein, Max Scheler, and Dietrich von Hildebrand), and devout Protestants (Hedwig Conrad-Martius). Husserl observed: "My philosophical effect has something remarkably revolutionary about it: Protestants become Catholics; Catholics become Protestants. But I have no intention of furthering either . . . , just a radical, uncomplicated way of thinking."[89]

Receiving at Freiburg the doctorate *summa cum laude* with a dissertation on the phenomenology of empathy, Stein became for a while a special assistant to Husserl: "Your work pleases me more and more; in fact it is outstanding; actually you are a very smart girl."[90] The entrance to a German university position was gained by a second dissertation, the *Habilitation,* but at that time no university would permit a woman to pursue the advanced degree, and Husserl, incapable of considering the idea of women as professors, did not support her vocational quest. In June of 1918 she wrote to Roman Ingarden: "This evening I went to Husserl in order to discuss your work with him. But on the doorstep I met the little Heidegger, so the three of us took a long walk — very nice — and talked about the philosophy of religion."[91] Przywara recalled: "There was certainly, if one can express it in this way, a charm in her intellectual being, something which so attracted her teacher and professor, Husserl, that he did not find her conversion an infidelity. Rather in the Catholic philosophy of Edith Stein he saw the pure incorporation of his ideas . . . [and hoped] that the Catholic church would emerge as the heir of his philosophy."[92] Stein was aware of the religious quest within her and had visited Catholic monasteries. In the summer of 1921 while visiting her Protestant friend Hedwig Conrad-Martius, a companion in phenomenological journeys, she randomly took down and read through the night the autobiography of Teresa of Avila: in the morning she decided to enter the church. On January 1, 1922, she was baptized. Przywara, however, reported a different turning point. "We were walking along the bank of the Rhein in Speyer when she told me that while still an atheist she found in the bookstore she frequented a copy of the *Spiritual Exercises*. It interested her first only as a study of psychology but she quickly realized that it was not something to read but to do. So as an atheist, she made, along with the little book, the long retreat and finished the thirty days with the decision to convert."[93]

Without prospects for a university position she taught German and history in the Dominican sisters' *Gymnasium* from 1923 to 1931 and lectured around Germany on the vocation and freedom of women. In 1934 she entered the Carmelites at Cologne and after fleeing to a Carmel in Holland in 1942 was arrested with her sister by the Nazis — they had been angered by a defense of the Jews recently published by Dutch bishops — and both were sent to Auschwitz. One might ask, what would her life and her philosophy have been if she had found a university position? What would her thought have been if she had stayed within phenomenology and not shifted her interests to John of the Cross and Aquinas? What changes in the church, theology, and the American Catholic Church would she have furthered, if after the seizure of power by Hitler she, like Paul Tillich or Dietrich von Hildebrand, had fled to America?

It was Dietrich von Hildebrand (1889–1977), son of the famous sculptor, disciple of Husserl, professor in Munich and early anti-Nazi, who first mentioned Erich Przywara to Edith Stein.[94] After 1925 they met and exchanged letters and visits over the next six years. It was the Jesuit, only two years older, who suggested that she write about her life in a Jewish family.[95] Przywara noted that he came to know Edith Stein at the time when he was "preparing with Daniel Feuling and Dietrich von Hildebrand a complete edition of the works of Newman in German. Von Hildebrand said to me at once that he wanted Edith Stein to work on the most important texts."[96] Przywara, already the author of two books on Newman — a collection of texts, and a philosophy of religion drawn from the English thinker — outlined the kind of translation he envisaged, advocating what he called a style of controlled liberalism that would keep something of Newman's word-order and stylistic rhythm. "She understood what I wanted and in fact fashioned a wonderful translation of the letters of the Anglican period."[97] That German edition of excerpts from letters and diaries of the Anglican years was published in 1928 (published, according to Przywara, by a

small publishing house because larger ones ignored it).[98] Apparently she
also translated *The Idea of a University*, which never appeared.[99]

She sought Przywara's advice on the direction of her interests
and accepted a further suggestion that she translate into German the
Quaestiones disputatae de veritate of Thomas Aquinas. This occupied her
from 1925 to 1929, time stolen from teaching, and the two volumes —
the handwritten manuscript had 2,400 pages — appeared in 1931. The
thought of Aquinas was not well known to her; she struggled to learn
a method different from that of phenomenology without depreciat-
ing either. Her mind was obviously not, as she put it, "a *tabula rasa*,"
and "the two philosophical worlds called for an encounter with each
other."[100] The great founder of medieval studies, Martin Grabmann,
wrote an introduction to the *De Veritate*. He noted how all great works
of philosophy have the same goal, the service of truth, and spoke of
the translation's display "of the language of contemporary philosophy
joined to a study of the thought-world of scholasticism,"[101] a translation by a gifted student of phenomenology but faithful to Aquinas, a
translation into real German where the words themselves mediated
between thinkers, something which is "for one who attempts it very
difficult."[102] Przywara evaluated the German version in *Stimmen der
Zeit* as successful in including a real "Thomas Aquinas in German" and
"the vitality of contemporary philosophizing." "German Catholic philosophy will hopefully realize that here in a dialogue between Husserl
and Aquinas a new way has been opened."[103] Critics described the German text as modern in its expression, although many agreed that it
contained an original, distinguished conversation between medieval
and modern thought.

Przywara asked her advice on his study, *Analogia Entis*. Wilhelmy nar-
rates: "This was a time of frequent intellectual contacts with Edith Stein
to whom he often showed his drafts to get her views. She must have
been a strict censor, for with the last draft he gave it directly to the
printer. When she received a copy of the book, she observed: 'The second part should have been the first, and the first the second.'"[104] In her
"Vorwort" to *Endliches und Ewiges Sein*, "a book written by one learning for co-learners," she inquired into the relationship of her book and
its author to Przywara's *Analogia Entis*. Both books were written during a time of "a vital exchange of ideas ... that influenced in an important way the problematic and presentation of both."[105] Stein's work, like
Heidegger's concerned with the "question of Being," follows upon the
published first part of the Jesuit's work and points to the sections he left

unpublished. There is, however, a difference in emphasis, for her think-ing is more situated in the subject. Consciousness is seen in its relation-ship to objects. There is a focus upon a teaching about being but not on a philosophical system; an essayistic attention to an area of thinking and not to the multiple relationships of knowing to being. Both are pursu-ing the thinking of the creature, and both agree on the relationship of Creator and creation, of philosophy and theology, on the great sources of Christian thought.[106] Stein's tone is unassuming but is perhaps also more independent and self-confident than Przywara's broad, demon-strative union of typologies and aphorisms.

Przywara saw in Edith Stein a varied personality, an analogical figure of spiritual and intellectual life: "the broadest feminine receptivity . . . , and at the same time a dry, masculine objectivity."[107] She found him a valuable companion although she kept her distance from his distinctive ontological analyses. As a student of phenomenology she had come to see that modern philosophy needed some outside infusion, for it had reached a series of empty stages. "Modern philosophy has discovered that it is no longer possible to stay on the path where it has been for three centuries."[108] Przywara's work had encouraged Catholics to employ, but not idolize, Aquinas, and a fruit of that perspective was Stein's essay on Husserl and Aquinas for the *Festschrift* honoring Husserl's seventieth birthday in 1929 (Przywara evaluated it as an "as-tonishing confrontation between Husserl and Aquinas").[109]

What do the two thinkers mean by philosophy and science and how do they approach reality? A *philosophia perennis* (a slogan of many neo-scholastics advocating their particular selection of axioms) is not a peaceful park where thinking can rest from facing a plurality of views but a many-sided inquiry into the being of all realities and the ground of all questioning.[110] Reviewing a book by Dietrich von Hildebrand, she observed: "Thomistic metaphysics is for us today not a deposit of metaphysics removed from all questions but a task. The philosophy of recent centuries should perform the same work which St. Thomas did in the past with Aristotle and draw out the perduring content of truth so that philosophy outside of Christianity might explore the founda-tions of Christian thought."[111] Her knowledge of Aquinas grew in silent study over a decade, but she was largely self-taught and not well acquainted with the different schools of neo-Thomism; some prin-ciples she might have known only in their rigid, manualist form. Was there a similarity to the Jesuit Suárez, an influence coming not from contact with Jesuits but from an emphasis upon human knowing?

Stein's thought had its Thomistic strains, although her writings remained eclectic and personal. Her thought did not remain with Aquinas but drew in some insights of Pseudo-Dionysius and Scotus and
entered, as the years passed, a further stage in which Augustine was
central.[112] Przywara saw the dialogue between Husserl and Catholic
thinkers as a fulfillment of "the real goal of the work of the research
group of Ehrle, Denifle, Bäumker, and Grabmann: to confront the
depth of classical scholasticism with contemporary intellectual life."[113]

The Jesuit and the future Carmelite were two quite different
people: the former began with Aquinas' metaphysics of being and the
latter with Husserl's intuition into essence amid the problematic of
human psychology and of evil.[114] Florent Gaboriau writes: "The
manner in which each proceeds, Przywara on the one hand, Edith
Stein on the other, suggests 'two kinds of spirit.' The former seeks the
means of gaining access to things from concepts already formulated
by others; the second prefers research directly inspired by the real. . . .
The phenomenologist [Stein] by nature tends to see a supra-historical
truth without denying an interest in the history of thought, while
Przywara has a central idea under which all is seen, a kind of fundamental law which touches every being."[115]

Przywara very much wanted for Stein to meet the poet and novelist Gertrud von Le Fort, also a recent convert. He was friend and adviser
to that woman of Westphalian Protestant patrician stock who now as
a Catholic writer lived south of Munich. Her *Hymnen an die Kirche* of
1924 had made her widely known as a poet and writer, and two years
after its publication she entered the Catholic church. Two novels on a
young woman's search for faith and identity at the turn of the century
and a retelling of the medieval story of a pope from the Roman Jewish
ghetto led to a presentation of the story of Carmelite nuns executed
during the French Revolution, the foundation for the opera by Francis
Poulenc, *Dialogues of the Carmelites*. An exchange between Przywara and
Le Fort went on for many years, as he reviewed her works and dedicated some of his own writings to her.[116] In 1930 Le Fort and Stein met
in Munich and corresponded with each other during the following
years. In 1933, Stein's permission to teach was withdrawn by the new
Nazi regime and in the same year she entered the Carmelites; three days
after her entrance she wrote, "My dear Gertrud von le Fort, I just read
in the quiet of my cell your beautiful hymn to Mary. Carmel is the
right place for it." The next year Le Fort visited the cloistered nun in

Cologne. In her own way she continued Stein's work of looking at the role of women in the twentieth century.[117]

In 1956 Przywara wrote an essay comparing Edith Stein and Simone Weil, both of Jewish background, both victims of the war. Stein had a German cultural background and Weil a French, liberal political one, and so at first glance they seem to be quite different. Weil is younger, not a child of the nineteenth century or of the years before World War I; she is concerned with social issues, with Bolshevism, while Stein is taken up with academic philosophy. Stein entered a cloister, Weil a factory; Stein was a calm and happy personality; Weil a rather uncertain and depressed one.

Edith Stein's thinking moves without any question in the realm of Greek antiquity whose maturity is Plato and Aristotle, while Simone Weil breaks out of this world into that of a primal myth like the world around Parmenides or Heraclitus. Stein even while interpreting and translating Aquinas remains the true disciple, the "daughter" of the phenomenological method (but not of a transcendental idealism) of Husserl. She leads all the real objects to the level of "essentials" but not to an "ideal world" closed in upon itself (not in an ecological or monadic way as the development of Husserl effected); she leads to a "free, ideal world" in which "connections" do not just occur but are "contemplated" in each individuality. Edith Stein uncovers in a basic way "free essentialities" out of a systematic approach, and this connects her in a parallel way to what Nikolai Hartmann did with the ideal world of Hegel, freeing it from the chains of the Hegelian systematic triad.[118]

This essay written after Stein's death offered some reservations about her writings. Was her understanding of analogy adequate? Did she see correctly the links of the eternal with the finite, or did she place too much emphasis upon mutuality? Was there too much essentialism and similarity? (Stein, of course, had posed the same questions to Pryzwara.)[119] Still, her "essentialism" is never a transcendental system, never an isolated perception and intuition; there is always a personal relationship to what is pondered and an openness to being contacted by it. "What in her teacher Husserl was the last, secret accent of his systematic transcendentalism, the epoché, is for her a holding of the self away from and towards the 'divine in the inner human being,'

that is, in a 'pure essentialism.' There is a true fulfillment of this ultimate depth of the epoché in the Carmelite despoliation of the worlds
of the senses and the spirit, in the night of the senses and of the spirit.
That is the real transcendental philosophy; all that is the divine presence in the bright night is experienced in a way without experience,
far beyond all experience (as the core of the theoretical writings of
St. John of the Cross and of Dionysius the Areopagite show)."[120] This
she sketched in the *Kreuzwissenschaft* where the Carmelite pursued
the dark night in the mystery of existence and in the prayer to the
ultimate, to the camp of death.

A further interesting view of Stein by her Jesuit friend comes from
an essay on the tenth anniversary of her death at Auschwitz. He talked
about going to Speyer to meet her for the first time, about her cultural
interests in the late religious songs of Max Reger, the paintings of
Simone Martini, and the prints of Rembrandt. Przywara saw her as a
thinker pursuing a single direction rather than a dialectic, someone a
little critical of his analogical thought, a personality led by the "*justitia*
and instinct of her race."[121] Unable to resist yet a further synthesis, he
saw Edith Stein as a transcendent union of the German and the Jewish.
She was, he wrote, "not particularly Jewish looking but reminiscent of
quintessentially Germanic statues in Romanesque churches. . . . That
was Edith Stein: pure, strict Jewish patrician blood and still a German
woman."[122] Edith was both philosopher and believer, a Catholic convert but a convert whose conversion led her spiritually and personally
to Carmelite spirituality—and did not that strict, cloistered regime sus-
tain in a varied way the legal format of the Hebrew covenant? "Her
mother's strict religiosity remained the religious model during her
life . . . [someone who] in an almost fiery participation shared in the
Zionistic attempts in Palestine."[123] Carmel and Israel came together
in Elias the prophet; the origins of the Carmelites in the land of the
prophets and the prophet taken up into heaven pointed to the recon-
ciliation of her Jewish family with the Christian community.[124] Pursued by an ideal of clarity, she belonged to no school. Her fidelity to
Husserl, her work with Aquinas, her life in Carmel, her deportation to
death—these were more than scholarship, more than the academic
fashions of phenomenology and existentialism.[125]

Przywara noticed that Catholic circles after World War II, apart from
the *Akademikerverband* and *Frauenbund,* did not adequately appreciate
Stein, while students of Husserl who had no religious inclinations
kept her memory alive. Her death at Auschwitz brought her to the

attention of German Catholics but as a "symbol of co-suffering with the Jews murdered in the time of the Nazis."[126] There was more to the philosopher and teacher, there was a depth, a multifaceted reality in Edith Stein. "The hour of the intellectual and spiritual mission of Edith Stein may still today not have arrived. . . . Every cult of Edith Stein which is too zealously undertaken is thereby still not the cult of the true Edith Stein."[127] She was for Przywara not so much a saint as a type of holiness inspiring people at work in philosophy, in contemporary liturgy, and in the theological renaissance of Thomas Aquinas.[128] Przywara's ideas and ideals found an echo in Stein's own words in captivity: "For now, the world consists of opposites, but in the end none of those contrasts will remain. There will only be the fullness of love. How could it be otherwise."[129]

MARTIN HEIDEGGER (1889–1976)

With Edith Stein we have entered the philosophical world of the philosophers after Husserl. Whether a world of existentialism or neo-scholasticism, of dialectical theology or philosophies of religion, it is very much the world of Martin Heidegger.

Heidegger drew on Meister Eckhart and Kant, Schelling, and also on Søren Kierkegaard. Przywara, too, studied at length the Danish religious thinker for dialectical theology and existential philosophy, for a general existential approach to life and God after World War I.[130] Przywara said that to struggle with the issues of his time was to engage in an open or secret struggle with Kierkegaard; "hardly a new direction can be found out of whose depth the Dane does not look."[131] Whether in Barth or Heidegger, in all that was existential, dialectic, ambiguous the newly discovered Kierkegaard was present. The Protestant theologian Hermann Diem wrote that the Jesuit's book on Kierkegaard was the most lucid book yet written on him.[132] He faced the issues of what led Kierkegaard so far apart from church and society, faced the tensions in the Dane's life where music, eros, depression, and death struggled with each other. Przywara's pages mix psychological interpretation with philosophical exposition: to write about Kierkegaard, he observed, is to struggle, to fight with him, and the road to the mystery of Kierkegaard lies through taking seriously Romanticism, late idealism, and dialectical theology.[133] The new psychological and philosophical analysis leads ultimately to religion. Was not the many-sided Kierkegaard a mystic whose

view of the abandonment of Christ and the uncertainty of life's darkness related him to John of the Cross?[134] The mystery of the writings
lie in their influence upon existentialism and psychoanalysis. The philosophy is about dialectic and ambiguity, about existence and life, about
a vital thought versus an abstract thought, about two forms of subjectivity, transcendental and existential: in the last analysis it is "dialectical
thinking in the living moment."[135] Although for Przywara Kierkegaard represents both a climax to and a passing beyond Luther, he
also shows a transition from Lutheranism into an interior Catholicism
marked by a theology of Mary that attempts to interpret and bless the
roles of women and the feminine in Kierkegaard's own life. This leads
on to themes of interpersonal conflict, tension with God, and the
struggle over vocation. While Przywara's book is marked by originality
and insight, it is also, curiously, an apology for a Catholic theology
to whose depths Kierkegaard points. According to the Jesuit's book on
Kierkegaard, Heidegger had taken part in the "resurrection of the *existential thinking* of Kierkegaard" by fashioning a phenomenology of the
Being of beings, an epistemology of every understanding of being
coming from the depth of self-understanding, and a concrete presentation of the reality of the human being in the existentials of care,
anxiety, guilt—forms and insights found in Kierkegaard.[136]

Heidegger and Przywara were the same age. Martin Heidegger grew
up in the family of the caretaker of a parish church in the Black Forest
and was educated in medieval and modern philosophies in Freiburg im
Breisgau, receiving a doctorate with a study of Scotist philosophy in
1913 and completing a *Habilitation* in neo-Kantian thought in 1916. He
was Husserl's assistant and a *Privatdozent* from 1918 to 1923, and after
five years in Marburg became the successor to the great phenomenologist. Przywara recognized Heidegger's Catholic roots—"a primal
Catholic family, a former Jesuit novice, onetime theology student of
the Freiburg seminary, student of the aggressively Catholic philosopher
Josef Geyser"—and also his subsequent individuality, emerging as "the
radical opposite (a role hidden at first in *Sein und Zeit*) to his teacher
Husserl, reducing the '*Cogito*' to the Being of beings."[137]

The Jesuit's lectures at Leipzig and a study on Kant run parallel to
Heidegger's book on Kant and *Sein und Zeit:* there are similarities in
the approach to knowing and being in terms of objectivity, and in the
analysis of subjectivity through its relationships to and realizations in a
world. Przywara reviewed *Sein und Zeit* when it appeared in 1927, an

early reaction by a Catholic intellectual to what would be one of the great works of philosophy.[138] *Sein und Zeit* can distract the reader by numerous detailed analyses, but the subject viewed as being and time remains throughout the book the vital reality of Being. "The specific problem [for Heidegger] is *the problem of life-being.*"[139] Going beyond Dilthey and Simmel and yet related to the religious metaphysics of Kierkegaard and Barth, what is proper and original to *Sein und Zeit* is a move to unify ontology and history in human temporality. The world of ordinary human life is a presentation of Being; understanding is a kind of seeing, a seeing into all that reveals life and being and truth.

Przywara reviewed Heidegger's first publications, joining him to Husserl and Scheler as giving the three great directions in phenomenology.[140] Scheler is a bridge from Husserl to Heidegger: the philosopher of life leads from Husserl's consciousness to Heidegger's existence. Martin Heidegger belonged to the direction of contemporary philosophy coming after Husserl and Scheler. Despite some personal contact at Davos and Freiburg, Przywara was critical of Heidegger's publications: he represented one of the important basic directions of phenomenology and yet was too much an opposing counter to Husserl, indeed, the annihilator of phenomenology.[141] Beyond Husserl, this was a philosophy of the tragic dimension of life in a metaphysics of existence, an affirmation of jagged empty finitude, an exaltation of nothingness. Original as they might be, Heidegger's existentials had an atmosphere of isolation opening on to tragedy and boded a rejection of religion. It is not enough to ask, as Catholic critics do, about idealism and subjectivity, about scholasticism and originality; are the divine and the human in some kind of interplay here?[142] At that time, however, few were asking, as Przywara did, does *Sein und Zeit* contribute to a philosophy of religion? A secularity shoves away religion and emphasizes the closed aspect of being-in-the-world; the mystery of Being is too much a nothingness—and yet in the last analysis perhaps its philosophy is "a secularized Mount Carmel,"[143] that is, it is about creaturehood and the negativity of the journey of life. If the analysis and prominence of existence offer few insights into religion, they do raise questions. On the other hand, is not his employment in theology by the Protestant exegete Rudolf Bultmann dangerous, since the Gospel becomes a religion of immanence and anxious existence? While patristic and medieval thinkers separated essence from existence in the creature, doesn't bringing them together make human existence the absolute? Is not God drawn into the divineness of time-being? The human person in a terrific solitariness is placed before the all-powerful but mysterious and not godly presence of Being, and Heidegger does not help (he even guides away) the subject before the choice of finitude or the infinite.[144]

In 1934 Przywara wrote a further response to the new existential-ism, a personal theological response combining meditations with the thought of great philosophical minds. It was an application of key ideas to contemporary life as interpreted by Heidegger's "facticity" and "being-in-the-world." Treating four modes of life — existential, Ger-man, Christian, and ecclesial—Przywara interpreted the simplicity, reality, and earthiness of existence in the first section. "Existence is a word of our age, and, above all, a sober word."[145] Existence is not nature and essence but realization, meaning, facticity of life. The Trinity and the Incarnation, however, are ways in which existence is realized, ways in which existence steps out from nothingness and moves to ecstasy and the demonic, to moral and artistic existence, totality, and vitality. *Existenz,* a German word, can represent what is tearing Germany apart even as it expresses that which leads the German mind to quest, longing, uncertainty, and tragedy. The section on German existence looks at earth, *Reich,* becoming, night, and music; German symbols like the grail and the *Kaiser;* German thinkers like Albert the Great and Meis-ter Eckhart, Luther, Goethe, and Nietzsche. Should not Heidegger be linked to idealist and Romantic, even medieval philosophies? Always quick to note that Heidegger is not as original as one might think, he concludes that Jacob Boehme and Hegel are the sources of Heidegger, while the emphasis upon historicity is only an attempt to breathe new life into Dilthey.[146] "Martin Heidegger and Nicolai Hartmann represent the attempt in today's philosophy to return to the classical tradition of antiquity and scholasticism, to interpret this tradition in terms of a phi-losophy of the ultimate closed modality of the world. In Heidegger there is a Scotist dynamic and energy; in Hartmann a more Aristotelian view of the movement of the world in itself. Of course, Catholic phi-losophers have undertaken parallel enterprises."[147]

Is there a Christian existence emerging from eschatology, an exis-tence that is service in the world and community? Life in the church celebrates both the impotence and the power of the Christian. A seem-ing ordinariness, a lowliness of faith vitalized by grace empower one's profession and vocation. Life ultimately faces the demonic and the divine. The temptations of Jesus up to the Resurrection are a *Kairos* not only for Jesus but also for the Demon. The scriptural readings and the liturgy of Holy Week (the full liturgy of Holy Week had not yet been restored) are the framework for the theologian's response to the fashionable theories of existence and to the gloomy upheavals of his time. The Jesuit's meditations, drawing existentialism into what is Christian and yet tense with suffering, were published in the year when Hitler became dictator of the Third Reich. They were not just an analysis of some terms from Heidegger but reflections on existence as suffering and temporality, and observations of how the German spirit in history furthers and responds to such forces.

After the war Przywara continued to write essays on Heidegger, for French as well as German journals. A review of Gustav Siewerth's study of Aquinas in light of Heidegger noted the "Catholic disciples of Heidegger" such as Max Müller, J. B. Lotz, and others in whose writings one finds not only the presence of Heidegger but of Joseph Maréchal, "the Thomist writer who was the first to have tried the genial enterprise of 'transposing' Kant and Hegel to the plane of Aquinas."[148] Neither Maréchal nor Heidegger, Przywara thought, advanced beyond Husserl and Scheler, and neither was as Thomistic as some think. "The Thomism of Maréchal has made a dynamic infinity into the principle of a system, while the phenomenology of Heidegger made a dynamic finitude into its system's principle."[149] Przywara insightfully noted the similarity of Heidegger's idea of truth as disclosure to Aquinas' truth of being in its varied, analogous modalities. If Heidegger is now theologically identified with Bultmann, in fact their origins show different theological worlds; later on, ignorance of Heidegger's theological and phenomenological sources made him appear almost as a "Catholic convert" leaving behind his employment by liberal Protestant theologians, a time when he took up anew being and history and his original interests in medieval mysticism reappeared. His time in the Jesuit novitiate and his doctorate on Scotus led him to view God and the world dynamically and to see the person as living between destiny and free choice. Was this a Scotist Ockhamism swinging between revolution and passive mysticism? The result is a powerful sovereignty of Being, an existence which though active seems at the mercy of greater forces; in short, a purely immanent theology.[150]

The early Heidegger's metaphysics of the really existing human later becomes a pantheism, a monist, secular salvation-history with its own eschatology that, nonetheless, is somewhat static and interior to the world. In fact, Heidegger is close, not to medieval Aristotelianism, but to Schelling. "This is almost Schelling redivivus—but without his authentic breadth and depth. It is a despairing attempt to break out of an age of austere technology into a new 'pneumatic' age of which the neo-Russian [Slavophile] gnosis dreamed."[151] This secular philosophy contains a "teaching about salvation resembling a cosmological theosophy": "An eschatological Christianity which at the same time is a pneumatic Christianity of being addressed—in Christian terms this is expressed by calling the Holy Spirit the 'paraclete'—that seems to be the recent message (even if it is quite carefully hidden) of this last German philosopher who became a mystical Magi."[152] Heidegger's thought, "an adventist mysticism of an arrival of Being,"[153] does not state an antagonism between Christianity and existentialism but establishes a secularity, a philosophy of a world closed in on itself, and takes on more and more the aspects of a myth, of a kind of immanent theology or a theosophy, a replacement of revelation. In Heidegger German philosophy comes to a terminal stage. "[One sees] the actual lack of success, the fundamental impossibility of achieving a phenomenology essentially distinct from every system, a direction with Husserl as its origin and Heidegger as its end which is slowly revealing philosophy 'in its last hour.'"[154] If there are Catholics as well as Protestants who find in Heidegger a new expression of the Bible and Christianity—*Sein und Zeit* called forth theological disciples without mentioning God[155]—that would be like "resuscitating a church lying on its death-bed through the viaticum of a single German philosophy."[156]

In his forties Przywara seemingly could not go much beyond the philosophers of his youth, Husserl and Scheler, and could not find in Heidegger's newer existentialism—it was also a turn to the objective, the human, the historical—the positive direction which many theologians were praising. There appeared too not only a critique of Heidegger but a tone of suspicion toward his Catholic contemporaries, even fellow Jesuits who were transcendental Thomists or moderate Heideggerians. Some point out that Przywara found it difficult to be sympathetic to a philosophy where form so dominates and where content, religious content, is so absent, while others wondered if Przywara's presentation of analogy did not approach Heidegger's Being. The dynamism, transcendental orientation, and the perspective of life places the Jesuit in a somewhat parallel position to Heidegger's.[157]

HANS URS VON BALTHASAR (1905–1988)

Hans Urs von Balthasar wrote two brief overviews of Przywara's life and thought in 1963 and 1966, essays written after Balthasar had left the Jesuits and before the postconciliar period.[158] "Erich Przywara was placed in a time which employed all its powers and interests in terms of the world and the human person, in a speculative-philosophical time for which world and human person were the reality and the theme; God was at best a 'horizon' of the being of the world, a boarder-concept of thinking, a chiffre of existence."[159] Those times were the years from 1920 to 1945.

Balthasar, born in Switzerland in 1905, a year after Karl Rahner and sixteen years after Przywara, pursued his gymnasium studies at Engelberg with the Benedictines and at Feldkirch with the Jesuits where Przywara prior to ordination had taught music. After time in Vienna for study of the psychological approach of Rudolf Allers and semesters in Berlin at the lectures of Romano Guardini, he moved from the field of music to literature. Enthusiastic for the poetry of Stefan George, he received his doctorate with a dissertation on Romanticism in German literature in 1928 and entered the Society of Jesus. After the two years of novitiate he was sent in 1931 to Pullach near Munich to study philosophy, and during that time of twenty months or so he had some contact with Erich Przywara, who in Munich was at work on *Analogia Entis;* Balthasar wrote a short dissertation on analogy for the licentiate in philosophy, material published in 1932 as an overview of Przywara's metaphysics in two articles.[160] From 1933 to 1934 Balthasar was at Lyon-Fourvière for his seminary studies in theology. Ordained and ready for ministry, he returned in the autumn of 1937 to Munich to join the staff of *Stimmen der Zeit;* during the next year and a half the volumes of his study of German Romanticism appeared. After tertianship at Pullach in the fall of 1939 he became the chaplain for students in Basel and soon encouraged Adrienne von Speyer, his later spiritual companion, to enter the church; in 1950 he left the Jesuits to be fully a part of her circle until her death in 1967.[161] His time of contact with Przywara was not extensive, two periods of less than two years with one of them being a time of living and working together. Gustav Wilhelmy writes: "Von Balthasar and Przywara in various periods of their lives remained joined in a faithful gratitude although there was no lack of reservations on both sides."[162] Balthasar through the 1950s found time for conversations with

Przywara, although in the view of Karl H. Neufeld "in the years of the Council certainly this contact died out."[163] Przywara was cheered by the three volumes of his *Schriften,* brought out in 1962 by Johannes Verlag, founded and controlled by Balthasar.

Balthasar proclaimed Erich Przywara to be original, distinctive, almost unique. He wanted him to be a special figure, a person distinct from other theologians of the age, even someone apart from his own times; he placed himself in an intellectual line coming from Przywara and sometimes praised him, a special mentor, in unusual, rhetorical terms, a figure not tarnished by uncertain times and movements of change. In 1945 he wrote that Przywara was "the greatest spirit I was ever permitted to meet,"[164] and in 1966 he concluded, "He alone possessed the language in which the word 'God' could be heard without the turmoil which the sly discourse of our mediocre theology has caused."[165] Balthasar indicated that Przywara was for him a special guide, although there was limited personal contact. Balthasar mentioned that modern philosophies received little attention from Przywara, who stood apart from the theological streams (he did not cite any of Przywara's books or ideas to support this position).[166] In 1966 he could still write that Przywara's thinking could be "*the* medicine [*pharmakon*] for the philosophy and theology of our age."[167] Was he thinking of essays from the 1920s, or did this imply a lack of sympathy for the vital theological milieu around the Council and thereby an attempt to draw Przywara into an anticonciliar group? The contacts between the two Jesuits were limited.

Balthasar described the form of Przywara's thought, noting the forms of polarity, intuition, the dialectic of Newman and Husserl, of Augustine and Aquinas. The basic thought-form of Przywara is that of a "dynamic thinking emerging in the most extreme tension between two oppositions of the process of thought," and this brings with it "an extreme will to style, to order in the presentation, a virtuoso letting voices be heard."[168] Przywara, on the other hand, evaluated Balthasar's writings as having their own analogical dialectic, a different direction from his, one evident as early as the *Apokalypse der deutschen Seele;* its form of analogy stands in distinction to the more metaphysical tension in the older Jesuit's writings, containing great similarity in greater dissimilarity.

As the years passed, Balthasar oriented his writings to an attractive reexpression of Christianity in biblical themes and in motifs from literary and philosophical figures. Both have an aesthetic interest — it may come from the influence of Platonic patristic ideas or modern philosophers—although in Przywara this is limited. In *Weg zu Gott* from the early 1920s the chapter on various mysticisms through the century has a certain similarity with the synthetic surveys which three decades later make up Balthasar's *The Glory of the Lord*.[169] Nonetheless, if Przywara's interests and writings touch upon the arts and literature, his theology is not extensively aesthetic, and his sources do not compose a mosaic but are integrated into a metaphysical stance. Przywara was not an eclectic; disparate sources were always drawn into his perspective; there is a strong tonality of harmony and universality and synthesis, as contemporary perspectives from all areas of culture are brought forth to help the self-understanding of ordinary Christians.

In terms of church and pastoral life, both theologians at times reduced charisms and ministries to types and biblical figures. Balthasar's ecclesiology is a spirituality of biblical figures who have little reference to the concrete problems of the church in this century,[170] and Przywara, after describing positively the new movements during and after Catholic Action and searching for an incipient theology of lay ministry, can end with an ecclesiology of a dialectical symbolism, of male and female, with active males and the abstract generic church as Eve or Mary Magdalene.[171] Przywara is more ecclesially realistic and engaged, for he knew the new movements by experience and saw them as part of the turn to the new.

In Balthasar's view, *Analogia Entis* is a watershed in Przywara's thought and is somehow different from what preceded or followed it. Few experts agree: Przywara's themes are present from the beginning, undergoing some maturing.[172] World War II brings for him a *caesura*, as he is debilitated by age, less energy, and illness: the creativity and value of the writings around 1960 are not of the same level as those of 1923. So Balthasar's enthusiastic remarks from 1966 do not fit the man then alive whose career lay some decades back and who has only a few years to live. The disaster of World War II and Przywara's illnesses were responsible for a diminished presence, while pastoral developments like ecumenism, social ethics, liturgical renewal, and the expansion of ministry meant that the Jesuit's accomplishments would be a part of a history of church and theology in the twentieth century that no one theologian could dominate, not even a Congar or a Rahner.

Balthasar with his overarching literary style does not simply give an interpretation to the analogy of being but fashions it into a new mode of faith. How does this mix of analogies of being and love (a love born

of faith which receives all of Being and which is a principle of interpretation of life) relate to the underlying principle of Przywara's
thought? Balthasar's thought-form is more subjective, not so much an
objective prism of reality but an aesthetic spirituality rooted in citations from metaphysicians. The Swiss priest asked whether Przywara's metaphysics does not suppress the figure and image, whether
the rhythm of analogy should not focus more on the Son manifesting the Father (a view limiting the independence of philosophy), and
whether the divine diffusion of love is more limited (a reaction to the
Catholic theologies of wider grace).[173] The continuance of the creative act of God into the redemptive cross is important to Przywara as
to Barth and Balthasar, but this does not mean he turns a metaphysical
and objective view of creation and incarnation into the gift of faith or
the act of love.[174] Przywara is knowledgeable and perceptive about
the thought of Thomas Aquinas, one of his venerated sources, while
Balthasar is much less influenced by Aquinas and, because of his
bad experience of neoscholasticism can be rather indifferent to him.[175]
Przywara emphasized the Aristotelian ordinariness of creaturely existence and causality and the interplay of a truly mysterious and infinite
but not otherly transcendence God and the creature dignified with
grace and being. The drift toward Barthianism in Balthasar is repeatedly rejected by Przywara, who finds Calvinist theopanism the opposite of Catholic thought.

Przywara situates the individual interpretation of the rhythm of
analogia entis explicitly in the dynamic meeting between God and the
human being, the heart of analogy under the sign of otherness—
even of a tension-in-antithesis. For Georges de Schrijver, Balthasar
found "his first inspiration there [in Przywara], but one need not conclude that he takes without critique all the analyses of Przywara."[176]
Never leaving behind the principle of the Fourth Lateran Council
affirming the ever greater difference between Creator and creature,
Przywara "introduced a constant mounting ascent of incommensurability between God and the creature, particularly just at the precise
moment where the creature is creature, and especially when the creature is admitted to enter into participation with God by pure grace
and in total abandon. It is from this that Balthasar begins to distance
himself."[177] Balthasar found Przywara's metaphysics of being and grace
somewhat lacking in a clear Christian word and center, for he saw in
Christ the expressive figure of the Father, someone and something
going beyond the oscillations of an analogy of being; not only the

Word of God but the suffering Redeemer of humanity.[178] Schrijver notes that the ideas of correspondence, expression, representation receive in Balthasar a different sense, not so much in a metaphysics of analogy which for Catholicism must serve revelation linguistically but in a "theological aesthetics."[179] The metaphysics of analogy as the form of creation and grace is somewhat different in the two, and Schrijver concludes that some of Przywara's approaches have "in fact no place in the thought of Balthasar."[180]

In the view of Manfred Lochbrunner, "The christological view of Balthasar, matured through the many years of intensive study of Barth, gives the conception of Przywara of the *analogia entis* a more concrete form and lets Christ emerge as the '*Universale concretum*'."[181] "Balthasar assumed a mediating and clarifying role in the struggle between Przywara's 'analogia entis' and Barth's 'analogia fidei'."[182] For Sturmius Wittschier, however, Przywara emphasized the dynamic swing, the difference of independent beings, and an approach from creation and society, while Balthasar looked at stable forms and biblical sources to serve the Word descending from above.[183] Julio Terán Dutari finds Balthasar to be less firm and traditional than Przywara in his view of nature within grace, less nuanced in describing the real and existential identity of human nature responding to grace as expressed in the new theologies. Second, Balthasar's emphasis upon the concrete and historical in Christ is severe, while Przywara is very much a theologian of the complexity and mystery of history.[184] Balthasar is less optimistic about grace in history and less interested in contemporary philosophy and science and church life.

Did not Balthasar frame Przywara as a figure apart in order to counter mainstream Catholic theology leading to and beyond Vatican II? Balthasar, when summarizing Przywara, not seldom locates him in a situation of isolation and decline in society and church, while Przywara's own writings have a self-assurance and interest in his age. Balthasar wrote in 1966 of Przywara's thinking process as polar and dynamic, but then he implies it is a mistrust of each system, an encouragement of the nonresolution of every movement of thought, and an antipathy toward every ontic principle; to read Przywara prior to 1940 is to find a sympathy toward systems and the hope of system, and a strong and cautious optimism.[185]

The opening lines of one of the sketches by Balthasar of Przywara runs: "Erich Przywara's enormous theological commission—in its depth and breadth not comparable to anyone else's in this time—might have been the decisive means of salvation for our Christian thinking today. The age chose the easier way, not to engage him. And he himself is not without guilt in this. He had from early on seen the opening of the church to all, an opening the Council brought but beyond that he held the corrective which in the tone and wide impact of the Council did not become influential."[186] At face value these views are not quite true. Balthasar does not give passages or themes to show either an anticipation of the Council or an insightful critique of the postconciliar period. Przywara is not incomparable; he engaged his own age but did not see so clearly the pastoral and future developments of his ideas. He had influence, and theologians did not reject him. Przywara was not a theologian of the Council. Like Guardini's, his writings were a remote preparation for the assembly but were for a while forgotten after 1960. He remained a metaphysician while the Council was about pastoral work; he did not easily imagine concrete pastoral changes, precisely the direction of the future.

Balthasar interpreted Przywara as he would like to see him. Someone special but on the margin, a thinker of one systematic idea, which is analogy, dependent above all else on Augustine;[187] an aesthetic arranger of ideas or a contemplative of themes from spiritualities; a theologian of the Logos in the cross; a conversation partner with Karl Barth—these figures are, of course, Hans Urs von Balthasar.[188] Przywara, however, is much more: a sympathetic reader of modern philosophy, a Thomist of secondary causality and grace, an Ignatian activist in the ministry, a sympathetic reviewer of European literature, someone involved in movements of church renewal.[189] Balthasar's exaggerated praise of Przywara may be a little self-serving, for it implies that what came after 1965 was generally deficient and the result of less gifted theologians, an observation no theologian involved in the council would have made. About Przywara, Balthasar had concluded: "He remains an incomparable teacher—every thinker must have thought through what he shows—who modestly lets all who have been fired by him pursue their own way."[190] Karl Rahner gave a positive interpretation to this: "I won't argue with him [Balthasar] but will only ask whether every theologian does not have his own task, whether it cannot sometimes belong to the first level of theology to say something for the second level, whether it is not required for the student to present the work of the teacher and to unfold it—whether that be in the church or to a Council.... But I think at a deeper level Balthasar is right. Theology in the future will learn much from Przywara."[191]

Regardless, both men remained theologians of the era before Vatican II: Przywara was old and sick, and, while he welcomed the project of the Council, his imagination could not assist it, while Balthasar had removed himself from exercising theological influence by leaving the Jesuits, by affiliating himself with a group around a private mystic, and by writing little of service to the Council.[192] Balthasar embraced a perspective very much his own, one different from that of his earlier philosophical mentor. Maréchal, Przywara, Rahner, and Balthasar are distinct figures with their own ideas, their own times, and their own lives. Neither Rahner nor Przywara drew extensively from previous German Jesuits. Balthasar and Rahner were correct: Przywara's personality and thinking made it unlikely he would have disciples or a school.

KARL RAHNER (1904–1984)

"One must not forget Father Erich Przywara. For the Catholics of Germany in the twenties, thirties, and forties he was considered one of the greatest minds. He had a great influence on all of us when we were young. He is now seventy-five; he is quite sick and can barely write." So Karl Rahner recalled his fellow Jesuit in 1965.[193] In one of his many interviews he spoke of an influence which touched an age as much as individuals: "There were also men in the generation of Jesuits just before me one should mention; they were already, in fact, forerunners or initiators of a breakthrough from the philosophy and theology of neoscholasticism. I'm thinking now of men like Peter Lippert, or even more of Erich Przywara."[194]

Born in 1904 in Freiburg im Breisgau, Rahner entered the Jesuits in 1922 at a novitiate just moved from Holland and located near the school of Stella Matutina where Przywara had taught in the Austrian Vorarlberg. While his philosophical studies were done in Pullach near Munich, Rahner's theological studies, as with Przywara, were done in Valkenburg in Holland. Ordained at the Jesuit center of St. Michael in Munich in 1923, he pursued doctoral studies in philosophy at Freiburg, attending the doctoral seminars of Heidegger and writing a dissertation on Aquinas and Kant under a conservative neo-Thomist. His rejected dissertation, *Geist in Welt,* was published to acclaim in 1939, and his philosophy of religion, *Hörer des Wortes,* applying in an original way contemporary philosophical reflections on person and history to Christian revelation, appeared in 1941. After pastoral work in Vienna during the war he became professor of theology at Pullach and then at Innsbruck, later assuming German university positions at Munich and Münster. Karl Neufeld wrote: "Przywara stayed in contact with Rahner up to the last year of [Przywara's] life as Rahner from time to time went out to Murnau. It was not surprising that Rahner represented him when the Silesian award was given him. . . . Rahner cannot, however, be seen as a student of Przywara—it is difficult to speak about students or disciples in this case at all. It's a question, rather, of friends, of people with a certain common approach but each with great individuality."[195] Przywara influenced Rahner in some general ways, but that there was marked influence is "not only unprovable but also unlikely." Neufeld continues: "Przywara lived in the Jesuit writers' house in Munich not too far from the philosophate in Pullach; still, the mutual contacts then were not very frequent; outside of official invitations to days of reflection or to occasional and rare lectures one cannot presume that Przywara was at Pullach. Naturally in the Jesuit houses the journal *Stimmen der Zeit* was at hand, and so Przywara was known and influential through his publications. When one reflects upon the customs of the German Jesuits at that time it is not conceivable that a student from Pullach would take the initiative to enter energetically into the thinking of someone other than those furthered by the official faculty for studies."[196]

When Przywara received the Upper Silesian Cultural Prize in 1967, Karl Rahner gave the *Laudatio*, observing that he had been in contact with Przywara and his work for forty years. "It is difficult to discuss this work with its extensive content and varied relationships to the intellectual history of Europe and of Christianity in the last fifty years. The task of his vocation came together with his cultural and intellectual mission: he belonged to no class, no clique, and fidelity to his personal mission never conflicted with fidelity to the Society."[197] Despite the broad appeal of his work he was profoundly Catholic, "Catholic in the sense of an effective, lifelong dialogue with the past and the present, with the totality of European intellectual history from Heraclitus to Nietzsche."[198] Przywara led Catholicism from the currents of the late nineteenth century through neoscholastic schools and antimodernist condemnations to the point where Catholicism could again fashion a theology which addressed the times rather than condemned them. Rahner wrote of the older Jesuit, "It is certainly he more than all other

Catholic thinkers of his age who brought the radical pathos of a *theologia crucis* of the Reformation into Catholic thinking without it ceasing to be Catholic. . . . He has developed for Catholic thinking the idea of polarity. He is for us the teacher of the radical openness of metaphysical thinking which he draws foward to its limits where one must decide to collapse or to transform one's attitude into that of the *Adoro te devote latens*. . . . Through him the *analogia entis* moves from being a small technical issue to being the basic structure of the Catholic reality."[199]

Rahner placed Przywara in the company of Pierre Teilhard de Chardin—a solitary pioneer, a person of dialogue between faith and science, an independent mind during a time of ecclesiastical condemnation. "We, the generation after him, and the coming generations still have important, beneficial lessons to learn from him. The total and true Przywara is yet to come. He stands at a point in the pathway which many in the church must still pass by."[200] Creative theologians could still be inspired by Przywara; timid and reactionary ones would still have to study his writings.

As we hear one Jesuit praising an older one, it may occur to some that Rahner is not without his similarities to Przywara. Both Jesuit theologians accepted and furthered an openness to philosophy in the twentieth century; both were gifted at bringing together German philosophies with older Christian theologies, understanding that idealism was turning to individual existence and temporality; and both had a deep understanding of Aquinas joined to a critique of neo-Thomism. Theirs was a gift for speculation and system joined to an involvement in practical issues. Przywara anticipated Rahner in the desire to fashion a philosophical expression of the inner core of Christianity and to lead theological motifs and church forms to their deeper roots. Both were deeply influenced by the Ignatian *Spiritual Exercises,* and both expressed anew that spirituality.[201] They distanced themselves from academic theology (from footnoted articles on marginal topics in little-read journals) and fled from "competition or envy in so-called scientific theology."[202]

Surprisingly, few pages comparing Przywara and Rahner have appeared.

In Przywara's lectures at Leipzig in 1925 one hears a tonality that will at times appear in Rahner's language, themes of the ineffable God and of mystery. The movements of an age search for God; the real and the concrete lead to mystery. If God is not easily reached, this is because "he is the mystery of mysteries, the primal mystery, the universal mystery."[203] Is God to be found in creation or high above it? Przywara answered: "But when God is the one above conceptualization, the mystery plain and simple (which we cannot just puzzle over), when we place everything good and beautiful in this world in an absolute mode, and even when we search in the last explosion of all suffering in the world for something primal . . . , then God is, one might say, the absolutized mysteriousness of human existence."[204] And similarly, when we read the following lines of Rahner, we are reminded of the older Jesuit: "The absolute incommensurability of God, the impossibility of reducing him simply to one element in man's universe so that human horizons fix God's limits—these are ideas which have never really taken root in devotional practice. This is not surprising, for this absolute God must at the same time become the concrete God of the tangible, explicit, and categorical enactment of our spiritual life. This concrete God, however, is first an absolute God, a radical mystery, an incomprehensible abyss from which everything originates, when he remains God in all of our concrete, categorical, religious life."[205] In his early philosophy of religion Przywara placed as the climax to his religious and metaphysical structures "the concrete self-sharing [*Selbstmitteilen*] of the Catholic God."[206] If creatures as beings have limited although relatively open relationships to God, the divine love has an inconceivable freedom vis-à-vis creation, which opens outward into the Incarnation. An essay of 1929 offering the interplay of existence and divine presence in history resembles the later Rahner: "Every emergence into the world will sooner or later be a secularization if it has not previously been a journey into God. . . . That means that there is for Catholics as concrete men and women no area which is neutral or interconfessional. That is the practical meaning of the Catholic teaching of the 'supernatural goal and sole goal.' Certainly the supernatural of the redemption and sanctification is in no way the inner property or function of nature . . . but is concretely a historical supernaturally redeemed and elevated nature, i.e., the concrete existing human being . . . the human being whose individual goal of life and meaning of life is to be one Christ in body and soul. . . . "[207] And a passage on the Incarnation recalls the Rahnerian dialectic of categorical and transcendental in human history: the Incarnation flows from a drive to participation. "The ultimate meaning of Incarnation lies not so much in a spiritualization of the corporeal as in a corporealization of the spiritual; it lies in a complete and thorough penetration by God of the spiritual world of the senses beginning with the Incarnation and proceeding in and through the mystery of the sacramental church, and completing itself in the resurrection of the dead."[208]

Occasionally lines in Rahner's popular essays—"So in every neighbor we accept and love that one Neighbor who united what is nearest and farthest from us"[209]—find an earlier variant in Przywara's words. "He is the one who illumines us when we keep our distance and when we approach; the infinite light which is always further the closer we come. Every finding is a commencement of a new search."[210] The theme of the relationship between the human person and the Trinitarian presence is central to both Jesuits. Using the language and categories of Scheler and Newman and not the later Heideggerian existential terms, Przywara's writings treat the intimate, active interplay of grace and existence, the theme of a supernaturally gifted dynamic. From his first writings Przywara often combined the motifs of mystery and self-communication. "What is first and foundational is precisely this towering distinctiveness of God. There is also the self-communication of God reaching from creation to the human person where . . . , as Thomas Aquinas says, there is a 'movement of God' in that which here emerges from God but is essentially 'other than God.'"[211]

Rahner wanted to make explicit in an incarnational theology transcendental divine presence active in concrete realizations in history, and in a general way this theme was in Przywara; the revelation behind the many types of theology and the grace behind movements and spiritualities are examples of it. "For Catholics," Przywara wrote, "there is no detailed list which makes up the essence of Christianity. Rather, the living church in its infallible teaching office is, in the last instance, the essence of Christianity. . . . From this it follows immediately that no 'theological schools or systems' can be equated with the church, but that the daily life of the church with its liturgy and devotions too belongs to the very being of Christianity."[212] The most basic motif in Rahner was the transcendental ground of revelation and grace manifest in the categorical and existential forms of historical ages.

Klaus Fischer sees Przywara's union of spirituality and metaphysical theology in *Deus Semper Major* as influencing Rahner not only as an interpreter of the *Spiritual Exercises* (at Pullach Przywara gave the Exercises in 1935 and Rahner directed them in 1936) but in his idea and realization of theology as inevitably personal and pastoral. Rahner's essay from the 1950s, "On the Logic of Existential Knowing in Ignatius Loyola," seeks to draw Przywara's program of the 'in-over' of the presence of the *Deus incomprehensibilis* into a theo-logic of an existential knowledge by means of a transcendental path, and Rahner mentions Przywara's commentary as an expansive beginning. Both Jesuits interpret the traditional *potentia obedientialis* as an opening, a question which is ontic and dynamic, an aspect of human nature; both lead spirituality to speculative theology by proceeding from the person, living in the contemporary world and discerning the meaning of an individual life, a hearer of the word, whose openness to transcendence and threat of nothingness is already surrounded by grace. "The language of Przywara, if somewhat softened, reaches through Rahner's writings including the ones on the spiritual life."[213] Fischer sees Przywara's thought and spirituality influencing the structure of Rahner's philosophy of religion, *Hearers of the Word*.[214] "What Rahner will call the mystery of the human being is evident in [Przywara's] interpretation of the creatureliness of the person seen as directed beyond, as a movement beyond the self, as restlessness out toward God."[215] History is bringing forth not only ideas but also new and old forms for human persons whose transcendence is realized in the worlds of church and liturgy. Rahner was certainly a theologian of the ordinary, a contemplative of the generous extent of God's grace, a priest of the liturgy of daily life, and Przywara held that "a Catholic is someone who is not rigid but is thoroughly relaxed, someone of happy ordinariness."[216] It is understandable why Rahner would speak of his good fortune in having Przywara as a guide for his own insight and synthesis. Nonetheless, the conclusion of the insightful Klaus Fischer must remain: "As much as a collective and comparative contemplation can find deep similarities between Przywara and Rahner, at the end to do justice to the relationship of the two theologians means to give up theories of dependency. It is more the vision, the spiritual-cultural optic which forms something common between the two than individual statement or terminological parallels."[217]

There are differences between the two theologians. Rahner looked very much at the transcendental ground of the knowing and living person as well as at a post-Kantian existential structure of the hearer of the word anchored in being and revelation; Rahner's quest was not for dialectical patterns of theologians, for a fundamental theology where Augustine and Aquinas are balanced, or for cultural movements, but for a Christian anthropology where the interplay of traditional Catholic thinkers (including Greek patristic thought) with philosophers (Kant and Heidegger, and not Husserl and Scheler) has reached an easier and more creative stage. Rahner was only generally interested in the course of philosophy in the twentieth century; it could assist a Christian anthropology to explain existence before and with grace. Although the supernatural existential is central, the human person is neither analyzed in the negative existentialism of the 1920s nor from time to time related to Protestant theologies of the cross.

Przywara could be critical of Rahner, although the criticism touched more Rahner's teachers or contemporary Catholic philosophers than his conclusions or insights. In 1940 when the younger Jesuit had published only *Geist in Welt*, Przywara mentioned him as a member of a school drawn from both Joseph Maréchal and Heidegger, a direction whose view of the dynamic projectivity of the knowing self challenged the simpler traditional forms of the analogy of being. Przywara saw Maréchal as excessively mental and criticized the next generation of German Catholic philosophers from the 1950s — Gustav Siewerth, Gustav Söhngen, J. B. Lotz, Max Müller, and Karl Rahner — as lacking a critical distance from the Belgian Jesuit and lacking Przywara's interpretation of analogy, knowing, or intuition. "The intellectual mentality of the German postwar period is unfortunately still an imitation without critique of the great phenomenologists (Husserl, Scheler, Heidegger), or a serene, also uncritical rebaptism into a so-called Catholic phenomenology of both the work of Joseph Maréchal and his circle of followers, poor in ideas; that marriage between Heidegger and Maréchal shows, [an absence of] . . . a clear and neat distinction between phenomenology and Thomas Aquinas."[218] That kind of transcendentalism is too mental, a philosophy where there is too close an identity between idea and thing, a Thomism which is too Platonic, too essentialist.[219] Rahner, following Heidegger, preferred "existential finitude over against essential infinity"[220] and had a sanguine attitude toward Maréchal, who offered an intellectual, transcendental dynamism, a conditional desire which does not take away finite or Infinite freedom but which is "fundamentally present in every spiritual act in the form of a longing for the absolute Being (without therefore being explicitly and conceptually formulated). It is the a priori condition of every affirmation and acceptance of any finite thing."[221] Rahner's recollection of Maréchal's influence only touches on the most general orientations of a transcendental and active person.[222]

Przywara wrote, "Certainly the theology of the 'Christian person,' as Rahner seeks to develop it, shows too much the traces of Heidegger and too little argumentation in favor of the efficacy of such an approach."[223] As the decades passed, the influence of Heidegger on Rahner did not expand but remained limited to the method of inquiring questions and a general understanding of an approach to salvation-history that was both transcendental and existential.

John M. McDermott has presented a careful study of some influences of Przywara's understanding of analogy upon Rahner. In *Geist in Welt* the theme of oscillation in Przywara (Rahner employs *Schwebe*) is present, and little by little the existing person is identified with this hanging in a balance. "By considering man a *Schwebe* joining the infinite horizon of being to the here and now of sensibility, Rahner was harkening back to Przywara's preferred word to describe *analogia entis*. . . . Rahner's dynamic oscillation was located primarily in the individual subject, or spirit, while Przywara emphasized the overall metaphysical structure of reality embracing while transcending human subjectivity."[224] This dialectical and dynamic consideration of the relationship of the human and the divine is present in the *Foundations of Christian Faith*. God can create beings and relate to them without being subject to their vast difference from him; he offers creatures being and graced life, each being as "a concrete dialectic in history."[225] "For Przywara the desire for the supernatural vision was not so urgent as in Rahner, and he was more concerned to show how the poles of each lower order correlate harmoniously to the higher order so that at the end the supernatural gift complements and crowns the open structure of infravalent tensions found in a metaphysics of being. In Rahner's interpretation the individual subject has a profound thirst for the supernatural revelation of God that must be given as a gift." God's being of grace presupposes created being while "God's Word presupposes the human word in which he expresses himself freely and intelligibly."[226] Being and grace, not only in concept and metaphysical or revealed expression but in judgment and reality, oscillate between nothingness and the infinite as both gift and realization.

Przywara was aware of Rahner's growing importance, and in 1961 he praised him for fashioning a theology of the individual within the community, a Christianity of "Christ in me." Rahner was "a real Jesuit, with a reflective, cool, sober detachment," a true disciple of the great Jesuit theologians, "one who knows how to open up the traditional tracts in a positive way and so within an 'old theology' find a new theology."[227] Those Jesuit emphases reveal qualities in the individual and are sources for what could appear as an "existentialism," a direction highlighting the individual as qualitatively unique. "What the 'new theology' draws out authentically, despite its over-enthusiastic style, Rahner has drawn out from the beginning in a true Jesuit simplicity, reflexive and hesitant. In contrast to the Dominican, almost icon-like 'truth in itself,' he is concerned with the 'veritas creata of Aquinas.' Truth is not a superterrestrial 'veritas aeterna'—this God alone has and is— but truth in the 'creaturely form' of 'becoming.'"[228]

Przywara reviewed the first four volumes of Rahner's Schriften zur Theologie, "quite rich volumes," authentically human, colored by special situations. "This is not simply 'old theology' which was and always has been engaged in producing a one-sided 'abstraction' ceaselessly opposed to all that is contemporary and concrete, and changing everything into an ideal, eternal existence. Nor is it simply 'new theology' which presents charismatic, pneumatic 'visions' in contrast to a pile of old junk. The theology of Karl Rahner opens up the 'old theology' which is discussed in detail and transformed into something living, and he offers as well a 'new theology' in which the old is transparent . . . in which the particular newness of a concrete situation presents itself as 'the old theology here and today.'"[229] Rahner is undertaking something daring, "to fashion a dogmatic theology (which has long been static) into something dynamic and existential, dynamic in its roots and in all its branches." He does this by unfolding with the greatest care the basic intentions of these sources and areas, of getting past frozen formulas to the original questions they once addressed. "Rahner is certainly the only dogmatic theologian today who does not simply hand out the old equipment but who thoughtfully creates original equipment for the coming new age in advance of its arrival. These volumes and essays have all gathered new impulses so that the old traditions are not bypassed but have risen as today's reality."[230]

As we will see in the next chapter, when Przywara looked at the problem of the relationship of Catholic faith and revelation to a world of religions, he too drew on the Catholic tradition of implicit faith and subliminal grace. He asked what is the least one must believe to belong to the "soul" of the church, if not to the public social reality of the community of the baptized, and his response was along the same line as the later one of Rahner. Catholic theology holds that the act and content of faith in a person in its dynamic center at least touches the reality described explicitly by the church's faith. Do not deep articulations of belief in God's existence and the readiness to receive revelation in some way relate to Trinity and Incarnation? "The religious constitution," Przywara wrote, "of the soul of this 'Least-Catholic' is that for his religious consciousness his faith-realizations signify a conviction of God's existence and a self-giving to faith. So throughout his life there might be a lack of knowledge or a rejection of Catholic or Christian teaching . . . but the 'salvation' of this 'Least-Catholic' depends on him striving with the best knowledge and conscience for truth."[231] In some way the "Least-Catholic" is an anticipation of the infelicitous (and set-aside) phrase of Rahner, "the anonymous Christian." The words in both Jesuits, and the ideas of Catholic theologians of the first half of the twentieth century and before (sometimes in a prolix or mechanical way) usually develop a positive realization of some implicit faith enabled by grace. Przywara, like Rahner, stands in the long theological line of numerous theologians considering the movements of faith and free will from and toward grace. Rahner gives a different emphasis, one increasingly less philosophical and more and more historical, more ecclesial, increasingly replete with pastoral insights in concrete areas. The two theologians certainly agreed on the infinite richness and nearness of grace, on the Christian reality as making near the incomprehensibility of God with and through Jesus the Crucified.

What an array of companions! They all drew ideas and inspiration from Przywara, and they all saw him in their own way. Karl Barth found him to be the articulate apologete for Catholic sacramentality, while Edith Stein knew him as a spiritual counselor and a metaphysical companion. Hans Urs von Balthasar praised him almost mythically, while for Karl Rahner his fellow Jesuit was an independent, challenging precursor. For all of them he was someone of a particular church, spirituality, and metaphysical theology; in various ways an inspiring teacher, an advocate of contemporary Catholicism dealing with modern problems, a person of a particular generation, a man of limitations and of great stimulus.

Chapter 5

The Christian in the Church

With these pages, a final chapter, we move from a consideration of Erich Przywara's contemporaries to his theological
ideas. If his theology frequently touched people he knew and
arranged philosophers and theologians of the past, it nevertheless explores three Christian realities, three contacts between
the searching human being and the Triune God: Christian life
and spirituality, liturgy, and church. Each of the three is related
to the others: a particular spirituality personalizes Christian
life; the liturgy is the public worship of the Christian; the
church is the collectivity of Christian lives. A thematic expression of Erich Przywara's is "God in Christ in the church."

In the 1920s Przywara saw new directions in Catholic life,
directions running parallel to those of the Protestant dialectical theologians, themes born of Aquinas and Newman and
developed by Karl Adam and Romano Guardini, movements
of symbol and community. Clearly the future lay beyond neoscholasticism, beyond the medieval and Baroque theological
schools of religious orders and universities. The challenge was
to escape the old subjectivism and the new existentialism, and
to find a unity of the objective and the subjective, of salvation
and faith; in short, to describe and employ the "Catholic primal
principle" of *analogia entis*[1] culminating in Incarnation.

Przywara's theology wanted to help both the modern seeker
and the Christian believer. There could be no dabbling in a science for which only mathematics existed, in a modern philosophy in which anxious existence had pushed away God, or in a
Protestantism where God did all. Polarity, that dynamic swing
between the divine and the human, was a way for men and

women to understand the depth and richness of God, to exist between the revelation of the Triune God and the phenomenologies of the present. Analogy, participation, and commerce joined the Infinite and the finite as theologies of grace active in humanity, making the Catholic tradition an equilibrium of polarities. Life in the church is a path to be walked, a path of transformation described by theologians and mystics, a path leading away from a sinful attempt to be like God. Life is the journey of the Christian paradox, losing life to save it.

CHRISTIAN EXISTENCE

After 1920 Przywara sought a contemporary and personal expression of the presence of God in the life of a man or a woman. As we mentioned, he was among the Catholic theologians who unfolded a theology of grace beyond the Baroque mechanics of actual graces and mortal sins pushing and pulling a neutral human person from day to day.[2] He explored how the transcendental personality called for, moved toward, received, was vivified by divine life. That active receptivity— he sought a synthesis of Molinist and Bañezian inspirations—freely received from a free God a higher life as a gift. Human transcendentality and history can be natural and supernatural, humanist and Trinitarian. How was Przywara's theology exemplified in the graced life of an individual, in the liturgical and ecclesial life of the community?

The life of grace leads at times to dramatic concretizations in what today are called "spiritualities." What is a spirituality? Spirituality is a theology made vivid in lives. Spirituality is the life of grace made personal. The word is only a century or so old, although the reality is ancient in the Catholic church. A spirituality is a group's particular arrangement of and emphasis upon aspects of Christianity, a way of life and a way of seeing life. Spirituality is doctrine in praxis, a tradition and a school, a cluster of beliefs about God and self. Where does a spirituality come from? A person living in a cultural era selects and emphasizes out of his or her faith ways of encountering the realms of the holy and of the revealed. That cluster of Gospel truths is the spirituality. Christianity is too rich to be fully presented by one monastery or school, by one age or culture, and so history and genius create spiritualities. A spirituality appears in a moment of history to present a vision or a path to grace. A spirituality comes into existence not to dismantle or criticize the content of the Gospel but to apply dynamically some facets of revelation which appear powerful and useful for this world or this movement, charisms of God embodied in a person first and next in schools and traditions.

Many articles and books have been written and continue to be written on how Ignatian spirituality formed and inspired Przywara's metaphysical theology, and how his theology led to an important interpretation and exposition of Jesuit spirituality. His work on the *Spiritual Exercises* lies prior to the interpretations of both Karl and Hugo Rahner, Gaston Fessard, Hans Urs von Balthasar, and Bernard Lonergan. Karl Rahner said of the older Jesuit: "He made Ignatius Loyola into an intelligible and great figure in Christian intellectual history and removed the Baroque and scholastic layers of paint covering his image."[3] In a single essay he could find new similarities between Aquinas and Ignatius or argue that the human being Nietzsche intended was the one nourished by the *Spiritual Exercises.*[4]

Przywara was an individual educated in a particular Catholic spirituality of one particular religious order, the Society of Jesus: that spirituality was deeply imbued with the vision of Ignatius of Loyola. Przywara, however, was comfortable with other spiritualities and with articulating traditional ones anew. His knowledge of the history of spirituality was extensive. Knowledgeable about the Rhenish and Dominican spiritualities (but less so about Cistercian and monastic ones), he was deeply drawn to the great figures of Carmel. Translations and paraphrases of the poems and hymns of John of the Cross, collections of writings by Augustine and Newman, the poetic presentations of psalms or the collection of prayers and readings from the feasts of the church year—these are texts in Hebrew, Augustinian, Carmelite spiritualities. And yet, a lasting spirituality is ultimately a philosophical theology, and real mysticism is "the setting aside of every mysticism."[5]

Przywara entered the Jesuits in 1908 and wrote down reflections during his formation and in the years after he was ordained in 1920. In 1925 he published a set of meditations on Ignatian spirituality, *Divine Majesty,* a book whose literary genre is personal questioning and whose reflections resemble free verse, pages decorated with references to biblical passages in the margins. Thomas Corbishley, S. J., described Przywara as "one of the ablest and most perceptive of commentators on the text of the *Exercises* . . . [whose work] brings out, then, not so much the basic structure of the *Exercises* as the varied aspects, one might almost call them the moods of the process which the retreat-maker undergoes under the direction of Ignatius."[6] The chosen themes are solitude, service, self-giving, and love. A finely written concluding essay discusses Ignatian piety as a spirituality bringing not a new content different from other forms of Christian life appearing in history but a particular stance and attitude. Like the German mystics who celebrated the procession of the human soul as a word of God born out into daily life in order to find God, Ignatian spirituality finds God in all things. If this sounds like Meister Eckhart and Jan van Ruusbroec in the fourteenth century, it differs from the Rhineland mystics, for their outward flow of the person from the Word remains in terms of soul and God still somewhat above ordinary life. Ignatius' respect before God was born of the experience of God's infiniteness and groundlessness, a sobriety that accepts existence as existence and earth as earth. "Through Ignatian piety there blows the wind of autumn, the autumn of the reality of earth, the community of earth, the aloneness of earth."[7] The *Exercises* fashion a path to new life: one aspect should not be taken for the whole. Aloneness is the presupposition for meeting the One who comes silently, while self-giving and ministry are the meeting's fulfillment. Being alone does not exclude community as family, society, and church, while the cycle of the liturgy nourishes the individual. Aloneness does not mean being apart, but being detached bestows toward all that God has created a detachment from all that is not God.[8]

Does Ignatian spirituality belong only to the members of one religious order? How can it offer insight to those who are not members? How can it avoid losing its identity in the Society when it becomes the ethos of organization or a formalistic obedience minimalizing free life? Bernhard Gertz sees Przywara moving away from a theology of "soul" ("not a word of antiquity, of the Old Testament, nor of European Christianity")[9] to a view of the Christian and the church, active in service.[10] Experts point out that Przywara was a pioneering force in transcending an Ignatian spirituality that was rigid and solely ascetic, timid and cold and concerned with sacrifice of any sort.[11]

In 1938, after five years of concentrated effort by Przywara, a multivolume theology of the exercises, *Deus Semper Major,* was published. Because the *Spiritual Exercises* aim at opening up the word of God in the revelation of the Old and New Covenants, it is a biblical theology and a speculative theology. That book on Ignatian spirituality is the complementary twin to Przywara's study *Analogia Entis.* James Zeitz writes: "In his whole programme Przywara explains the *Exercises* in their material and formal dimensions, using the texts of Ignatius to show their coherency. His originality is to elevate the commentary-genre of the *Exercises* to a theology, to the 'God-logic' that the *Exercises* contain and express."[12] Przywara wrote at the beginning of his book, "The inner 'logic' of the *Exercises* should disclose itself as 'theo-logic.'"[13] Volume 1 considers the opening prayer of the *Exercises,* the *Anima Christi,* commenting on key phrases and sketching the foundation of the spirituality, and then turns to the first week. Two subsequent volumes treat the further weeks. Przywara wrote of drawing together three interpretations of the exercises. The first focuses on salvation through acts of personal freedom drawn toward the future, and it saw the exercises as a religious school of the will; the second draws more on the glory of God and the detachment of the creature seeking and finding the glory and plan of God; the third unfolds the foolishness of the cross, the humility and modesty of the creature, and the various deaths encountered in the contradictions of this world, deaths which are, however, paths to life.[14] The work in various parts is not a crowning synthesis but often blocks of notes, and its direction and integration are not always evident.

We must let experts in this area guide us. Michael Schneider has studied three interpretations of the *Spiritual Exercises:* those of Przywara, Karl Rahner, and Fessard. The approach of Przywara he names "the call unto the other," a focus on the human believer with a human face. "The movement of theological thinking in Przywara is a quest for the 'ungraspable' point where world and humanity meet the living God. . . . What is decisive in Christian theology is clear: it can point out the way to God through crises and efforts of differentiation."[15] A central exercise is the discernment of spirits, the personal meditation upon the direction life should take at this moment. Przywara gave *discretio spirituum* three meanings. First, it embodies a theocentric crisis, a need to look beneath all systems of thought and being (this spirituality furthers a contemplative metaphysics of thought and being), and thus the *Spiritual Exercises,* which is not a book of information or method, not really an exercise or a set of exercises, offers a theological program for life or philosophical reflection.[16] Second, discernment of spirits takes place in light of the incarnate Word and the paradox of the cross. Third, this capability of discernment accompanies the individual on the path of existence and assists the disciple in discerning the plan and invitation of God.[17] Thus the Ignatian path of discernment is a theology of discipleship involving experiential knowledge of the divine will. What will be lived out in daily life appears in an exemplary way in the knowledge of God, and so religious reflection and existential life belong together. For

Przywara discernment and life draw on the incarnation of grace in the person. To begin is to enter upon a journey penetrated by the *commercium*, by an incarnational exchange where analogy is interpreted as participation in divine life; next, that incarnational theology interpreted in light of the Ignatian "*Deus semper major*" involves foundation, explanation, vocation, union, mission, and resolution; finally, while the act of discernment and the theology of commerce lead to finding God present in all things, they also bring the rule of sensing and living with and within the church.

The experience[18] of knowledge and love, of being known and loved by God calls forth a respectful distance and yet a closeness of self-giving service in the world. The Word of God descends into the existential reality of an individual life, and each life assumes the form of a journey, a path of self-change with the transcendent commandment of love in the foreground, a journey pre-indicated in Exodus and the Acts of the Apostles, a journey sustained by the tradition of the church. For Friedrich Wulf, Przywara's Ignatian spirituality is philosophical and theological, incarnational and active. The Christian life of reflection and action exists within not only faith but theories of the world of beings. "Przywara cannot speak of religion and spirituality without speaking metaphysically."[19] Theo-logical discourse tends to the always greater God who as mystery and intimacy is present in our history. Balancing this metaphysical theology is the descent of the incarnation into history and the cross, the emptying of Philippians. The believer's response in humility is "a leap into not knowing," "a foolishness with Christ."[20] "There is a difference in language between Przywara's metaphysical-theological style of speaking and that of most of his contemporaries. Particularly in the later phase of his work he speaks more as a visionary and prophet, peering into the now of time to see its relationship to the end. . . . This is the *summa* of the spirituality of Przywara: God and the human person as one in love despite everything, the greatest of all mysteries because in it there is a hint of who God is."[21] The journey of spirituality could be put succinctly: "The way of the Christian is a transformation from a religious life of outward observance and mechanical exercises into a truly personal life with God and creator."[22]

Is God's will for us attractive? Does God's call shatter us? Are we only blunt, lifeless tools? If there is a limitation in the German Jesuit's writings on Ignatian spirituality, it is that the existential and personal dimensions remain abstract; and second, that the profound issues of divine and human freedoms (that venerable field of dispute between Dominicans, Jesuits, and Jansenists) are not penetrated very far. The Jesuit, however, is distinctive: he belongs to no "religious family" but labors everywhere in the world to bring the Gospel to all; without new name or special clothes he belongs to the church.[23] The teaching of Ignatius Loyola on the instrumentality of service is central. The goal of the Christian's ministry was not to be nothing nor to replace God but to follow the Spirit in a service that could only be incomplete.

As part of his view of Catholicism faced with a changing society, Przywara wrote of the new importance of women. Does society exist through an opposition of men and women or is it above that? It is the same human life in those two forms. The Jesuit, however, contrasts the woman's intrinsic characteristic of life with the orientation of men to things. The world of life is the world of the house and not of science, and yet the house is a kind of prison for a woman. "The issue is for the woman in her manner to draw all professions into the warm nearness of life and for this characteristic of the woman to be given its due in society and culture."[24] And yet there is a danger that the woman will become a man—a development which is all too clear in the pressures put on women ("the neuroses and psychoses which many psychologists described in students and women in the workplace").[25] Some of this is a problem of society, for all work is executed in the style of the man. Can Catholicism contribute to this situation? God is beyond male and female; God is father as a term in the inner-divine filiation, and not in contrast to a mother (whom God is also). Catholicism does not divinize the male, and it puts a woman at the beginning and center of its faith. Nor, he continues, should the priesthood turn the man into an idol aloof from women, for the ideal of the priesthood is a unity of man and woman in the form of virginity.[26] Przywara ends his essays, nonetheless, with the typical characteristics of active and passive, agent and recipient, Jesus and Mary at Calvary—an eschatology of equality. These views, even the clear discussion of the problem, may have been progressive for 1930, but it is curious that his experience with Edith Stein and her struggle to find a university position—he prized her advice in abstract metaphysical issues—did not show him the limitations of his position.

Spirituality did not exist for itself but reached from the Trinity to mundane service. A spirituality of Catholic Action, a spirituality of the liturgical movement, a spirituality of women—in the 1920s Przywara praised their emergence and then often located them in the milieu of

an Ignatian spirituality which was also modified by the new understanding of the reciprocity of nature and grace. "There is no point in
being excited about Catholic activity if it has not been preceded by
Catholic life of prayer. . . . Every emergence into the world will sooner
or later be a secularization if it has not previously been a journey into
God.This kind of Catholicism of the absolute service of God must be
a Catholicism encompassing all. That means that there is for Catholics as
concrete men and women no area that is neutral or interconfessional.
That is the practical meaning of the Catholic teaching of the 'supernatural and sole goal.' Certainly the supernatural reality of redemption
and sanctification is in no way the inner property or function of nature:
nature retains its proper causality and laws. Nature is not a 'pure nature'
but is concretely a historical supernaturally redeemed and elevated nature, i.e., the concrete existing human being . . . the human being whose
individual goal and meaning in life is to be one Christ in body and soul,
the *una sancta catholica.*"[27] Every spirituality is deeply personal, highly
metaphysical, and yet destined for service in the world.

After World War II, in 1960, Przywara published a book which he
must have seen as a contribution to a spirituality for postwar German
Catholics; it was not a further description of Augustine's *Confessions*
or of Ignatius' *Spiritual Exercises* but a consideration of three virtues:
humility, patience, and love.Those chapters were written during and
after the war, and they hold the tonality of a defeated and occupied
country. "The three studies are a contribution to the relationship
between classical and Christian teaching on virtue.Within Christianity
there is sometimes an attempt to present a typology of the teaching on
virtue, to work out a certain dialectic. Ultimately we want to see here
real examples of the morality, the asceticism, and mysticism of revelation that are necessary forms vis-à-vis human, speculative morality."[28]
The Przywara method was present (Max Scheler's *Zur Rehabilitierung
der Tugend* is mentioned as an inspiration) and each virtue was considered in its form in classic Greek philosophy, in the revelation of the Old
and New convenants, and then in Christian spiritual classics ranging
from Augustine and Benedict through Aquinas to Thérèse of Lisieux.
In that book written forty years after his early considerations of philosophical theologies and spiritualities, the same patterns appear: contrasts
and harmony, polarity and opposition.

Writers on Przywara presume that the Ignatian source of his theology remained central throughout his life. Free activity, the relation-

ship of freedom to the cross in an individual's journey, contemplation becoming love and love becoming service — these are important in all the genres of his work. The existential dimensions of Przywara's writings flow from a young man's introduction into a spirituality that is practical, one where the spiritual life is drawn from religious experience and pursued concretely. At the same time, his views on the liturgical movement suggest that a spirituality of Baroque interiority hindered the Jesuit a little from appreciating new directions for the liturgy rediscovered in the patristic church (ranging from icons to solemn ritual), and from imagining new movements in society and church destined to alter the status quo of parishes and sodalities.

The personality of Erich Przywara sought spirituality in abstract theologies and yet expected theologies to be personal. Drawing on a metaphysics encompassing faith as well as knowing, he sketched a life-journey to the divine through being and grace. Mysticism and prayer were the insight-born gifts of knowing, as Joseph Maréchal had worked to show.[29] Contrary to the approach of many schools of spirituality developed in the Baroque period and after, Przywara did not separate the spiritual life from communal liturgy, nor the ordinary life of virtue from grace. Ascetic practice and contemplation nourish each other. Thus his perspective unifies prayer and service as do the theology of Aquinas or the ministry of Ignatius Loyola. In those theologies the soul sought not to be lost in the Godhead but to be present to God in ministerial activity. Przywara composed a theology for the church and the world; he sought to be an evangelist of graced life as ordinary: "The Catholic is the fully relaxed, unconstrained person, the person of serene ordinariness ... In his direct and ordinary development and activity the Catholic lives in a true holiness as one among many and in this consciousness is essentially already someone influential. Catholic virtue means 'holy ordinariness.'"[30]

THE LITURGY

The thinker of transcendence and analogy was also a participant in the reappearance of theologies of liturgy and church that ultimately would lead to Vatican II. Early on, Przywara wrote popular books on the Eucharist (1917) and the church year (1923), and his writings on the Bible often used a liturgical perspective.[31] He arranged liturgical texts for publication and modeled poems on the hymns of the divine office. A selection of texts (translated from Hebrew, Greek, and Latin) led the reader through the liturgical year, *Nuptiae Agni. Liturgie des Kirchenjahrs* (composed in 1934 but published in 1948), while *Hymnus* (1936) offered poetically formed translations of Latin liturgical fragments. His writings about the church year were not summaries of the history and meaning of liturgical feasts but meditations for the individual attending the daily Mass of different feasts. The church year is about life overcoming death, memory and childlike composure, community and aloneness, in short about polarities. That "ultimate idea of the liturgical movement"[32] did not, however, unfold the historical origins of the various cycles of feasts nor unlock the interplay of readings and prayers but drew the liturgy into a philosophical spirituality, into a succession of polarities and personal attitudes, and unlike the liturgical movement did not study the biblical and historical sources.[33]

As we have seen, the Jesuit had a certain reserve toward the liturgical movement as it looked to patristic and monastic models, to the objective historical rituals within community celebration making present the Risen Christ, and he focused more on interior prayer. Odo Casel, Ildefons Herwegen, and Romano Guardini composed liturgical theologies of presence and symbol anticipating the divine, as the liturgical movement shifted attention from rubrics (precisely fulfilled to summon forth a mechanics of divine grace) to the understanding of the symbols and rites. The nature of liturgy itself, its interesting and varied origins, its relationship to the Bible and to the historical and risen Christ were central to Pius Parsch, Odo Casel and many Benedictines, Romano Guardini, and Josef Jungmann, and Franz Xaver Arnold.[34] Did they, Przywara asked, run the risk of losing Catholic objectivity? Were they influenced by contemporary sociologists such as Georg Simmel, scholars of the history of religions school such as Richard Reitzenstein, and by liberal Protestant theologians such as Adolf von Harnack? Przywara was opposed to an understanding of liturgy focused greatly on Easter and the Risen Christ because they might neglect the suffering Christ and the suffering Christian. "What is clearly Catholic is the crucified Risen One and the risen Crucified."[35]

The liturgical movement "has a historical continuity with the organic theology of Romanticism, with Johann Adam Möhler's idea of church . . . [flowing] from the Romantic primacy of community" and comes too "from Dom Guéranger's idea of the church year, from

the abbeys of Maredsous and Maria-Laach, from the retrieval by Adam
Müller and Romano Guardini of tradition."[36] It echoes the Tübingen
school with its ideas of church as organism and organization as a dialectic between a church of love and a church of law. Przywara's attitude toward German Romantic theology was positive and critical;
as a young teacher in Feldkirch he had learned much from the writings of Joseph Görres and Martin Deutinger, from the mystical systems of Franz von Baader and from the ecclesiology of Möhler. The
Romantics, going beyond the arrogant Enlightenment, struggled to
join life with reality but failed sometimes to keep the transcendence
and presence of God distinct, to separate mysticism from magic. In
the 1930s Przywara was slightly reserved toward ecclesiologies redolent
of Romanticism, for they ran the risk of idealist pantheism. He feared
an emphasis on mystical interiority at the expense of the external;
Romanticism's true mission was to retain dialectical forces which,
exploding closed, rational systems, would draw the human person
to depth and expanse. "The Romantic sees the eternal only in the
medium of time."[37]

Enthusiasm for patristic homilies and medieval architecture was
spreading. Was the historical rediscovery of liturgy a repristination, too
symbolic and ecclesiastical in a Byzantine way? Certainly there are
important forms and sources from the first centuries of the church—
Przywara admits that they have a superior theology and style in prayers
from those centuries over against prayers for feasts of saints composed
after 1700—but the course of history brings legitimate changes and
variety: no one period, no matter how ancient, can be the paradigm. "It
is the Catholic view that the Holy Spirit is active in the church in all
ages. No level of time is immediately 'Primal Christianity' since Christianity is not an ethos which blooms in a particular time and in the
following ages fades, but Christianity is in all ages Christ living on.
The patristic age is no closer to Christ than is our age."[38] Are the personal spiritualities of Francis of Assisi and Ignatius Loyola not inspiring
today? Liturgy immersed in the psalms is more than eternalized forms,
the forms of certain classical centuries (he does not mention concrete
changes in rites and texts). Perhaps his difficulty lay in a shift away from
metaphysical language into biblical language, a consideration of forms
leading to aesthetic issues, an emphasis upon transformation and eschatology in light of Orthodox liturgies. Do they threaten his perspective?
The analogy of being is not mainly concerned with the empowering

visibility of symbolic movement and form. His articles and reviews, generally repeating the same points, approved of development and change but wanted liturgy to fit into a metaphysics of God and subjectivity. There was a difference between a theology of transformation and his own perspective of polarity. The former gave Christ, the liturgy, and the Christian too transfigured an identity and paid too little attention to the cross and the human (and also too little attention to an inner spirituality of devotions). Przywara had in terms of liturgy been formed in other worlds—Tridentine liturgy and Baroque spirituality.

What is curious is that his criticisms of 1960 repeated the ones of 1925, while the liturgical movement with its many theological centers and journals had expanded and varied its approaches and was no longer only the ideas of Casel and Guardini.

From 1923 on, nonetheless, he saw the liturgical movement as one of the distinctive forces in a renewed Catholicism: it challenged what he called the extensive exteriorization of society, the reduction of life to classes and to possessions. A look at the liturgical movement in 1930 proclaimed: the liturgical movement is a "No" to an individualistic church, a gathering of individuals, and a "No" to a bureaucratic church in which the individual is not a real, active member but just an object.[39] The liturgical movement has links to the new ecclesiology of the Body of Christ which stands over against the previous theories of "church militant," legal entity, perfect society, organization.[40] In any interplay of personal spirituality and community, devotion is inseparable from the real sacramental forms of the community and is distinct from the Enlightenment and modernity because it proffers both an eschatological viewpoint and a transformative viewpoint. He recognized that making the symbolic forms of liturgy understood and meaningful is not accidental to liturgy, although forms do not exist for themselves and are themselves mediating between the Creator God and our lives.[41] Gertz selects the following as characteristics of Przywara's theology of liturgy: a union of spiritual and ecclesial life with liturgy; the lasting activity of the spirit in a creature who has similarity and dissimilarity with God; the rejection of the ideas that community and liturgical life set aside personal spirituality or that the form of the liturgy is the measure of the Gospel; a critique of the overshadowing of the reality of the cross by symbols and rites.[42]

Przywara's writings came from the same milieu as those of Guardini, and in the mid-1920s he praised Guardini's program for liturgy, a program that was not just an aesthetic or a general religious ethos but was the result of philosophical theology. With respect for the ethos of a God who is apart from history, it holds that cult is the correlate of logos and that liturgy differs from mysticism.[43] Nonetheless, throughout his life a general critique of Guardini was present. Liturgy is not primarily about the morality of the self but about the honor of God; if highly personal, it aims at transcendence. In Hanna-Barbara Gerl's view, Przywara found in Guardini's liturgical views a particular ethos, a "program": form over against free life, community over against individualism, monastic and symbolic life over against active life. He feared a too solitary mystical space of the renewed church, an aesthetic symbolism, the primacy of the word, the danger of a liturgical or priestly aristocracy and experience and moment over journey and mission. "The authenticity and health of the liturgical renewal depends above all on the ultimate comportment of *service*."[44] He asked in the 1930s whether Guardini took seriously human nature, injured and injuring human existence. Was his well-known dialectic of opposites too quick to remove opposition or pain, too "caught up in aphorisms"?[45] Guardini's thought ran the risk of being too personal, of neglecting the tension between nature and grace.[46] Faber concludes: "Przywara does not understand sacramentality in Guardini's two-dimensional form of symbol in which the inner reality works out through the external form and becomes the expression of itself. Rather, the Jesuit connects the divine and human reality in sacraments within the *commercium* through which God has an exchange with the creature, totally other to God."[47]

In 1960 — the fulfillment of the preliminary stages of the liturgical movement at Vatican II could not yet be foreseen — the Jesuit reviewed positively Cipriano Vagaggini's *Theological Dimensions of the Liturgy*. He noted the impoverished celebration and theology of liturgy before the movement began. Vagaggini's approach is one of history, not one of mystery in the line of Casel and Herwegen, and it stands in contrast to Guardini's "game of the Muses" leading to an "aestheticization of liturgy obscuring the death and resurrection, the cross and glory, the enormous mystery of the redeeming exchange."[48]

Przywara's perspective changed little over forty years: he advocated a historical dimension for liturgical renewal, feared the aestheticization of the liturgy, and emphasized service along with symbol.[49] Still, it cannot be said that his critique, born of a more individual spirituality and profound orientation to metaphysics, offered its own theology or practice of liturgy.

THE CHURCH

The church is persons and places where not only officeholders but religious worldviews and interplays of life and grace occur. The 1920s saw the emergence of new directions in the theology of the church that were historical and biblical, patristic and modern. That new ecclesiology focused upon community and not just on membership, upon ministries other than authority; it was a true theology and not the usual ineffective apologetics based on the four marks of the church.[50]

Przywara's early philosophy of religion mentioned the church briefly: a continuance of the incarnation, an organization within sacramentality, a place of spirituality. In the Catholic church cult offers a divine and unchanging liturgy, while Catholic mysticism and praxis grasp God as the formal ideal of holiness.[51] The Leipzig lectures showed how Platonic and Aristotelian metaphysics, Reformation and Idealist philosophies fashioned different ecclesiologies; for instance, there were political theories and historical occurrences where Christianity was subject to political authority, whether in Constantinople or Vienna, and, at the other pole, there are small enthusiastic sects rejecting every civic and ecclesial form. Modern subjectivisms too — the rigorist Christian sectarian, the linguistic analyst, the academic theoretician, the ethician of duty — have their dangers.[52]

The dialectic of immanence and transcendence developed in light of God and Christ is also true for the church. Incarnation and its continuance in the liturgical church exist over against two extremes: first, an immanentism where a self-disclosing God dwells solely in the human being for whom the word "god" is only the name of creation's unfolding; second, the transcendentalism of the moribund, static worship of an eternal god existing in eternity for whom the self-changing life of humanity has no inner religious meaning and is, at best, a purely negative self-offering.[53] Ultimately Przywara's ecclesiology flows from theoretical foundations of the interplay of the human and the divine: it is incarnational, sacramental, and somewhat individualist. Could he draw it into the new movements of church life?

What Is the Church?

Throughout Europe after World War I ecclesiology was leaving the constraints of apologetical arguments over the sole validity of the Roman Catholic church. How is the church related to the reign of

God? As participation or as fullness, as a moment in time or as the eschaton? Is God present in the individual or in society?

The fashion since 1900 had been to seek out the essence of religion or of Christianity—the books by Karl Adam, Leo Baeck, Adolf von Harnack, and Daniel Feuling (Przywara's coworker in the translation of Newman) all present "an essence," a *Wesen*.[54] A Catholic, however, belongs not to a religion, not to a collective idea or theory, but to a church. "For Catholics there is no detailed list which makes up the essence of Christianity. Rather, the living church in its infallible teaching office is, in the last instance, the essence of Christianity.... From this it follows immediately that no 'theological schools or systems' can be equated with the church, but that the daily life of the church with its liturgy and devotions too belongs to the very being of Christianity."[55] The reality of Christianity is not solely a transcendental subjectivity; Catholicism's nature finds various objective realizations. "This is the Catholic correlation between faith and church: the church overshadows faith, objective holiness overshadows subjective holiness."[56] The church is more diverse than a religious ethos, more social than a decisive human existence. Not rejecting existential and vitalist motifs, Przywara expected the church to be a place where grace occurs in activity, where modes of monastic life flourish in mysticism and liturgy (mysticism relates to knowing, while liturgy relates to life), and where new movements draw strivings and feelings to the mystery which is God. "In Catholic interiority there is a radicalism of an 'immediacy before God' which can be viewed as the highest level of mysticism, as 'immediate vision.' In Catholic cult there is the radicalism of a divine, unchanging liturgy which is the authentic but creative change of the cultic forms in the course of the centuries."[57] Praxis complements interiority, and in Catholic praxis there is the radicalism of a supernatural ethic and culture which can grasp God as the formal ideal of sanctity.

Przywara began with a critique of a church of pure interior experience, or of "cultic hierarchy" or "heavenly court."[58] The church is a community of the redeemed who are also sinners; its liturgy employs signs and sacraments for simple realities. Should religion be utterly interiorized, exchanging any objective realm of religion for existential inspiration; or, on the other hand, should the community, demeaning the individual, become a "God-community," a theocracy containing everything? One cannot help but notice that in some writings the specter of totalitarianism is unrealistically portrayed as remote, while a critique of individualism is more forceful than the critique of a too domineering ecclesiastical directorate. Pauline texts reject a church of riches and power: there is in history "a scandal of an un-Christian Christian people, a scandal of an unpriestly priesthood, scandals of unmonastic monasteries, of clerical envy and ambition among the ordained; there are even scandals concerning the papacy itself."[59]

Catholicism is quite distinct from Protestantism. Przywara saw the Protestant churches as vulnerable when they move away from their Reformation roots and embrace the religious expressions of modern philosophy. Luther and Calvin are a Protestantism "from above" while modern Protestantism is "from below." The Protestant churches, because they do not struggle with the forms of being a church, find it difficult to fashion a union of the expression of faith and the life of the church.[60] In ecclesiology Przywara shied away from an Augustinian theology where God and the soul converse, and away from its variation in Protestantism. "In Catholicism there is no either/or between quest and tradition, and it is erroneous when one exalts one of the two as the Catholic position. Being-in-tradition is the discipline and ethos of the Catholic quest, and that religious quest is the inner life of Catholic tradition. The severance of either side is Protestant, whether it is a Protestantism of the absolutized seeker or that of the divinized authority."[61] In the mid-1920s Przywara said that contemporary theology was not simply speculative and philosophical but also "ecclesiocentric," and he inquired into the ideal of community for Catholicism. What was the future church to be? Was it to be a contemporary group of full freedom, or an idealized Gothic past? Regardless, the structures of the church should not remain as they are, a deformed tapestry of aristocratic customs. Ultimately ecclesiology for Przywara is a series of variations on the underlying swing-tension of immanence and transcendence, God and the individual and the community.

The Ecclesiology of the Body of Christ

One new ecclesiology emerging in Europe during the 1920s was biblical, the Pauline Body of Christ: for instance, it is present in Guardini's *The Church and the Catholic* (1922) emphasizing the "we" of the church beyond ecclesiastical servitude and ignorance. In 1940 Przywara published an overview of the ecclesiological literature on "*Corpus Christi Mysticum,*" treating at length the pioneering work of the Dominican, Dominikus Mannes Koster, *Volk Gottes im Werden,* whose motifs of Body of Christ and People of God influenced the encyclical of Pius XII, the theology of Yves Congar, and the texts of Vatican II.[62] Rudolf Michael Schmitz in his survey of ecclesiologies from 1918 to 1943 joins Przywara to Guardini and Adam, because all three see world and church as two polarities from which a unity should emerge.[63] What is characteristic in the ecclesiology is ontological-theological underpinnings for church issues. The primal structure is two unmixed realities, as God and the human were in Christ, and these enter into the historical forms of church life; the church is "the sole concreteness of God in Christ."[64]

The church is "the ultimate form," of salvation-history, of the ongoing presence of the Spirit,[65] but this sacramental organism needs to rediscover its full activity. One source of this new theology lay outside ecclesiology: Max Scheler's essay on the sociological orientation of Catholics after the First World War and their mission in the contemporary world. It called for an ecclesiology which included more than the hierarchy, for a theory and praxis of a church that was more than the church militant.[66] Przywara also saw Husserl's turn to the object and Heidegger's philosophy of existence in the world implied in the Pauline theme of "pneumatic existence." The Apostle's "communal we" is not a modish phrase but an essential description of the church, implying neither the "perfect society" of post-Baroque Catholicism nor the Lutheran state-church but the theologies of the Body of Christ, old and new. There are legitimate legal structural aspects in the church, but theology stimulated by Scheler asks how does an intellectual and ethical community become one of liturgical and personal sacrifice, and what is the difference between a general love and Christian ministry.[67] Still, the liturgical movement and the new ecclesiology of the Body of Christ are advances over the previous theories of church militant, legal entity, society, organization—and in modest ways they too are born of the new philosophical directions.[68]

Pius XII issued his encyclical *Mystici Corporis* in 1943. Yves Congar in his history of ecclesiology, when discussing that papal letter, mentioned favorably the critique by Przywara of "a tendency to a certain vague romanticism, a tendency to conceive the Mystical Body simply as the domain of grace, an inclination to see the consequent aberration of imagining a permanent physical presence of Christ in each Christian."[69] Nevertheless, Przywara wrote, the encyclical avoids two extremes: the church as a mystical milieu, and the church as a rational or legal institution. The real church seeks in a dialectic of history to overcome the one-sidedness of a church of immanent life or a church of law and authority. "The accent lies on the visible, divine majesty in the church, on the here-and-now of God in the living word of the church."[70] Inevitably the church has four modalities: (1) the collective person receiving the presences of the Trinity, (2) the Body of Christ, (3) an organization of visible offices, and (4) a Christian spiritual company of individual members "who are formed by the church and who enter into the world, a church of sent laity, a church of people and of the world."[71] If today's ecclesiology begins with biblical metaphors for the church and the Pauline "charismatic order" in the church, it ends with a community made concrete in external services for church or society; it will not be a church solely of Jesus or solely of itself but of a people contacted by all three persons of the Trinity, an ecclesiology which is incarnational exchange and analogy of participation.[72]

Eva-Maria Faber in her study comparing the ecclesiologies of Przywara and Guardini devotes to the topic of mission a large section on Przywara's ecclesiology. "An institutional and hierarchical constitution should render the church not a form resting within itself, with itself as goal, but should structure the church as essentially a church in mission. The institution takes the church and each Christian into an instrumental service as mission."[73] The pulsing structure of the analogy of being joined to the missions of the Trinity support this ecclesiology, while from another direction a theology of mission is inspired by the Ignatian *Spiritual Exercises,* in which spiritual union with God leads to mission. The Lord of mission is the Word incarnate, and Pentecost contains grace lasting through time and throughout the world for service. The church exists not to present perfect theology and liturgy but to assist the work of Jesus and his Apostles. In a tension of analogy Christians effect the growth of the kingdom of God, but they always retain their dissimilarity to the Holy Spirit in nature and grace.[74] The church is sent to all peoples, to perform many ministries.

New developments like the liturgical movement and Catholic Action call forth groups where Catholics take part as mature individuals working for the improvement of society and governments. In 1924 Przywara appealed to the Catholic associations not to overlook a political and social role, not to remain active only within the church, and for the liturgical movement to pass out into the world after the *Ite missa est.* Przywara did not envisage new monastic orders emerging but saw the

future ministerial direction to be the laity and clergy in society. His theology of mission, however, did not escape the presumption of his time:
the ordained are active in liturgy, the laity in the secular word. "The
mission and power of the 'hierarchical church' finds its goal in the mission and empowerment of '(ordinary) people in midst of the (profane)
world' through the sacramental characters, while the 'sacramental
life' of the 'Body of Christ' has a 'secularized world' as its goal."[75] This
was progressive not in its unimaginative separation into secular and
clerical but in the consideration of the activity of the laity at all. The
continuance of the church in history is not simply a juridical organization nor an interior sanctification but a sovereign mission grounded
in the externalization of God into human life, both visibly and supernaturally.

Pursuing his theology of the church we will look at his ideas on
authority, teaching office, laity, ministry, and ecumenism.

Authority
The Roman Catholic church implies authority. What is the reason for
that authority? Where is authority in the church? The rhythm-structure
of the faith-world of revelation in the two covenants has been en-
trusted to the church.[76] The ground and form of hierarchy is incarnation; there can be no docetism in the church and no reduction of
the church to a charismatic sect. An institutional side with an intrinsic authority is binding, although in the hierarchy the divine source of
life is not a code or a prince. "God is not an idea and also not simply
a power, not a will or a lonely person; God is the personal divinity
where Majesty in a heavenly realm becomes a human being. The
totality aimed at by the incarnation is an incarnation of this God of
majesty in the court of heaven. The holy and kingly — this is what the
word hierarchy ('holy' [*hier*] and 'ruling' [*archia*]) says — realizes itself
in this way: God in Christ appears in the church."[77] In 1941 a sketch
of a theology of the church showed how the analogy between God and
creation points to an analogy between a hierarchical church and the
Body of Christ. The Letter to the Ephesians grounds in the Trinity
the Body of Christ with its hierarchy, and the realization of the hierarchy lies in a community of those born of the Spirit, in a church of
sacraments and grace, in a church destined to grow. The hierarchy of
the church has a primacy to the extent that the creative will of God is
the primal ground, but the communion of believers has the primacy

as the revelation of God's love. Ultimately there is not one authority
but forms of authority coming from the Spirit working visibly in the
church.[78]

What is the role of the teaching office of the church? It is concerned not with transtemporal truth but with truth in revelation in
history. Contrary to the currents of the twentieth century, doctrines
are true because they represent revelation, not because they suit the
aspirations of religion and humanity in general.[79] Yet, the magisterium and the individual stand at a distance from the divine act of
self-revealing. Przywara is critical of those who would find countless
examples of infallibility or who would use past dogmas to solve new
questions. Dogmas come through long processes, through fraternal discussions attending to the Spirit, but now, in the hands of the zealous,
agitated and disturbed, they become "canon shells whistling through
the air."[80] Faber concludes: "Ultimately what concerns Przywara is not
the dogmas themselves but their link to God. They do not impose a
calming certitude through infallible decisions—being in the possession of unconditioned truth—but imply some immediacy to God
bringing peace."[81] In Zeitz's view, the discussions of magisterium and
dogma, of primacy and infallibility, were not about particular dogmas
but were research into "the principles of ecclesial discernment."[82] Thus
difficult issues of ecclesial structure led to spirituality, just as dogmatic
issues were to theological metaphysics. Church authority does not serve
formulas but life.

Influenced by a Jesuit spirituality, Przywara linked obedience to
church authorities with obedience in Christ. He expected obedience to
the church, although the church is human, weak, and deficient. "Przywara explains office mainly as 'a representation-in-descent.'. . . [Still]
the office bearer is a member of the church composed of people needing redemption. The specific and almost exclusive function of office
is to represent Christ, to represent divine sovereignty. A representation
of the wider church beyond offices is only described slightly."[83] The
objective realization of office lies not with authority and display—
bishops should not cultivate "a mysticism of office"—but with service, and ministry is not something purely juridical but involves a
willingness to serve. The personal characteristics of a bishop can at
times interfere with his ministry, just as the Hebrew prophets and
Christian apostles failed in their mission; still, God can work through
weakness and foolishness, through fallible instruments. At the end of

time forms of power will meet a catastrophic eschaton, and authorities who preyed upon people will be severely judged.[84]

The Incarnation is the ground and reason why the body and head of the church are bearers of that truth. The Jesuit warned of the dangers of isolating the papacy from the totality of the church, and he expected limits in the Petrine primacy.

The hierarchy lives in a dialectic. "There is neither the directness of an 'episcopalism'—no council can stand above the pope—nor is there the directness of a 'papalism,' for an individual bishop is not a papal bureaucrat; rather each bishop has a ministry with ordinary and immediate jurisdiction and is placed there by the Holy Spirit as a follower of the Apostles, and, vice versa, the pope, bishop of Rome, is like other bishops. . . . The living sovereign church is thereby most vital when it (empowered by the infallible rejection of both episcopalism and papalism) can move between those two poles of tension."[85] If the bishop of Rome has a primacy, the bishops are "immediate successors of the apostles placed by the Holy Spirit.[86] "The totality of the bishops must be again particularly emphasized. Pure papalism and pure episcopalism are false directions. The jurisdictional primacy of the pope and the immediate jurisdiction of the bishops, as the Vatican Council defined both, are the foundations of a true dialectical movement between possible theories."[87] Roman centralism is "an inner-ecclesial heresy."[88]

The papacy, presented in the New Testament by images of shepherd and by the rhetoric of service, is to be respected and listened to with the hope and expectation that the popes would serve the universal church. The theologian discussed the Pian popes. Pius V had failed to understand the Reformation in England and, unlike the Jesuit thinkers and missionaries of the sixteenth century, acted with a bitter rigidity. Pius IX, who had originally shown progressive tendencies, became "a pope of rejection, rejecting new political directions, rejecting theologians, rejecting all modern ideas."[89] Naturally the Jesuit could not openly criticize popes, but Pius X received an ambiguous description mentioning his severity toward Catholic intellectuals (sacrifices to antimodernism) as well as his advocacy of frequent communion and the erection of new parishes in Rome. He was and is a pope of divisions, a shattered pope who had made "bitter demands of the truest sons of the church." Przywara lets the oppositions remain, dramatic holiness and dramatic authoritarianism, as he describes the

pontificate of the one beatified in 1951.[90] Pius XI, Achille Ratti, a
pope of simplicity and sympathy, escaping from being a political pris-
oner of the Vatican and setting aside some feudal aspects of the papacy,
understands that he is called to minister in an age of activity and freedom, and to form Catholics in a theological atmosphere of corespon-
sibility for a new age, the age of the objective. "Out of a mysterious
subjectivity, out of a mysterious flight from history and into movements
wanting to renew time, the providential character of Pius XI emerges as
'the pope of Catholic Action,' a movement not of more clerical authority but in Germany a development of Catholics to be active in a
new age, in civil responsibility within the state."[91] There will always be
a danger of papalism when the pope continues to name all bishops and
cardinals; that political format neglects the theology of the bishops
grounded in the Spirit and the Apostles. When the church joins universal jurisdiction to Vatican offices (an "ecclesial office-machine") and
ignores the inner life of grace of individuals it becomes a kind of "secret subjectivism."[92] And yet, in an ecclesiology that a few decades later
would be recognized as untraditional, nonepiscopal, and dangerous,
the Jesuit compared the leadership of the pope to the superior general
of a religious order.

The bishop of Rome—why do Catholics venerate him so much?
Is he a "pope-king"? Przywara noted that the veneration concerns
itself with a human, earthly person, not with an angelic spirit. In an
observation unusual at that time in ecclesiological discussions but one
quite Thomistic, he notes how the papacy is a manifestation of sacramentality, of grace acting through human nature. If the pope has an
independent claim on grace, nonetheless, this comes through his natural gifts. The pope should image and serve the idea of Catholicism,
the idea of the sacrament which can draw *ex opere operato* on grace,
but upon a grace which is conditioned *ex opere operantis*. His grace
and activity correspond to that of Christ who leaves the godhead to
be among sinful people in order to offer to God a new humanity.[93]
Authority, then, for Przywara—he experienced its encroachment
directly in the examination of his writings[94]—is not solitary, not divine
in a monophysite form, not apart from the human or the divine, or
their analogous commerce.

The Laity
How do the laity live in the church? Does the church offer them
more than a place for communion with God? Przywara did not want

to divide the church into hierarchy and people, did not want to separate its members into officeholders and laity. Rather, he began with the church as a totality.[95]

A severe distinction between clergy and laity is not biblical: all Christians are "clerics," that is, "heirs" of God's reign according to the Greek biblical word. The clerical state of the ordained is not one of privilege, nor are the laity purely secular; clergy exist to serve the laity and all have a place of active ministry in the kingdom of God. The use of the word "deacon" in the New Testament indicates that all, brothers and disciples, are "deacons."[96] Since office is not a secular reality of authority but a role existing to serve the church and the reign of God, the division between secular and spiritual is erroneous. All Catholic owe a first obedience to God and Jesus Christ, as do bishops, who are also members of the church.

A Christian is not a passive object of parish care but a member of a royal priesthood and thus an active cooperator in ministry. Each baptized man or woman is not beneath or simply in the church but is the church; laymen and laywomen have an office that is a ministry of cooperation with grace, an office which is essentially marked by service.[97] The early church expressed itself in familial, fraternal terms, in the language of an organic family, in the horizontal as well as the vertical. The Pauline mention of many charisms and ministries indicates that in the church there is room for diversity; the church, like Mary, is receptive and active. If in the pattern of analogy the church contains a dissimilarity from its head and source of grace, Christ and his Spirit, nonetheless, the more Christ is perceived concretely the more the historical church pursues its own patterns.[98]

Przywara, however, did not have any concrete ministries in mind, did not forecast that important public activities of parish and diocese would be given to the baptized (ministries which would appear after Vatican II). His mind was drawn to Benedictine or Discalced Carmelite contemplative life or to the general empowerment of the laity through Catholic Action.[99]

Sacrament was a link between ministry and the baptized woman or man. In Germany theology stimulated by church and liturgy was suggesting a broader understanding of sacrament, and this had important ramifications for ministry, laity, and social action. There are more spheres of the sacramental than the seven sacraments in a Christian's life. In the theology of the seminary textbooks in the late nineteenth and early twentieth century, the church was a juridical largely involved in

administering the seven sacraments. The rediscovery of a sacramentality beyond the seven sacraments and of the church as more than a
juridical institution, as itself a sacrament manifest in word and sacrament grounded in Jesus Christ, was significant. The church is sacrament
for Christians and a sacrament for all who are not personally and
visibly part of the Catholic church. In 1953 prior presentations of
the church as primal sacrament (*Ursakrament*) were enhanced by a
book of the Jesuit theologian Otto Semmelroth. Przywara's review
of the book, nonetheless, after noting how important that rediscovery
of church as sacrament is, mentions that the theology had been present in his own writings from the 1920s on, although Semmelroth refers
to none of them, nor to a key line from the liturgy for Holy Saturday
(*totius ecclesiae tuae sacramentum*).[100] Przywara thought that this new
work focused too much on "image" and neglected the sense-realities
of the sacraments, exhibiting thereby a certain "Alexandrine withdrawal from the human and material into the spiritual and the divine,
a neoscholastic Aristotelianism, and an Eastern iconic theology where
the interplay and exchange of grace and human nature are weak, as
are the foundations for the church as primal sacrament."[101] The wider
implications of a theology of sacrament remain: the sacramentality
of Christ and the church grounding both seven sacraments and varieties of ecclesial sacramentality draws the believers to the sacramentality of grace in the world, anticipating a number of theologians and
theological perspectives more influential after 1960. "The phrase 'sacramental world' is right to the extent that [this sacramentality] is as
instrument entering the world, as is the mission into the world from
the form of the 'hierarchical church.'"[102]

The sacramentality of the church joins invisible grace with the
visible signs and externals. If every Christian partakes in this sacramentality through baptism and confirmation, baptism does more: it brings
a ministerial coworking in the mystery of redemption. In the church
of the sacramental characters of baptism and confirmation and orders, the Body of Christ and the hierarchical church meet.[103] The new
ecclesiology, reacting against the church as a sacral enclosure, locates an
active laity as well as a hierarchy within the Body of Christ. The life
and mission of all members of the church, the maturity of the baptized in the lay apostolate, wider modes of serving a world not fully
profane, persons receptive to the grace of the Trinitarian persons—
these are returning Catholics to the mysteries of sacrament and incar-

nation and mission. Ecclesiology must become "Christian-ology" where the baptized are active in both church and society, where the symbol of the washing of the feet becomes reality. These calls to reality, stimulated by the theology of the Body of Christ in the 1930s and after Word War II, are an ecclesial application of an active interplay of human person and divine grace. While Przywara could not see the new (and old) metamorphoses of the ministries of the local church that would appear after the Council his instincts were that the future lay in that direction.[104]

Ecumenism

Przywara was involved personally in ecumenical dialogue during the years when ecumenism was new and when formal interchurch dialogue was forbidden to Catholics. Public dialogue with Paul Tillich, meetings with Karl Barth at the University of Münster in 1929— Barth called them "the first coming together of theologians of both confessions since the Reformation"—built upon contacts with the *Una Sancta* movement and with such ecumenists as Hans Asmussen and Otto Karrer.[105] In 1941 Przywara inquired into the relationships of Catholicism to the Reformation and to the Eastern Churches. "The East separated in the name of 'tradition,' while the Reformation separated in the name of 'conscience.' Thus the eastern schism is something purely objective and the Reformation is something purely subjective, both aimed against the Roman institution as Schism and Reformation."[106] Luther emphasized what is historical while Calvin looked at the interior, at free conscience and spirit, as did Jansenism, that final stage of the Reformation. Protestant sects and modern philosophies have difficulty bringing together the sacred and the profane, for sectarianism pits the sacred against the profane and flees from the Spirit in the pneumatic Christian and the church active in the world, while modernity sees the profane, the worldly, as solely necessary or given, a closed system.

In 1940, as the Gestapo was beginning to threaten the offices and files of *Stimmen der Zeit,* Przywara was giving in the Baroque Bürgersaal, headquarters of the large Marian Congregation of laity in Munich, a series of lectures on understanding Protestantism and furthering an ecumenical Catholicism. After World War II those treatments of topics like reformation, freedom of conscience, service, law and gospel, dogma and hierarchy were published, an example of increased Catholic ecumenical sensitivity working to make its own reality attractive and to take seriously the concerns and emphases of Luther and Eastern Orthodoxy. Catholicism always remains a sacramental church, incarnational in its hierarchical leadership and forms: thereby it stands in contrast to the church of the Reformers where many forms of the churches are sacrificed to the transcendence of God and where justification of the sinful by faith bypasses church and dogma. The 1950s showed a new ecumenical situation.[107] On the Protestant side there is an honest attempt to reconsider and appropriate Catholic positions, even the primacy of Peter, in the considerations of Oscar Cullmann and Joachim Jeremias; on the Catholic side there is a new view of the Reformation as an experience of the Spirit in the community of the church, even a desire to limit the presence of Rome and to have the liturgy in the vernacular. Luther, also a dialectical theologian, was not a moralist but a theologian of councils and dogmas, and the commentaries on Romans and Galatians and the Psalms show his real intention, which was not the multiplicity of iconoclastic churches.

Should this lead to a third reality, a third church as Joachim of Fiore or Schelling imagined it? No. An evangelical Catholicity integrates the intentions of the Reformers, and Protestants are coming to understand the medieval sources of the Reformation. Przywara—he could refer to his early meetings with Karl Barth in this regard—saw no purpose in a unity of externals among churches or in a unity sweeping away real, remaining differences. A "dialectical ecumenism" meant drawing together all that was faithful to the Gospel and transparent to grace in all churches East and West. The one-sidedness of Protestantism could not survive and the unnecessary aspects of the Counter-Reformation had to fall away for the all-encompassing wholeness of what is Catholic to appear.[108]

In 1961, Przywara, old and ill, could be both prescient and hesitant. He mentioned in an essay two perspectives that might be accepted after Vatican II: the church passing beyond a narrowly European Catholicism and transcending the Counter-Reformation.[109] But, as Protestant-Catholic ecumenism was entering a time of expansion and intensification, he was uncertain: he criticized Hans Küng's revolutionary study on justification in Barth, and the dialogue around Petrine primacy furthered by Cullmann, although he was sympathetic to the work of Max Lackmann, Lutheran pastor and author of an

important book on the Augsburg Confession and Catholicism, whom
he praised for emphasizing Luther's theology and acknowledging the
lack of Lutheran ecclesiology.[110] Should one see here a tendency to
be less able to relate to the theology of the decade before Vatican II than
to the earlier time of his own efforts?

By 1960 there was a new variation on the theme of ecumenism, a
wider ecumenism treating Christianity and its relationship to the long
history of human religions. Is there a reality of grace and revelation
existing outside of Christianity?

In his book on Scheler and Newman Przywara wrote that Christianity is not a particular religion but absolute religion, supernatural
and not the result of nature-worship. At the same time its expression
is not limited to one age or philosophy or language. The individual, a
people, a race are possible cultural vehicles and forms in which the
unchanging nature announces itself, for Christianity is a fullness, not
a constraint.[111] Theologians in Germany had been aware of this issue
for some decades — the new theologies of Vatican II had been prepared for in the 1920s.[112]

Already in 1924 an article stated that "Catholic Ecumenicity" did
not mean that "all the various confessions and religions retain their
own faith-content (dogmas) and yet through one overarching faith-
meaning hold all those various and competitive faith-contents as
symbols or peripheral concretizations."[113] This approach asked about
what is the least, the minimum, one must believe and do to belong to
God's community, to be prophetic in one's reference to the content of
Christ. Long ago Justin Martyr had spoken of the seeds of the *Logos,*
just as the scholastics spoke of the *votum ecclesiae* and Newman of
primal certainties. Przywara distinguished the "soul" of the church
from the formal reality of the baptized. Catholic theology holds that
the faith-content of a person apart from a mainly European church
"basically has for him a meaning of faith which in a kernel at least is
the meaning of the church's faith."[114] Those deepest realizations of
belief in God's existence and a readiness to receive revelation are in
some way related to Trinity and Incarnation. "The religious constitution of the soul of this 'Least-Catholic' is such that his religious consciousness and his faith-realizations signify a conviction of God's existence and a self-giving to faith. So throughout his life, although there
might be a lack of knowledge or a rejection of Catholic or Christian
teaching ... the 'salvation' of this 'Least-Catholic' depends upon a real

search through knowledge and conscience for truth."[115] There is no theory of relativism here but one of movement from what is in the complexity of human life not fully or well-expressed to the clarity of revelation (which also remains incomplete and richly mysterious). "Catholic teachings are a positive reflection of the not fully conceivable meaning of faith which outside of Catholicism is absolutized into one piece of this reflection."[116] The faith-sense of Catholics is a reality that in its divine depth includes a richness of revelation because it comes from and proceeds to the suprahuman and suprapersonal God. That term, the "Least-Catholic," is an anticipation of the infelicitous (and set-aside) phrase of Karl Rahner, "the anonymous Christian." The words in both Jesuits reflect the ideas of Catholic theologians in the first half of the twentieth century which (sometimes in a prolix and mechanical way) study different theories and realizations of implicit faith enabled by grace as the means of salvation.

Writing in 1961 Przywara finds an interior church, an inner Catholicity, which is not always identical with the collectivity of forms but is more than a realm of values or the phenomenon of the holy: it is an objective Catholicity. God in the church, however, does not mean mainly that God is located in the structures of this one church. God is present from the beginning of humanity and wishes to be among all peoples to the end of time. "A visible, institutional church limited in space and time is at least surrounded by an invisible 'church from the beginning' and 'a universal church' and 'a Christian ecumenicity.'" The presence of God furthers what is properly intended for Catholicism and also what nourishes the invisible "organic unity" between all "churches and religions."[117] Because Przywara saw the church as the realization of the presence of the Incarnation, of the Trinity, he spoke at times as though the church's limits were narrow ones for the presence of grace, although his theological mentality distinguished clearly between the reign of God and its church.[118] The lines mentioned above, however, indicate a theology of grace present in various ways in human history and salvation-history. His opposing dialectic was not between the Catholic church and other believers but between grace and secularity, because some churches and religions in the 1920s were in danger of becoming secular philosophies. "Every emergence into the world will sooner or later be a secularization if it has not previously been a journey into God. . . . That means that there is for Catholics as concrete men and women no area which is neutral or interconfessional. That is the practical meaning of the Catholic teaching of the 'supernatural goal and sole goal.'"[119] In the last analysis, he wrote at the end of his first philosophy of religion in 1927, the deepest meaning of Catholicism is God as all in all and as the totality of creation and humanity and meaning oriented toward God: this was "the positive and essential meaning of 'ouside the church no salvation.'"[120]

Przywara opposed the direction in some philosophies of religion which search for a single, vague religious core underlying the most varied religious forms and ideas; revelation in Catholic dogma is presented as true, and contradictory viewpoints are false. For Protestantism and the world religions, their "falsehood" lies not so much in clear opposing assertions but in a lack of completeness, an emphasis on one side of a profound religious issue, a lack of affirming a deeper richness. Religions are not just an expression of humanity, and what brings salvation is not anthropology but a form of the act of faith.

Toward Vatican II

What was Erich Przywara's attitude toward the call of Pope John XXIII in 1959 for an ecumenical council? His health was deteriorating and the activity of turning great ideas into writings was difficult. What did he think of the approaching council, Vatican II? Did he greet converging pastoral directions with the same enthusiasm with which his early lectures and books described the "turn" and its "movements"? In the 1920s he had proclaimed the church to be at a crossroads, needing new movements, caught between theologies of a static past and something new.[121] In a sermon published in 1948 there was a description of an old church and a younger church. The young church wants to be free of political involvements and cultural devotional forms and to dedicate itself to faith and worship; it wants a church where Christ is the center of a personal and existential faith (and wonders about the lasting control of the theologies of Augustine and Aquinas); the young church puts community and church at the center, puts the Spirit and ministry there too. Przywara asked whether this could become too communal and too active, perhaps sectarian and Protestant—he had made those reservations about the same directions twenty-five years earlier—and yet the Council should not be a static restorer of the past nor can it be something other than what the advocates of "the young church" want. Something new will come, although Przywara's words and ideas end not in a "complete program" but in a prayer for the arrival of the Holy Spirit in love and fire.[122]

In 1962 Przywara published his book *Kirche in Gegensätzen* looking
ahead to the council beginning in October of that year. To study the
history of ecumenical councils is to see that the coming Council, like
earlier assemblies, has a pre-history. There has already been "a preconciliar time of movements" in the time after 1900, a time of "a new
Catholicism over against the old Catholicism." In those theologians,
charismatic figures, and movements lay a struggle between modernism
and reactionary integralism, between the church as organism and the
cult of the organization, between word and sacrament, and the immanent and the transtemporal. The kind of questions in this preconciliar
time allows a look into the general direction of the coming council."[123]
The history of ecumenical councils shows a drive toward the new. In
contrast to many in the church in the English-speaking parts of the
world, and in Italy and Spain, Przywara held that the Council could
not be an exercise in recent canon law and neoscholasticism. He again
spoke favorably of the theology of the Tübingen school which would
influence Vatican II: because of its view of the totality of the church
active through various charisms and ministries, the theology of Paul
continued by Möhler, the organic theology of past and present theologians teaching in the Catholics faculties in Munich and Tübingen,
is needed again. A juridical church is too limited, too constrained; a
reactionary church is static and stagnant; the tensions between an
excessive Pauline theology and a rigid Petrine one, have already been
criticized by Cardinal Newman, whose spirit will certainly be influential in preparing for this council.[124] "Ecclesial life is to be fashioned
within a moving dialectic, an oscillation, a swing which does justice
to Pauline and Tübingen theologies."[125] An ecclesiology solely of the
Spirit or a theology of the church as lay organism are too free, too
loose, and need structure and obedience. "The true 'love' and the true
'community' and the true 'Pneuma' of the New Testament *are,* then,
this obedience. It is thus clear how Möhler and Vatican (the first council of that name) relate to each other. The 'mystical dynamism' of *Unity
in the Church,* in contrast to the rationalism and ethics and personalism
of the Enlightenment, was the first step to a life in the church and
from the church, but this mysticism of the church was fulfilled when
the Vatican Council [Vatican I] unfolded itself as a mystery of obedience in the definition of papal infallibility, where every mysticism
of the mystical Body of Christ first receives its criterion."[126] Ecclesiology and pastoral praxis find their ultimate, concluding mystery—

ultimately the mystery of God—in the tension between continuing human history and a supra-temporary-eschatological Christianity: in short, in the pattern of 1923: God in and over all.[127] *Kirche in Gegensätzen* is prophetic in general vision but thin in concrete ideas. The basic attitude and themes of the philosopher of religion of the 1920s empowered him to welcome something new, and his experiences of church life in the 1920s told him that something new would come. Bernhard Gertz collected articles by Przywara—the Jesuit wrote some lines of introduction to the collection in 1967—to show that his work moved toward the renewal of Vatican II. "Erich Przywara has an illuminating message in that he recalls the history of the development of German Catholicism and shows how one particular way led to the climax of the Council."[128] His theology has a number of general similarities with the themes of the documents on the church and on the liturgy: an attention to the reality of church life, the prominence of service, a critique of a purely hierarchical church, a grounding of the church in the Trinity and not in canon law, salvation-history.[129] Karl Rahner spoke of Przywara's theological ideas that emerged in the time of "breakthrough" after World War I finding "official" realization at Vatican II.[130]

Schmitz observes in Przywara the hierarchical church and the ecclesiology of the Pauline Body of Christ drifting apart.[131] Perhaps the continuing incarnational typologies, a spirituality of one religious order, devotional and psychological structures in place of pastoral and social forms impair him.[132] Gertz observes that his theology "lacks the reference to the concrete person in the concrete world,"[133] a way of stating that his theology of the church and the pastorate remains abstract and tentative. Did not Przywara see the church in a somewhat secondary, mystical, or impoverished way? His interests were the individual's existence or the mystic's prayer. While not wanting to interiorize its institutional nature, Przywara was at home in discussing the church in metaphors: the Advent of the Lord, the Israel of God, the Fullness of Mary.[134] The church of laity and hierarchy seeks to correspond to an ideal that is more spiritual than pastoral, and his ecclesiology culminates in metaphors and strings of biblical citations.

Przywara remained caught in various polarities. To bring them together, to go ahead of their slightly outdated tensions seems to him to involve the sacrifice of one or the other. For the worldwide church, synthesis lies a few years ahead, in a freer, more pastoral mode of consideration, something not connatural to the thinker of great metaphysical and theological systems in history. The too often repeated dialectic brought an unsatisfactory mentality, more psychological than theological. Must one choose either the cross or an enthusiasm for the new in both spirituality and philosophy?[135] If a certain anxiety and strictness entered with the approach of the Council, still Przywara argued against two extremes: an illusionary merging of the differences between Catholicism and other religious groups, and the reluctance to leave behind a particular past devotion or theology.[136]

The gift of intuition still appeared sporadically. Przywara mentioned three of the expanding perspectives bestowed by the event of the Council. One was the end of the Counter-Reformation; the second, a movement to a church that is more than European. The third might be Karl Rahner's "world-church." Pope John XXIII had spoken of a "new Pentecost," and in 1964 Przywara echoed that call: "Now is the true hour of Pentecost for Europe, passing out of the upper room of Europe out into the real breadth of a true world-church, or better a church of the cosmos."[137]

Conclusion

Son of an immigrant, a seminarian educated in exile, an ascetic Jesuit, a disciple of abstract thinkers, frail and yet owning an impressive mind and voice, Erich Przywara was engaged during the period from World War I to the Third Reich in a dialogue with church and culture, philosophy and Christian revelation. Martha Zechmeister concluded, "The rising of God as the inconceivable and intangible takes place for Przywara in the night of historical reality. He does not belong to the thinkers whom one can understand sundered from their historical hour. His work with its rifts and gullies mirrors the tensions, oppositions, and collapses of that time."[1] His lifetime theme was not a logic of concepts or biblical phrases but the dynamic interplay of the Created and the uncreated. At the Ulm lectures of 1923 he announced: "What we need, and what we propose as our program, is a philosophy of balance, a balance not of 'today and always' but more a balance of 'further into the infinite' . . . of dynamic polarity."[2] Faith and intuition touched an analogy of realities: the human, the cosmic, and a special real world brought to a climax by the Incarnation and continuing on in graced people. His ministry and mission sought to address and go beyond modern questions within the Catholic church and the German Catholic ethos. Speculative theology was not abstract theology, for Przywara contemplated, as Bernhard Gertz puts it, "the festive exchange of analogy which is the inner concept of all biblical and positive theology."[3]

Those who commented on Przywara's personality and style, as Karl Barth did, found him sympathetic and engaging but also clear and certain in his positions. A youthful independence led him to go beyond scholasticism, psychologism, and transcendental monism to Husserl and Scheler, to go beyond philosophies that were academic and thus indifferent to living religion. Enlarging his knowledge of contemporary directions in philosophy and religion, he rejected the willfulness, the isolation, the irrationality of modern society. At the age of twenty-seven he had written, "In a vital unity with the past, the present moment becomes living future."[4] His life and thinking and writings belong together.

This theologian, although increasingly distant from us as time moves ahead in this new millennium, is, nonetheless, somewhat of our own time. Catholicism after two world wars, and especially after Vatican II, still struggles, in theory and in praxis, to express the Gospel to a modern world. There are still a few voices that denounce all that is secular, idolize a neoscholasticism or a recent devotion, and complain about modernity. These pages have described how one man struggled to further the Catholic church's contacts with the twentieth century. His work in the periods after 1920 and after 1945 prepared for Vatican II. Like any history or story within Catholicism in the twentieth century, Przywara's narrative proceeded on various levels: the philosophical and the cultural, the theological and the political, the ecclesiastical and the spiritual. To learn something of his life and thought is to understand that European Catholicism was not moribund between Pius X and Pius XII but contained the seeds of the renewal to come. Karl Rahner expressed what had always been known in German and French circles but had been left unexpressed in much of the rest of the church: "What was manifest and officially received at Vatican II is effectively present in the Catholic church during the time between the two world wars."[5]

Few Catholic thinkers in the first half of this century studied contemporary culture so intensely and openly as Przywara did. At a time of a rigid retrenchment, when even reading a work of philosophy after Kant was morally suspicious, Przywara and some of his Jesuit confreres dared a Catholic encounter with modern German philosophy. He furthered at the same time an early Catholic ecumenism, one of meetings with important figures representing a new, dynamic Protestantism, with Karl Barth and Paul Tillich. The man who was obviously a speculative spirit enjoyed liturgical renewal, youth movements, the cultural world of Jews in German cities, and the aspirations of women as artists and academics. Karl Neufeld writes: "Przywara presented himself as the analyst of the moment; more precisely, as the examiner of spiritually and culturally influential streams of the moment. That is the foundation of what he has to say. He belongs to the pioneers of a conscious and encompassing analysis of the age. It was, at that time, at least in ecclesial and theological circles, something new."[6] It would be a mistake to invoke him as a dilettante, an aesthete, a metaphysician; or as an outsider, or a Barthian. He was a scholar, a philosopher, but, above all, a dedicated friend to many.

The dynamics, the themes we find in his work came from careful study, dialogue, respect for tradition, and from a conviction that theology could influence life. Przywara understood Aquinas better than many neoscholastics, while his interest in Newman led him to long-range projects furthering the introduction of the writings of the English thinker into Germany. His sources compose a curious mosaic: yet, he had a detachment toward each, a contemplative reserve which permitted the study of further thinkers, old and new. He was a committed Christian; while sailing confidently through the open waters of transcendental systems, he noted the needs of churchgoers. He pointed the way to a ministerial and philosophical interpretation of Ignatian spirituality, an interpretation that influenced directly or indirectly hundreds who gave the *Spiritual Exercises* and tens of thousands who made them.

He was certainly an apologete for Christianity. As a modern philosophical theologian he labored to show that the deepest realities of Catholicism are a kind of fulfillment of modern subjectivity and history. Although he was Catholic in a vital way, he was not apologetic in the meaning of that branch of theology and preaching that so dominated Catholic theology since the sixteenth century. He was ecclesial but not sectarian; not in favor of dividing the sacral from the secular but supportive, in religion, of intuition, analogous imagination, a polar and incarnational history of divine presence. "For this reason Catholicism holds this Christian root-term, *oikonomia,* to be its most fundamental term."[7] Analogy, incarnation, divine economy, the commerce of grace and personality flowed from Przywara's fundamental term.

His basic perspective, incarnational and polar, remained. He took as his own Cardinal Newman's phrase, "My only stability is stability in change."[8] The research of Julio Terán Dutari shows how Przywara's thought remains during five stages, from entry into the Jesuits to the end of World War II, within its original interests and insights: the single great theme is metaphysics and Christianity discussed through forms of analogy.[9] The ideological misdirection of the twentieth century is not an atheism or a pantheism: it lies deeper in a "theopanism" which is the source of either the rejection of all except the material and human, or the rejection of all except when it is asserted to be God. The problem of modern ideologies is not that they deny God but that they replace him, and the alternative is not a strict theism of Calvin, or the Enlightenment, but the Incarnation, in Jesus as the paradigm, and in men and women as graced images.

Przywara influenced—more in general directions than in precise ideas—the generation following him: J. B. Lotz, Emil Coreth, and Rahner, and to a lesser extent Gustav Söhngen, Joseph Pieper, and Max Müller. With Romano Guardini, with whom he had some approaches in common but who was a quite different writer, theologian, and personality, he was a precursor of Catholics expressing their faith to wider groups. Rahner asked: What did Przywara do for the church today? He gave the church a "capability for dialogue with its own time, a new direction."[10] Przywara had called this "the way of Easter."

Przywara's personality burst forth in the twenty-five years after World War I. The course of his life was marked by suffering and fragmentation, and it was not easy to find new directions after 1946 (although some argue for such, and future scholarly research may reveal them). He saw the parade of philosophers move on, leaving Georg Simmel, Hermann Cohen, and even Edmund Husserl behind and in their place presenting Martin Heidegger and Karl Jaspers, and he dismissed too facilely some new philosophical and theological worlds. A thinker rarely exceeds his original inspirations, rarely has a proper originality for more than two or three decades.

His limits came from a metaphysical personality whose style sometimes became distractingly rhetorical or poetic, while as the decades of the twentieth century passed, European Catholicism moved more and more toward the pastoral and the concrete. He could see the Trinitarian source of the church and the dignity of the baptized but could not follow those themes into a future expansion in ministry, liturgical renewal, or collegial authority. Did a lurking fear of past pantheisms keep him from seeing history—Western history, world history, salvation-history—in new ways, from seeing it as more than a gallery of thinkers? Did a fear of Protestant sectarians or liberal academics keep him from appreciating what Heideggerian existentialism and hermeneutics had in common with Origen or Bonaventure?

Erich Przywara's life and work remained, and remains, incomplete: first, his personality was both metaphysical and poetic; second, outside factors modified the normal course of his life—a totalitarian regime, a world war; and third, illnesses, physical and emotional, blocked his work. After World War II Przywara alluded little to the collective catastrophe of the Third Reich, to individuals like Edith Stein whose tragedies concerned him. "The life work of those three," he wrote, "ended in tragedy: the tragedy of Husserl behind whose coffin, when the great pride of Freiburg died, no one dared walk; the sadness of Scheler whose volcano-like temperament blew him back and forth between various intellectual fronts; the life work of Georg Simmel scattered, blown away by contradictory winds."[11] But had history witnessed only tragedy or freely chosen violence? Illness kept him from witnessing and comprehending the conciliar period with its ecclesiology and ecumenism. We do not know how a healthy or younger Przywara would have addressed the 1960s, encouraging an ecumenical council whose masterpiece was a theology of the church in the modern world. So, while he remained spiritually open and welcomed Vatican II, the precursor was not able to greet the fulfillment of his work.

In some ways, the 1920s resembled the 1960s and 1970s, and so Przywara could have been of considerable assistance in the years immediately after the Council, although in fact his efforts anticipating and inspiring conciliar theologians were little known outside of Germany. Denis Biju-Duval asks: "Who does not see the need still to de-absolutize subjectivity and to give in a new way its authentic meaning to God and to the reality of others? This is one of the major challenges posed by modern critical thought and metaphysics to Christian thought."[12] A teacher for today? Martha Zechmeister writes that "contrary to all external appearance in the work of Przywara there is actually the power of a 'saving means' for today's theology stuck in various crises, and that even in the situation of issues which were dramatically altered by the council it has a high degree of contemporaneity."[13] There are limitations to Erich Przywara's work: despite the stated intention to keep the human and the divine separate, his interpretation of the analogy often leaves the relationship, the precise exchange of being and grace, unclear; the relationship of a theology of the cross to Incarnation and Resurrection is too often presented in terms of poetry and metaphors. Przywara does not see far beyond the philosophical currents of only the first third of the twentieth century, and he has difficulty, not in supporting, but in courageously imagining new directions for concrete pastoral directions in the church.

On the other hand, his attention to the rich history of Christian reflection and culture, and his optimism that the core of Catholic faith could be made attractive to Catholics of every generation and every country, could urge them to reflect upon their vast and rich heritage and not to yield to extra-Catholic or ecclesiastical pessimism. He has a sensitivity to the divine Source, to the ultimate meaning of the Gospel, and to the Spirit's word to Christians today. His ability to approach and draw people to some degree of perception and faith, to befriend a wide range of men and women in and out of the church, offers a modern theology of the analysis of the presence of grace. The graced are not always the churched: those who question doctrines or leave the church, or who have never known by name their own grace, still have a hidden conversation with the Spirit and their own discernment of spirits for the directions of their lives. Przywara brought together center and diversity, dogma and life; in various philosophies he saw life as a theater of exciting possibilities. The phrase which Karl Rahner made famous, "the world-church," Przywara had used in 1964. "Now is the true hour of Pentecost for Europe, passing out of the upper room of Europe into the real breadth of a true world-church, or better a church of the cosmos."[14]

Today, however, it is not clear what his contribution would be other than to show the history of Catholic thinking in this century and to state, often in striking and pregnant terms, ways in which a literal meaning of the Gospel can be expressed in modern thinking. This theologian's presence remains usually in abstract insights, or in principles no longer immediately seminal for concrete issues in liturgy, ecclesiology, and ethics. Paradoxically, his earliest writings and ideas hold our attention: his project of pondering and not condemning his own age, his interpretation of Newman and others in terms of intuition, the wide circle of men and women he inspired, a union of theological perception with artistic and aesthetic sensitivity, an emphasis on the proper causality of creatures against the world-demeaning fundamentalists of his time, a critical and encouraging view of a church whose forms were open to renewal.

Commentators of recent years are correct: the Jesuit from Silesia and the writer in Munich proffers not a system or conclusions but a way of thinking that is *Durchgang,* transition, passageway.[15] Convinced that life is a journey, a way, a transformation, Erich Przywara saw his numerous train trips taking him to give lectures as an imitation of Ignatius Loyola. He too was "a dust-covered and dust-surrounded messenger on the world's roads in service to the world, or a modest waiter at the meal which God was offering to the world."[16] For his thinking and lecturing and writing, always in the service of the divine, he found a summation, a consolation in a line recalled from Newman: "All is but a whirling of the reason, and a dazzling of the imagination, and an overwhelming of the feelings, reminding us that we are but mortal men and he is God."[17]

Notes

Preface

1. Paul Imhof, ed., *Karl Rahner in Dialogue. Conversations and Interviews, 1965–1982* (New York: Crossroad, 1986), 14.

2. Karl Neufeld, "Kategorien des Katholischen. P. Erich Przywara—100 Jahre," *Catholica* 43 (1989): 297.

3. Friedrich Wulf, "Christliches Denken. Eine Einführung in das theologisch-religiöse Werk von Erich Przywara SJ (1889–1972)," in *Gottes Nähe. Religiöse Erfahrung in Mystik und Offenbarung,* ed. Paul Imhof (Würzburg: Echter, 1990), 353.

4. Zechmeister, "Przywara, Erich, SJ (1908)," in *Lexikon für Theologie und Kirche,* 3d ed. (Freiburg: Herder, 1999), 8:688; a detailed biographical essay is Gustav Wilhelmy, "Erich Przywara. Ein Überblick," in *Erich Przywara, 1889–1969. Eine Festgabe* (Düsseldorf: Patmos, 1969), 6–34.

5. Przywara, "Christian Root-Terms: Kerygma, Mysterium, Kairos, Oikonomia," in *Paul Tillich in Catholic Thought* (Dubuque: The Priory Press, 1964), 197ff.

Chapter 1.   Erich Przywara: His Age and His World

1. Siegried Behn, "Wer ist's?" in Siegfried Behn, *Der beständige Aufbruch* (Nuremberg: Glock und Lutz, 1962), 7–9; that volume contained greetings from Karl Barth and Karl Rahner, and essays on Le Corbusier and Meister Eckhart. A public discussion with Brunschwicg took place in Prague in 1934 (*Actes du huitième Congrès international de philosophie à Prague, 2–7 Septembre 1934* [Prague: Comité d'organisation du Congrès, 1936], 373ff.).

2. Peter Wust, "Ringen der Gegenwart. Zu Erich Przywaras gleichnamigen Buch," *Literarischer Handweiser* 66 (1929–1930): 2f.

3. Collins, "Przywara's 'Analogia Entis,'" *Thought* 17 (1942): 119.

4. Friedrich Wulf, "Christliches Denken. Eine Einführung in das theologische-religiöse Werk von Erich Przywara, S.J. (1889–1972)," in *Gottes Nähe*, ed. Paul Imhof (Würzburg: Echter, 1990), 364 (published in a French translation, "Przywara (Erich)," in *Dictionnaire de spiritualité* [Paris: Beauchesne, 1985], 12:2493–2501).

5. A detailed bibliographical essay is Gustav Wilhelmy, "Erich Przywara. Ein Überblick," in *Erich Przywara. 1889–1969. Eine Festgabe* (Düsseldorf: Patmos, 1969), 6–34, containing a brief English section. Denis Biju-Duval discusses his absence from French philosophy and theology in "La pensée d'Erich Przywara," *Nouvelle revue théologique* 121 (1999): 240–53.

6. See Michael Brenner, "Beyond Naphta: Thomas Mann's Jews and German-Jewish Writing," *A Companion to Thomas Mann's Magic Mountain,* ed. Stephen Dowden (Columbia: Camden House, 1999).

7. Przywara, "Thomas von Aquin heute," in *Humanitas. Der Mensch gestern und morgen* (Nuremberg: Glock und Lutz, 1952), 740f.

8. Neufeld, "Kategorien des Katholischen. P. Erich Przywara—100 Jahre," *Catholica* 43 (1989): 295.

9. "Ein Gang durch die Zeit," in *Ringen der Gegenwart* (Augsburg: Filser, 1929), 1:222–39.

10. "Oberschlesien," in *In und Gegen* (Nuremberg: Glock und Lutz, 1955),14f.; Martha Zechmeister, "Die 'Erde' Przywaras," in *Gottes-Nacht* (Münster: LIT, 1997), 51–57.

11. Cited in Bernhard Gertz, "Erich Przywara (1889–1972)," in *Christliche Philosophie im katholischen Denken des 19. und 20. Jahrhunderts,* ed. Emerich Coreth (Graz: Styria, 1988), 2:572; on music and Przywara's youth, see Zechmeister, *Gottes-Nacht,* 57–63.

12. See E. Soderini, *Leo XIII und der deutsche Kulturkampf* (Vienna: Tyrolia, 1935); J. Heckel, "Die Beilegung des Kulturkampfes in Preussen," *Zeitschrift der Savigny-Stiftung für Rechtsgeschichte, Kanonistische Abteilung* 19 (1930): 215–353; Rudolf Lill, *Die Wende im Kulturkampf* (Tübingen: Niemeyer, 1973).

13. Lill, "Der Kulturkampf in Preussen und im Deutschen Reich," in *Handbuch der Kirchengeschichte,* ed. H. Jedin (Freiburg: Herder, 1968),VI:2:77.

14. Some historians have seen the contra-constitutional treatment of the Jesuits, with expulsion rather than mass death as a significant difference, as a rehearsal for the Nazis' program for Jews: "Scandalous and deformed developments of recent German history were thereby given their foundation" (Lill, "Der Kulturkampf in Preussen . . . " 41).

15. Wilhelmy, "Przywara," 10.

16. The hymnbook was *Unsere Kirche* (Zechmeister, *Gottes-Nacht, 57*); the book of meditations, *Eucharistie und Arbeit* (Freiburg: Herder, 1917), appearing as articles in 1914 and 1915, was arranged around four themes—

work, interior work, exterior work, the community of work—and opened with a quotation by the Munich university theologian Martin Deutinger from 1851: "The question of the age is in its deepest source a religious one, and politics and society are only the cloaks of its hidden existence." The book appeared ten years later in a revised and expanded edition in *Christus lebt in mir* (Freiburg: Herder, 1929).

17. Gertz, "Erich Przywara (1889–1972)," 573.

18. Ibid.

19. Wilhelmy, 13. Przywara describes the energetic and diverse community of Jesuits at *Stimmen der Zeit,* with such members as Peter Lippert and Constantin Noppel, in "Hermann Bahr," *In und Gegen,* 96.

20. For other years, see James Zeitz, *Spirituality and Analogia Entis according to Erich Przywara, S.J.* (Washington, D.C.: University Press of America, 1982), 4. See the chart of Julio Téran Dutari, continued by Wilhelmy, of books and essays and lectures for the years from 1922 to 1941 in the Przywara *Festgabe;* Martha Zechmeister counts 25 monographs and 277 essays for the time between 1922 and 1941 (*Gottes-Nacht,* 74). The two volumes—over a thousand pages—of *Ringen der Gegenwart* contain surveys of German philosophical, theological, and cultural life from 1922 to 1927; see as a further example the review of books on ancient, medieval, and modern philosophy in "Philosophisches Werden," *Stimmen der Zeit* 118 (1929–30): 462–71.

21. Walter Dirks cited in K.H. Neufeld, "Vertiefte und gelebte Katholizität. Erich Przywara, 100 Jahre," *Theologie und Philosophie* 65 (1990): 170.

22. Karl-Heinz Wiesemann lists a number of cities including Geneva, Lucerne, Utrecht, Amsterdam, and Groningen (*Zerspringender Akkord. Das Zusammenspiel von Theologie und Mystik bei Karl Adam, Romano Guardini und Erich Przywara als theologische Fuge* [Würzburg: Echter, 2000], 285).

23. *Logos* (Düsseldorf: Patmos, 1963), 169.

24. Wilhelmy, 18.

25. Leo Zimny, *Erich Przywara. Sein Schrifttum 1912–1962* (Einsiedeln: Johannes, 1963); see *Erich Przywara, 1889–1969. Eine Festgabe* (Düsseldorf: Patmos, 1969); Zechmeister, "Przywara, Erich, SJ (1908)," 688.

26. Wilhelmy, 23.

27. Christian Lagger, "Durchkreuzte Ästhetik. Zum Verständnis des Schönen bei Erich Przywara SJ," in *Gott-Bild,* ed. G. Larcher (Graz: Styria, 1977), 8.

28. Wilhelmy, 24.

29. Wilhelmy, 25.

30. Reinhold Schneider, *Pfeiler im Strom* (Wiesbaden: Insel, 1958), 300–301.

31. Przywara, "Der Ruf von Heute," 103, 91f.

32. *Analogia Entis* (Einsiedeln: Johannes, 1962), 10.

33. "Integraler Katholizismus," *Ringen der Gegenwart* 1:142f.

34. *Logos,* 169.

35. Przywara, "Essenz- und Existenz-Philosophie. Tragische Identität oder Distanz der Geduld," *Scholastik* 14 (1939): 544.

36. "Um Hölderlin," *In und Gegen,* 132.

37. *Alter und Neuer Bund. Theologie der Stunde* (Munich: Herold, 1956).

38. Eva-Maria Faber, *Kirche zwischen Identität und Differenz: Die ekklesiologischen Entwürfe von Romano Guardini und Erich Przywara* (Würzburg: Echter, 1993), 246.

39. *Vier Predigten über das Abendland* (Einsiedeln: Johannes, 1948). Przywara presented the catastrophe of World War II as continuing somewhat after 1950 (the following references are to articles and radio addresses collected in *In und Gegen*). There seems to be in his writings after the war no clear statement of how he viewed the effects of the Nazi regime and its relationship to the German people and culture or to the role and sufferings of the German church, although there was much rhetorical discussion of catastrophe, collapse, end, etc. Are there any positive statements about the United States, which had ended the Nazi terror in Europe and was now rebuilding Germany? Przywara's information on America—his remarks were often ideas taken from authors discussing America between the Civil War and the First World War— is drawn from critical passages from a few books (Thomas Wolfe, Henry James, L. L. Mathias, Simone de Beauvoir, Eugene O'Neill) and stresses the vast and disorganized nature of the United States. America, "a purely technological and mathematical giant" (271), is no "nation" at all, lacking culture and history, full of leftist intellectuals and eschatological Calvinists. America is an abyss, a secular disaster, doomed to collapse further into the ruins caused by the tension between materialism and Protestant idealism (205). Its coupling with Marxist Russia ordained by destiny (176f.) lets America's "absolute industrialization" now be realized by Stalin in Russia and used by him to ruin the Baroque culture of Poland (183). Simply an inverse form of Marxism, American democracy is supported by religious myths and so tends to its own fascism and is certainly not the model for European democracy (232); Przywara had linked Russia and America already in 1930 ("Bolschewismus als religiös-geistiges Phänomen," *Schweizer Rundschau* 31 [1931]: 939–43). The theme that America and Russia are similar mass societies, lacking culture and overly concerned with technology, is found in Martin Heidegger's lectures in 1942: "Gigantic excess . . . of quantity over quality . . . is the principle of what we call Americanism; Bolshevism is only a distortion of Americanism . . . dangerous because it enters in the form of bourgeois democracy mixed with Christianity" ("Die Deutung des Menschen in Sophokles' Antigone [1942]," in *Hölderlins Hymne 'Der Ister'* [Frankfurt: Klostermann, 1993], 86, and in *Einführung in die Metaphysik* [New Haven: Yale University Press, 1959], 46); similarly, Karl Adam wrote in 1926: "A look at the cultural and psychological effects of

Calvinism in the United States shows what would happen basically when this Calvinism in the intensified form of Karl Barth's theology takes root in the masses of people" ("Die Theologie der Krisis," *Hochland* 23 [1926]: 270–86).

40. *Alter und Neuer Bund,* 67.

41. Zimny, *Erich Przywara. Sein Schrifttum,* 25–27.

42. Friedrich Wulf, "Christliches Denken. Eine Einführung in das theologische-religiöse Werk von Erich Przywara, S. J. (1889–1972)," 354. For a description of that residence in terms of its library and books, see Rudolf Adolph, "Die Bibliothek eines Gelehrten," in Siegfried Behn, *Der beständige Aufbruch,* 18–21.

43. Wulf, 358.

44. Gertz, "Erich Przywara (1889–1972)," 575; for a helpful arrangement of the publications, see Friedrich Wulf, "Christliches Denken."

45. Wilhelmy, 27; see his subsequent pages for a detailed presentation of work in the postwar years.

46. "Karsamstag. Zu einer Theologie des Gott-vermissens," in *Vom Wagnis der Nichtidentität* (Münster: LIT, 2000), 74.

47. See Hans Wulf, "Erich Przywara. Zu den gesammelten Werken," *Stimmen der Zeit* 171 (1962/63): 401–11.

48. Review of Hans-Georg Gadamer, *Wahrheit und Methode,* in *Les Études philosophiques* 17 (1962): 258f.

49. "Laudatio auf Erich Przywara," *Gnade als Freiheit* (Freiburg: Herder, 1968), 266.

50. "Die Idee des Jesuiten nach der Liturgie des Festes Allerheiligen der Gesellschaft Jesu," *Zeitschrift für Aszese und Mystik* 8 (1933): 252.

51. Nieborak, *'Homo analogia.' Zur philosophisch-theologischen Bedeutung der 'analogia entis' im Rahmen der existentiellen Frage bei Erich Przywara S. J. (1889–1972)* (Frankfurt: Lang, 1994), 5.

52. Przywara offered a kind of motto—"to meet the real as well as the contemporary" ("des Sachlichen wie des Heutigen treffen")—in "Thomas von Aquin, Ignatius von Loyola, Friedrich Nietzsche," *Zeitschrift für Aszese und Mystik* 11 (1936): 257.

53. Przywara, *Ignatianisch. Vier Studien* (Frankfurt: Knecht, 1956), 135.

54. Zeitz, *Spirituality,* 24f.

55. *Analogia Entis,* 57.

56. Przywara, "Ahasver," *Stimmen der Zeit* 121 (1931): 152.

57. In a lighter vein, C. C. Martindale in his introduction to the collection of texts by Newman wrote: "The name of Fr. Przywara—quite apart from its somewhat alarming spelling—has become synonymous with deep thought and difficult diction—we remember that his German was once said to be so difficult that not even Germans could understand it!" (*An Augustine Synthesis* [New York: Sheed & Ward, 1936], v).

58. Przywara, "Edith Stein und Simone Weil—Zwei philosophische Grund-Motive," in *Edith Stein—eine grosse Glaubenzeugin*, ed. W. Herbstrith (Anweiler: Thomas Plöger, 1986), 231.

59. Wulf, "Christliches Denken," 361.

60. Zeitz, "Erich Przywara, Visionary Theologian," *Thought* 58 (1983): 145.

61. Nieborak, 5.

62. Nieborak, 551; see the survey of analogy as a theme beginning with the earliest works, in Julio Terán Dutari, *Christentum und Metaphysik. Das Verhältnis beider nach der Analogielehre Erich Przywaras* (Munich: Berchmanskolleg, 1973).

63. Zeitz, *Spirituality*, 37, 143, 23–26; see "Der Primat der Praxis und des religiösen Denkens," in Julio Terán Dutari, *Christentum und Metaphysik*, 87–95.

64. Mann, *Gladius Dei*, in *Sämtliche Erzählungen* (Frankfurt/Main: S. Fischer, 1963), 157.

65. Bahr, *Expressionismus* (Munich: Delphin, 1920); see Przywara, "Hermann Bahr," in *In und Gegen*, 96f.

66. See Michael Phayer, *The Catholic Church and the Holocaust, 1930–1965* (Bloomington: Indiana University Press, 2000); John Cornwall, *Hitler's Pope: The Secret History of Pius XII* (New York: Viking, 1999).

67. Przywara, *Religionsbegründung, Max Scheler—J. H. Newman* (Freiburg: Herder, 1923), 94.

68. Cited in a review of Robert Musil's *Diaries 1899–1941*, in *The New Criterion* (March 2000): 67.

69. R. Aubert, "Modernism," in Karl Rahner, *Sacramentum Mundi* (New York, 1968), 4, 99.

70. A collection of the main documents issued by the Vatican against Modernism can be found in A. Vermeersch, *De modernismo* (Bruges: C. Beyaert, 1910). Typical of the severe prejudice of the Vatican is: "As a result of the dominance of the erring and careless arguments of the unreflective, an atmosphere of ruin has been created, penetrating all and spreading like the plague" ("Pascendi dominici gregis," *Acta Sanctae Sedis* 40 [1907]: 626); for a broader interpretation of Modernism in Germany at that time, see Otto Weiss, *Der Modernismus in Deutschland* (Regensburg: Pustet, 1995).

71. "Sacrorum Antistitum," *Acta Apostolicae Sedis* 2 (1910): 655f. In 1931 Pius XI prescribed it for those attaining advanced ecclesiastical degrees and assuming positions in seminaries. Neither the Code of Canon Law of 1917 nor the recent Code mentions the antimodernist oath, although the oath remained in force until Vatican II.

72. Adam, "Der Antimodernisteneid und die theologischen Fakultäten," *Katholische Kirchenzeitung für Deutschland* 1 (1910): 83f.; see H. Kreidler, "Excurs über Karl Adam und die kirchliche Autorität. Der Modernismusverdacht," in *Eine Theologie des Lebens* (Mainz: Grünewald, 1988), 296ff.; J. Mausbach, *Der Eid wider den Modernismus und die theologische Wissenschaft* (Cologne: Bachem, 1911). Typical of a strict ecclesiastical defense of the oath are Reginald Schultes, *Was*

beschworen wir im Antimodernisteneid? (Mainz: Kirchheim, 1911) and K. Wieland, *Eine deutsche Abrechnung mit Rom* (Munich: Rieger, 1911).

In the months before the oath against Modernism, a strange document was being readied by the Vatican, one more anti-German and anti-Protestant than antimodernist. *Editae Saepe* was issued formally on May 29, 1910, to commemorate the 300th anniversary of the death of St. Charles Borromeo. The exaltation of this Milanese church leader of the Counter-Reformation was to be a lesson for Germany at the turn of the twentieth century, implying that once again the German church created a dangerous, extraecclesial movement: this time, not the Reformation but Modernism. Even more than other measures, this text illustrated an absence at the Vatican of accurate knowledge about theology and church north of the Alps and an ignorance of German culture and ethos. In late May 1910, the encyclical appeared in Italian on the pages of *Osservatore Romano* (it was published in *Acta Apostolicae Sedis* in early June). The pope linked the modernists to Protestant Reformers and viewed both, according to *Philippians* 3:19, as "enemies of the cross of Christ . . . whose god is their stomach." The success of the Reformation was due to corrupt princes and peoples, and now centuries later the Protestant church continued to distort faith and morals. Naturally, the encyclical caused an uproar in Prussia; Wilhelm II found it annoying, while Adolf von Harnack responded to its view of the Reformation. Communications and delegations on the letter reached the Vatican quickly even though the document had not yet been formally issued in Germany, the country of its destiny. In Berlin 6,000 people assembled to protest the letter, and politicians suggested a new *Kulturkampf,* one realizable in more subtle steps, like freezing the salaries of Catholic priests; several *Länder* forbade the publication and public reading of the encyclical which was printed in *Acta Apostolicae Sedis* 2 (1910): 357ff.; see G. Knopp, "Die 'Borromäusenzyklika' Pius X als Ursache einer kirchenpolitischen Auseinandersetzung in Preussen," in *Aufbruch ins 20. Jahrhundert. Zum Streit um Reformkatholizismus und Modernismus,* ed. G. Schwaiger (Göttingen: Vandenhoeck und Ruprecht, 1976), 56ff.; M. Hage, *Die Borromäus-Enzyklika und ihre Gegner* (Wiesbaden: Rauch, 1910); J. Schnitzer, *Borromäus-Enzyklika und Modernismus* (Berlin: Winser, 1911).

73. "Zwischen Religion und Kultur," in *Weg zu Gott,* 91.

74. "Sendung," in *Ringen der Gegenwart,* 2:961.

75. Gertz, "Erich Przywara (1889–1972)," 578.

76. "Modernismus," *Staatslexikon* (Freiburg: Herder, 1929), 3:1374.

77. *Religionsphilosophie katholischer Theologie* (Berlin: Oldenbourg, 1927), 65.

78. *Gottgeheimnis der Welt, Schriften* (Einsiedeln: Johannes 1962), II:150.

79. Przywara, "Besprechungen," *Stimmen der Zeit* 54 (1923): 69.

80. Przywara, "Verklärung und Polarität" (1924), in *Katholische Krise* (Düsseldorf: Patmos, 1967). The quote is from *Studiorum Ducem* in *Denzinger-Schönmetzer* (26th edition), 3667. "Is not the entire development of Catholic

movements up to Catholic Action a startling example of what concerns us
German Catholics so often and so negatively: namely, every interference of
the church which here and there first seems like pure destruction or at least
confusion of what has been achieved but then again presents itself as a liberation from chaos to form, from bubbling activity to maturity, Rome actually
seeking the salvation of Germans" ("Katholische Bewegung und Katholische
Aktion," in *Katholische Krise,* 70).

81. Rahner, "Laudatio," 269.

82. *Gottgeheimnis der Welt,* 146–47.

83. Letter in *Karl Barth — Eduard Thurneysen. Briefwechsel* (Zurich: Theologischer Verlag, 1974), 2:652.

84. Simmel was "the one who opened in terms of the pairs of opposites,
life and content, most profoundly the abyss" ("Ahasver" *Stimmen der Zeit* 121
[1931] 152); see Przywara, "Simmel-Husserl-Scheler," *In und Gegen* 33–54; on
Georg Simmel, see Ralph M. Leck, *Georg Simmel and Avant-Garde Sociology:
The Birth of Modernity, 1880–1920* (Amherst: Humanity Books, 2000).

85. *Gott* (Munich: Oratoriums-Verlag, 1926), 18.

86. *Gottgeheimnis der Welt,* 215.

87. Gertz, "Erich Przywara (1889–1972), 576, 584.

88. Przywara, "Tragische Welt?" *Stimmen der Zeit* 111 (1926): 183.

89. *Gott,* 9.

90. *Alter und Neuer Bund,* 539.

91. "Oberschlesien," in *In und Gegen,* 12f.; Wilhelmy, 9; his thought in this
regard resembled that of Thomas Mann and Lion Feuchtwanger in com-
ments on their novels. Striking is the rhetorical sweep of praise relating Przywara's style of thinking to both Asian mystical texts and to Bach's *Art of the
Fugue,* in Siegfried Behn, "Wer ist's?" in Siegfried Behn, *Der beständige Aufbruch* (Nuremberg: Glock und Lutz, 1962), 7–17; see the concluding pages of
Gertz, *Glaubenswelt als Analogie,* 449f.

92. Zechmeister, *Gottes-Nacht,* 58; see Wiesemann, "Musikantische Form:
Strukturmomente der Fuge. I. Sprache und Denkarchitektonik," in *Zerspringen-
gender Akkord,* 314ff.

93. Przywara, "Umschau: Neuer Thomismus," *Stimmen der Zeit* 138
(1941): 302.

94. Przywara, "Dionysos, Prometheus, Christus," *Stimmen der Zeit* 137
(1940): 369; in a literary piece Przywara contrasts tradition with the nihilism
and subjectivity of modern philosophers and ends with a poem by Gertrud
von Le Fort ("Tradition," *Stimmen der Zeit* 135 [1938–1939]: 302–18).

95. Przywara, "Der Mensch des Abgrundes," *Stimmen der Zeit* 121 (1931):
266ff.; a note mentions that Sinclair Lewis's *Babbitt* and Julien Greene's
Adrienne Mesurat might also have been treated in that article. After Undset,
the writings of Gertrud von Le Fort in such works as *Hymnen an die Kirche*
and the novel *Der Papst aus dem Ghetto* are considered.

96. Przywara, "Der Mensch des Abgrundes," 262.

97. *Gott*, 188–92. On music and dance in Kierkegaard and Przywara's interpretation of them as forms of "sounding chaos," see *Das Geheimnis Kierkegaards* (Munich: Oldenbourg, 1929), 4, 6, 7. Berthold Wassmer's "An Weihnachten" is a text by Przywara set to music for mixed choir and organ.

98. Neufeld, "Kategorien des Katholischen," 299.

99. Guardini, *Hölderlin. Weltbild und Frömmigkeit* (Leipzig: Hegner, 1939).

100. *Hölderlin* (Nuremberg: Glock und Lutz, 1949), 13.

101. Ibid., 73; "For Erich Przywara the Christ of Hölderlin is the Johannine and Apocalyptic Christ, Pantocrator, cosmic. Christ is the first and the last in the poetic *oeuvre* of Hölderlin, undergoing an eclipse or a transition, tainted by Hellenism. But the Hellenic Hölderlin cloaks the Johannine and Apocalyptic Hölderlin" (Emilio Brito, *Heidegger et l'hymne du sacré* [Leuven: University Press, 1999]: 200). "Along with his, [Przywara's] published volumes of poetry Rudolf Adolph mentions two thousand unpublished poems in manuscript form" ("Die Bibliothek eines Gelehrten," Behn, *Der beständige Aufbruch*, 21).

102. *Hölderlin*, 177–80; see Thomas F. O'Meara, "Martin Heidegger and Liturgical Time," *Worship* 59 (1985): 126–32.

103. "Oberschlesien," in *In und Gegen*, 12.

104. Przywara, "End-Zeit," *Stimmen der Zeit* 119 (1930): 353.

105. Gertz, "Kreuz-Struktur. Zur theologischen Methode Erich Przywaras," *Theologie und Philosophie* 45 (1970): 560f. Gertz observes that he pursued his studies of Przywara because he found his ideas useful in parish ministry (*Glaubenswelt als Analogie* [Düsseldorf: Patmos, 1969], 3).

106. "Kantischer und katholischer Geistestypus," *Ringen der Gegenwart*, 2:750; see Zechmeister *Gottes-Nacht*, 24ff.

107. See Biju-Duval, "La pensée d'Erich Przywara," 240ff.; *Foi chrétienne et philosophie de la connaissance: Étude d'Analogia entis' de Erich Przywara, et contribution théologique au débat* (Rome: Gregorian University, 1994), 245.

108. Terán Dutari, "Die drei Ebenen des Verhältnisses von Religion und Kultur," in *Christentum und Metaphysik*, 147–67.

Chapter 2.   The Challenge to Be a Catholic

1. Przywara, *Religionsphilosophie katholischer Theologie* (Berlin: Oldenbourg, 1927), 25.

2. *Karl Rahner in Dialogue* (New York: Crossroad, 1986), 258.

3. "Katholische Totalität," in *Ringen der Gegenwart* (Augsburg: Filser, 1929), 2:579.

4. Ibid.; see Zechmeister, "Przywaras 'Katholizität,'" *Gottes-Nacht* (Münster: LIT, 1997), 75ff.

5. See the sections on Karl Barth and Paul Tillich in chapter 4.

6. *Gottgeheimnis der Welt,* in *Religionsphilosophische Schriften* (Einsiedeln: Johannes, 1962), II:162. "Przywara repeatedly calls his writings in a subtitle a 'construction' or a 'foundation' or an 'outline'" (Neufeld, "Kategorien des Katholischen. P. Erich Przywara—100 Jahre," *Catholica* 43 [1989]: 300).

7. Neufeld, "Kategorien des Katholischen," 299.

8. *Reformkatholizismus,* also called "Contemporary Catholicism" or "Critical Catholicism," was not a single organization but a term including various programs for change where the most diverse issues came together in their causes: late idealist philosophy and the question of clerical celibacy; natural science and religious art; social reform and the role of the laity; see Joseph Müller, *Der Reformkatholizismus. Die Religion der Zukunft* (Würzburg: Göbel, 1899), and O. Schroeder, *Aufbruch und Missverständnis. Zur Geschichte der reformkatholischen Bewegung* (Graz: Styria, 1969).

9. See Przywara, "Katholische Totalität," in *Ringen der Gegenwart,* 2:579–608; "Die geschichtlichen Richtungen katholischer Religionsbegründung," *Religionsphilosophie katholischer Theologie,* 66–98.

10. *Analogia Entis* (Einsiedeln: Johannes, 1962), 54–71.

11. Przywara, "Katholizität (1925)," in *Katholische Krise* (Düsseldorf: Patmos, 1967), 20.

12. Przywara, "Katholizität," 21.

13. Ibid., 30.

14. Ibid., 38.

15. Przywara, "Die religiöse Krisis in der Gegenwart und der Katholizismus" (1925), in *Katholische Krise,* 47.

16. "Katholische Bewegung und katholische Aktion" (1929), in *Katholische Krise,* 54. Is what the Catholic Church offers inevitably something from the past? A renewed Catholicism emerged from Romanticism in the years after 1800 and so did not continue a minor Catholic period of theology drawing on the Enlightenment but furthered "an inner universality of the Catholic spirit" (Przywara, "Der Ruf von Heute," 91).

17. K. H. Neufeld, "Vertiefte und gelebte Katholizität. Erich Przywara, 100 Jahre," *Theologie und Philosophie* 65 (1990): 163; see Zechmeister, "Krise und Ende der Neuzeit," *Gottes-Nacht,* 235ff.

18. Przywara, "Die religiöse Krisis," 52f.

19. Ibid., 61.

20. "Katholische Bewegung," 55.

21. Przywara, "Der Ruf von Heute" (1930), in *Katholische Krise,* 94 (originally published as articles in *Stimmen der Zeit* from 1924 to 1926, "Situation und Aufgabe im deutschen Gegenwartskatholizismus").

22. Przywara, "Der Ruf von Heute," 91.

23. Ibid., 103, 92f.

24. Przywara, "Alter und neuer Katholizismus" (1941), in *Katholische Krise,* 167–71, 180.

25. Zechmeister, *Gottes-Nacht,* 79; "Oberschlesien," in *In und Gegen,* 14f.

26. "Laudatio auf Erich Przywara," in *Gnade als Freiheit* (Freiburg: Herder, 1968), 268.

27. "Kantischer und Katholischer Geistestypus," in *Ringen der Gegenwart,* 2:753; Zechmeister, *Gottes-Nacht,* 83ff.

28. "Laudatio," 267. "Leading Catholic theologians like Przywara could count on a large circle of readers for their publications" (W. v. Loewenich, *Der moderne Katholizismus. Erscheinung und Probleme* [Witten: Luther, 1956], 9).

29. See *Ulmer Tagblatt* (August 13, 1923): 910; also see Emmanuel von Severus, *Idelfons Herwegen, Person und Wirkungen* (Mainz: Landesbank Rheinland-Pfalz, 1979).

30. *Gottgeheimnis der Welt. Drei Vorträge über die geistige Krisis der Gegenwart, Schriften* (Einsiedeln: Johannes, 1962), II:145, 148 (originally published by Oratoriums-Verlag in Munich in 1923).

31. Hanna-Barbara Gerl, *Romano Guardini* (Mainz: Matthias-Grünewald, 1985), 150; see Robert Krieg, *Romano Guardini. A Precursor of Vatican II* (Notre Dame: University of Notre Dame Press, 1997).

32. *Gottgeheimnis der Welt,* 124.

33. Ibid., 156. In Plato the tendency is from realism to idealism, while in Aristotle the move is from the ideal to the real (164ff.).

34. Ibid., 124.

35. Ibid., 133.

36. Ibid., 141.

37. Ibid.

38. Ibid., 144.

39. Ibid., 238, 151.

40. Ibid., 242.

41. Przywara, "End-Zeit," *Stimmen der Zeit* 119 (1930): 346.

42. See Angelus Walz, *Andreas Kardinal Frühwirth (1845–1933)* (Vienna: Herder, 1950); Thomas F. O'Meara, *Church and Culture* (Notre Dame: University of Notre Dame Press, 1991), 184, 256.

43. Erich Pzywara, *Gott. Fünf Vorträge über das religionsphilosophische Problem* (Munich: Oratoriums-Verlag, 1926). The first eight notes covering seven pages survey several dozen figures in the philosophy of religion, while notes 21 to 23 indicate a remarkable knowledge of modern German philosophy. Interestingly one finds thanks expressed to Josef Pieper (page 8) for helping to prepare the manuscript. The work was reprinted in *Religionsphilosophische Schriften, Schriften II* (Einsiedeln: Johannes, 1962).

44. *Analogia Entis* (Einsiedeln: Johannes 1962), 56.

45. Erich Pzywara, *Gott,* 9 (page numbers for further citations are given in text).

46. Eduard von Hartmann (1842–1906) sought to provide a synthesis of Schelling, Hegel, and Schopenhauer. He developed an idea of the "unconscious" and in the tradition of Schelling related the idea or reality of God to persons freely becoming themselves. Przywara sometimes described modern German philosophy as lodged in the difference between Jakob Böhme, the Protestant mystic of the seventeenth century, and Hegel; Böhme himself has two diverse sources: Luther is focused on sin, while the Dominican Meister Eckhart is focused on Being and so has a wider field (38). "The philosophy of Böhme is the transposition of Lutheran theology, based exclusively on Scripture, into a metaphysical theosophy of a dialectical form: in this theosophy the opposition between the *Deus irae* and the *Deus misericordiae* is blurred in the obscure abyss of the *Ungrund* in God" (Przywara, "Thèmes anciens et modernes de la philosophie allemande," *Les Études philosophiques* 11 [1956]: 647).

47. In a review of Karl Jaspers's study on Schelling, Przywara spoke insightfully of a modern Johannism, a new Russian theognostic, an anthroposophy. Jaspers showed too that Schelling is a true source of what in a more Western mode we call existentialism. Heidegger's existentialism is a dialectic of Kierkegaard and Schelling. "Schelling becomes the true source of today's philosophy and theology, reaching from the secular adventism of Heidegger (the secularization of an eschatological Christianity) to a 'metaphysics of revelation' (according to which, in the schema of de Lubac, a speculative Aristotelian theology is 'de-Aristotelianized' to the point of a [metaphysics of] becoming as had already appeared with Origen and Augustine" (*Études Philosophiques* 11 [1956]: 135); see the review of the 1927 edition of Schelling's works in *Stimmen der Zeit* 115 (1928): 223–24.

48. "Neue Theologie," in *Ringen der Gegenwart,* 1:352f; see Thomas F. O'Meara, *Romantic Idealism and Roman Catholicism* (Notre Dame: University of Notre Dame Press, 1981); on the influence of Romantic idealism, see Przywara's views on that movement and the relationship of organic philosophy to the Body of Christ in chapter 5.

49. "Die fünf Wenden," 109.

50. See Bernhard Gertz, *Glaubenswelt als Analogie. Die theologische Analogielehre Erich Przywaras und ihr Ort in der Auseinandersetzung um die analogia fidei* (Düsseldorf: Patmos, 1969), 106–10.

51. "Theopanism," a word drawn from Rudolf Ott, indicated in the Leipzig lectures a general Protestant theology where all finite and human activity, whether of nature or grace, is caused solely by God (Bernhard Gertz, "Erich Przywara [1889–1972]," in *Christliche Philosophie im katholischen Denken des 19. und 20. Jahrhunderts,* ed. Emerich Coreth [Graz: Styria, 1988], 2:579).

52. *Augustinisch* (Einsiedeln: Johannes, 1972), 9, 11; on the conversation of Przywara with Augustine through the years, see Zechmeister, *Gottes-Nacht*, 145f.). *Augustinus, Die Gestalt als Gefüge* (Leipzig: Hegner, 1934) is a collection of texts under fourteen headings preceded by a valuable hundred-page introduction; it was published in English as *An Augustine Synthesis* (New York: Sheed and Ward, 1936) and in a reprint from Harper Torchbooks in 1958 without the Introduction by C. C. Martindale.

53. Scotus was not a theologian of the will empty of knowledge but a theoretician of the illumined will and of the creative power of the individual. Later Scotist directions are a source of aspects of modern thinking that can devalue creation and create too personal a mysticism as well as a will entranced by nothingness (*Gottgeheimnis der Welt, Religionsphilosophische Schriften,* II:192; "Mystik und Distanz," *Weg zu Gott, Religionsphilosophische Schriften* (Einsiedeln: Johannes, 1962, 74).

54. *Augustinisch,* 25.

55. *Kant Heute* (Munich: Oldenbourg, 1930), 5.

56. *Religionsbegründung. Max Scheler—J. H. Newman* (Freiburg: Herder, 1923), 260ff.

57. *Augustinus,* 236.

58. *Religionsphilosophie katholischer Theologie,* 72f.

59. *Augustinisch;* one chapter was published in English as "St. Augustine and the Modern World," in *A Monument to Saint Augustine* (London: Sheed and Ward, 1934), 251–86; this English commemorative volume includes essays by Blondel, Gilson, Maritain, and Rolland-Gosselin.

60. "Das Gnoseologisch-Religiöse bei St. Augustin," *Analogia Entis,* 432.

61. "Augustinus," in *In und Gegen,* 306.

62. "Thomas von Aquin," in *Ringen der Gegenwart,* 2:923.

63. *Religionsphilosophie katholischer Theologie,* 84ff.

64. Zechmeister, "Augustinus—Zerbrechen des 'Idealen' in durchlittener Geschichte," in *Gottes-Nacht,* 183–86.

65. "Zwischen Religion und Kultur," *Weg zu Gott,* 98.

66. "Thomas von Aquin heute," in *Humanitas,* 741, 887.

67. Grabmann, "Neuscholastik," *Lexikon fur Theologie und Kirche,* 1st ed. (Freiburg: Herder, 1935), 7, 522. On Leo XIII and the restoration of Thomism, see G. McCool, "The Nineteenth-Century Heritage" in *From Unity to Pluralism. The Internal Evolution of Thomism* (New York: Fordham University Press, 1989), 5ff. Otto Hermann Pesch, "Thomismus," in *Lexikon für Theologie und Kirche,* 2d ed. (Freiburg: Herder, 1965), 10:160–65; chapter 4 in this book and the bibliography in Thomas F. O'Meara, *Thomas Aquinas Theologian* (Notre Dame: University of Notre Dame Press, 1998); James Athanasius Weisheipl, "Thomism," in *The New Catholic Encyclopedia* (San Francisco: McGraw-Hill, 1967), 14:126–38; G. McCool, *Nineteenth-Century Scholasticism: The Search for a*

Unitary Method (New York: Fordham University Press, 1989);T. O'Meara, "The Two Directions of German Catholic Theology (1864–1914)," in his *Church and Culture* (Notre Dame: Notre Dame University Press, 1991), 25–53. Ultimately, static neo-Thomism involved several shifts: the texts of Aquinas and Thomists rather than the "books" of science and the Bible were central; the teacher was a commentator on speculative writings rather than one who explained revelation; an open spirit of research and dialogue became one of exposition of work already done; new questions and new sources (usually adversaries) were avoided.

68. "Wege zu Newman," in *In und Gegen,* 28f.; Przywara, "Thomas von Aquin deutsch," *Stimmen der Zeit* 121 (1931): 385. He spoke in an early work of a Thomistic piety of God in creation, nature, and grace (*Weg zu Gott,* 49).

69. "Thomas von Aquin Heute," *Humanitas,* 741.

70. "Thomismus and Molinismus," *Stimmen der Zeit* 125 (1933): 32. "Thomism draws everything from God's will, while Molinism draws it from God's knowledge. Thomism knows the individual only as the point where general laws are applied, while Molinism wants an eternal oscillation of individual ideas before God's eyes." Przywara, "Verklärung oder Polarität," (1924) in *Katholische Krise,* 12; on Molinism, see "Einheit von Natur und Übernatur?" *Stimmen der Zeit* 105 (1923): 436; on the influence of Suarezian Thomism on Przywara, see Julio Terán Dutari, "Die Geschichte des Terminus 'Analogia entis' und das Werk Erich Przywara," *Philosophisches Jahrbuch* 77 (1970): 164f.; and the same author's *Christentum und Metaphysik.* "Precisely in the anonymity of the 'No' to nothingness is Przywara a Jesuit Molinist and here again comes the proper tension-ground of his thinking into view. For to protect pure transparence and instrumentality from its worst danger of sinking into nothingness, to become the dialectical opposite pole of the divine emergence and thereby indirectly . . . to introduce the demonic identity of the contrary, created freedom must be retained. The unity and concreteness of the Jesuit Suarez, individuality as such, emerge from the night of anonymity. Molinism is different from Thomism (or better, Bañezianism) in the way in which the religious takes form, in the image behind the plan of thought: the ideal of the monk apart from work versus the worldly member of the Society of Jesus . . . , the difference between a mystical unification and a radical going out into the world" (Karl Heinz Wiesemann, *Zerspringender Akkord. Das Zusammenspiel von Theologie und Mystik bei Karl Adam, Romano Guardini und Erich Przywara als theologische Fuge* [Würzburg: Echter, 2000], 298f.).

71. Przywara, "Hauptrichtungen der katholischen Theologie und Philosophie," reprinted as "Die fünf Wenden. Eine Grundlegung," *Katholische Krise,* 108.

72. "Die Problematik der Neuscholastik," *Kant-Studien* 33 (1928): 73–98.

73. "Mystik und Distanz," in *Weg zu Gott,* 74.

74. Przywara, "Thomas von Aquin als Problematiker. Ein Versuch," *Stimmen der Zeit* 109 (1925): 199; on Dominicans before and after Aquinas, Albert, and Meister Eckhart, see *Christliche Existenz* (Leipzig: Hegner, 1934), 62ff. Strangely, Richard Schaeffler in his magisterial survey of modern philosophy and theology sees Przywara "as particularly exemplifying on-going Catholic scholasticism" (Schaeffler, *Die Wechselbeziehungen zwischen Philosophie und katholischer Theologie* [Darmstadt: Wissenschaftliche Buchgesellschaft, 1980], 42ff.).

75. "Thomas und Hegel," in *Ringen der Gegenwart,* 2:950.

76. "Tragische Seele," in *Ringen der Gegenwart,* 2:902, 897; "Thomas von Aquin," in *Ringen der Gegenwart,* 2:909–24.

77. "Neue Religiosität," in *Ringen der Gegenwart,* 1:57.

78. "Thomas von Aquin als Problematiker. Ein Versuch," 197. J. Martin-Palma in his history of the theology of grace holds the debatable view that Przywara is more Augustinian than Thomist because the theme of dynamic dialectic is more prominent than that of the relationship of beings (*Gnadenlehre. Von der Reformation bis zur Gegenwart* [Freiburg: Herder, 1980], 182). "In Augustine there is the longing for bridal love, while Thomas presents its tranquil celebration (Thomas is influenced by the liturgical ecstasy of the Areopagite): so in Augustine, there is the burning, the anticipation, the anxiety, and the transcendence of that longing (through heights and depths), while in Aquinas there is the impersonal style and the sobriety of a liturgy, almost of a static ceremonial . . . of prayer and confession" (*Augustinisch,* 111).

79. *Religionsphilosophie katholischer Theologie,* 74.

80. "Thomas und Hegel," in *Ringen der Gegenwart,* 2:948ff.

81. Przywara, "Thomas von Aquin deutsch," 385. Interestingly, Przywara was stimulated to give special attention to Aquinas by Martin Luther, by the fourth centennial of the Lutheran Reformation in 1917, by the Reformers' stress on *solus Deus* (Gertz, "Erich Przywara [1889–1972]," 578).

82. "Katholischer Radikalismus," in *Ringen der Gegenwart,* 1:82; see *Analogia entis,* 71–202; Julio Terán Dutari, *Christentum und Metaphysik. Das Verhältnis beider nach der Analogielehre Erich Przywaras* (Munich: Berchmanskolleg, 1973), 141ff.

83. "Thomas von Aquin," *Ringen der Gegenwart,* 2:929.

84. Aquinas, *Quaestiones disputatae, De Veritate,* 22, 4.

85. Przywara, "Der Grundsatz 'Gratia non destruit, sed supponit et perficit naturam.' Eine ideengeschichtliche Interpretation," *Scholastik* 17 (1942): 183; see Klaus Fischer, "Die Aussage, 'gratia non destruit,' und ihre Bedeutung für das Geheimnis des Menschen (E. Przywara in memoriam!)," *Der Mensch als Geheimnis. Die Anthropologie Karl Rahners* (Freiburg: Herder, 1974), 265ff. Przywara can also draw from Aquinas the Platonic strains of Pseudo-Denis and Nicholas of Cusa where hierarchical levels or divinely resolved

opposites reign, theologies which though present to Aquinas are not proper to him ("Thomas von Aquin, Ignatius von Loyola, Friedrich Nietzsche," *Zeitschrift für Aszese und Mystik* 11 [1936]: 287).

86. "Der Grundsatz," 184.

87. See "Einheit von Natur und Übernatur?" 428ff.

88. *Religionsphilosophie katholischer Theologie*, 75. Zechmeister traces the course of Przywara's study of Aquinas (*Gottes-Nacht*, 130–34).

89. *Kant Heute* (Munich: Oldenbourg, 1930), 106, 6.

90. Gertz, "Erich Przywara (1889–1972)," 580; citing Przywara, "Sendung," *Ringen der Gegenwart*, 2:961.

Chapter 3.   Philosophies of Religion in the Service of Theology

1. "The philosophy of religion is a creation of modern thinking" (Karl Eschweiler, "Zur Krisis der neuscholastischen Religionsphilosophie," *Bonner Zeitschrift für Theologie und Seelsorge* 1 [1924]: 313).

2. Hans Urs von Balthasar, "Erich Pryzwara," in Leo Zimny, *Erich Przywara. Sein Schrifttum 1912–1962* (Einsiedeln: Johannes, 1963), 5.

3. "Das Religiöse als Form des Denkens," *Stimmen der Zeit* 121 (1931): 15–27.

4. *Weg zu Gott, Religionsphilosophische Schriften* (Einsiedeln: Johannes, 1962), 24–26 (originally published in *Ringen der Gegenwart* [Augsburg: Filser, 1929], 1:389–539).

5. Nikolai Hartmann (1882–1950), not to be confused with the earlier Eduard von Hartmann, separated himself from neo-Kantianism and sought to grasp external reality through the experiencing self. He composed works on being but began with the individual penetrated by real and ideal worlds, anticipating both Husserl and Heidegger.

6. *Weg zu Gott*, chapters 4 and 5.

7. *Weg zu Gott*, 102–6.

8. Przywara, *Religionsbegründung. Max Scheler—J. H. Newman* (Freiburg: Herder, 1923), 257–60; the censor on behalf of the Jesuits was Augustin Bea, later to be a pioneer of ecumenism and a theologian at Vatican II.

9. Przywara, *Religionsbegründung*, 169.

10. Przywara, *Religionsbegründung*, 225–27.

11. "Zwischen Religion und Kultur," in *Ringen der Gegenwart*, 1:502ff.; on the role of Georg von Hertling, see Przywara, "Religiöse Bewegungen," in *Ringen der Gegenwart*, 1:3ff.; Thomas O'Meara, "Georg von Hertling," in *Church and Culture* (Notre Dame: University of Notre Dame Press, 1991), 155–60.

12. *Gott* (Munich: Oratoriums-Verlag, 1926), 13, 15, 21; see "Zum Problem Max Scheler," *Stimmen der Zeit* 108 (1924): 78–80.

13. Przywara, *Religionsbegründung,* 53, 75, 171, 191, 225.

14. Eschweiler, "Zur Krisis der neuscholastischen Religionsphilosophie," 325. "All the writings of Scheler beginning with the doctoral dissertation up to the recent publications are carefully drawn into [Przywara's] presentation" (Eschweiler, 317); for a negative view on Scheler by a Catholic, see Heinrich Lennerz, S. J., *Schelers Konformitätssystem und die Lehre der katholischen Kirche* (Münster: Aschendorff, 1924).

15. Przywara, *Religionsphilosophie katholischer Theologie* (Munich: Oldenbourg, 1927). The translation of this work by an Anglican professor at Oxford, A. C. Bouquet's *Polarity. A German Catholic's Interpretation of Religion* (London: Oxford University Press: 1935), one of the few works by Przywara in English, is both occasionally inaccurate and stylistically curious. In the opening pages, "Frömmigkeit" is translated not as devotional realm or spirituality but as "religious zeal," and "Gott" often emerges quaintly as "Deity"; words like "Godward" are fashioned, and some German phrases don't receive any nuanced English version; the text veers toward views that are extreme and not those of the author.

16. Letter of September 30, 1923, in *Karl Barth—Eduard Thurneysen. Briefwechsel* (Zurich: Theologischer Verlag, 1974), 2:259f.; Emil Brunner, *Religionsphilosophie evangelischer Theologie* (Munich: Oldenbourg, 1928).

17. *Religionsphilosophie katholischer Theologie,* 94.

18. Ibid., 94f.

19. Heinrich Fries, *Die katholische Religionsphilosophie der Gegenwart. Der Einfluss Max Schelers auf ihre Formen und Gestalten* (Heidelberg: Kerle, 1949), 23.

20. Ibid., 30.

21. Ibid., 358f.

22. Ibid., 372.

23. Przywara, "Essenz- und Existenz-Philosophie. Tragische Identität oder Distanz der Geduld," *Scholastik* 14 (1939): 517.

24. Ibid., 516.

25. "Ende oder Anfang der Philosophie," *Stimmen der Zeit* 127 (1934): 46–49. For Przywara, the contemporary existential and searching individual has some relationship to the Reformation. That division in Western Christianity during the sixteenth century made the dramatic exaltation of the cross into the sole image of Christianity but at the same time removed the cross from the spiritual life of the Christian. So eventually in post-Reformation Germany the Christian embraces rather than overcomes the tragic.

26. Przywara, "Essenz- und Existenz-Philosophie," 521. Peter Lippert, a member of the staff of *Stimmen der Zeit* who wrote on Jesuit spirituality and the psychology of the Society of Jesus, published in 1927 *Die Weltanschauung des Katholizismus* (Leipzig: Reinicke, 1927); the book looked at the content, origin, and characteristics of a Catholic worldview; at sin, renewal, and end of the world, and finally at Catholicism as a metaphysics, a religion, and an

ethos. He added a survey of recent literature on this theme, and on apologetics and dogmatics; he also wrote a theology of the church. See Joseph Kreitmaier, *Peter Lippert, der Mann und sein Werk* (Freiburg: Herder, 1938); O. Köhler, "Peter Lippert," *Stimmen der Zeit* 208 (1990): 745–51. Przywara saw him as an explorer of life, always finding more layers of its magical confusion (Przywara, "Die fünf Wenden. Eine Grundlegung," in *Katholische Krise*, 108), while Hans Urs von Balthasar described him as "someone of encouragement amid those languishing of thirst in the desert of neoscholasticism" (Emmanuel Bauer, "Hans Urs von Balthasar (1905–1988)—Sein philosophisches Werk," in *Christliche Philosophie* [Graz: Styria, 1990], 3:286).

27. Przywara, "Essenz- und Existenz-Philosophie," 544.

28. *Logos. Logos, Abendland, Reich, Commercium* (Düsseldorf: Patmos, 1963).

29. Paolo Molteni's study, mainly on analogy, lists thirty articles and books written on this aspect of Przywara's thought (*Al di là degli estremi. Introduzione al pensiero di Erich Przywara* [Milan: Ares, 1996], 103–5); see particularly Bernhard Gertz, *Glaubenswelt als Analogie. Die theologische Analogielehre Erich Przywaras und ihr Ort in der Auseinandersetzung um die analogia fidei* (Düsseldorf: Patmos, 1969); R. Stertenbrink, *Ein Weg zum Denken. Die Analogia entis bei Erich Przywara* (Salzburg: Pustet, 1971); Julio Terán Dutari, *Christentum und Metaphysik. Das Verhältnis beider nach der Analogielehre Erich Przywaras* (Munich: Berchmanskolleg, 1973); E. Naab, *Zur Begründung der analogia entis bei Erich Przywara. Eine Erörterung* (Regensburg: Pustet, 1987); Stefan Nieborak, *'Homo analogia': Zur philosophisch-theologischen Bedeutung der 'analogia entis' im Rahmen der existentiellen Frage bei Erich Przywara S.J. (1889–1972)* (Frankfurt: Lang, 1994); G. Copers, *De analogieleer van Erich Przywara* (Brussels: Palais der Academiën, 1952); S. Holm, "Religionsfilosofien paa grundlag af analogia entis, Erich Przywara," in *Religionsfilosofien in det tyvende aarhundrede* (Copenhagen: Nyt Nordisk Forlag, 1952), 199–224; in English there are the writings of James Zeitz.

30. St. Thomas Aquinas, *Commentary on the Metaphysics of Aristotle* (Chicago: Regnery, 1961), 1:215ff.; Aristotle, *Metaphysics* IV, 6, 1016B; see R. Antilla, *Analogy: A Basic Bibliography* (Amsterdam: J. Benjamins, 1977).

31. Lotz, "Analogie," in W. Brugger, *Philosophiches Wörterbuch* (Freiburg: Herder, 1964), 9; Gustav Söhngen, "Analogie," in *Handbuch theologischer Grundbegriffe* (Munich: Kösel, 1962), 1:49. Söhngen, an intellectual compatriot of Przywara, also goes beyond the logic of words to an analogy that is "the basic structure in all the regions of being and knowing," a motif in many cultural and intellectual areas, a theme he traces back to Cardinal Newman ("Analogie," 50).

32. Aquinas, *Summa theologiae* 1, q. 13, a. 5.

33. Julio Terán Dutari, "Die Geschichte des Terminus 'Analogia entis' und das Werk Erich Przywara," *Philosophisches Jahrbuch* 77 (1970): 164f. On the

influence of Jesuit scholasticism and Suárez, see Eschweiler, 320–30; for a history of analogy in treatises and manuals from the sixteenth to the nineteenth century, see Gertz, *Glaubenswelt als Analogie,* 53–87.

34. "Gotteserfahrung und Gottesbeweis," *Stimmen der Zeit* 104 (1923): 12–19; on the early development of the term in Przywara, see Gertz, *Glaubenswelt als Analogie,* 237f.

35. *Nicomachean Ethics* V, 7, 1131B11, in *The Ethics of Aristotle,* trans. J. A. K. Tomson and Hugh Tredennick (New York: Penguin, 1976), 180.

36. Adam's theology, according to the Jesuit, was typical of "an extreme Thomism which had no place for nature and philosophy but then drew them back in through the form of a strong Scotism of the person facing the irrational in the flow of history" (Przywara, "Die Reichweite der Analogie als katholische Grundform," *Scholastik* 15 [1940]: 339f.).

37. "Zwischen Religion und Kultur," *Weg zu Gott,* 93.

38. See *Glaubenswelt als Analogie,* 209; 222–32.

39. *Analogia Entis. Metaphysik. Ur-Struktur und All-Rhythmus* (Munich: Kösel, 1932) reprinted in Erich Przywara, *Schriften* (Einsiedeln: Johannes, 1962), III:253.

40. Wilhelmy, 16.

41. "Neue Theologie? Das Problem katholischer Theologie," *Stimmen der Zeit* 111 (1926): 443. "In 1923 I introduced the expression '*analogia entis*' in my philosophy of religion in dialogue with Scheler and in 1925 in dialogue with Karl Barth, making it the central point of my metaphysical and controversial theological writings and of my philosophy of religion. . . . It did not, however, become the point of departure of fruitful discussion but the point of departure for a great conflict" ("Tradition," *In und Gegen. Stellungnahmen zur Zeit* [Nuremburg: Glock und Lutz, 1955], 177). There were critical reviews by scholastics and Protestants but the impact of the theology, in contrast to the work of Guardini or Henri de Lubac preparing for Vatican II, was modest. "Przywara's main work found beyond a narrow circle of specialists no reception corresponding to its import. Its thought-process is too difficult. Moreover, a second volume was announced in which one expected a precise commentary, but it never appeared" (Friedrich Wulf, "Christliches Denken. Eine Einführung in das theologische-religiöse Werk von Erich Przywara, S. J. (1889–1972)," in *Gottes Nähe,* ed. Paul Imhof [Würzburg: Echter, 1990], 358). Richard Schenk, citing the support of Richard Schaeffler, observes that "the reason why Przywara's thought lacked to a large extent reception among philosophers lay in the narrow ordering of philosophy beneath theology. Przywara's treatment of the axiom about grace leaves too little autonomy to philosophy" (*Die Gnade vollendeter Endlichkeit: Zur tranzendentaltheologischen Auslegung der thomanischen Anthropologie* [Freiburg: Herder, 1989], 373).

42. *Analogia Entis,* 297, and the subtitle of the work; see "'Analogia Entis' als Denkform," in Terán Dutari, *Christentum und Metaphysik,* 225ff.

43. *Religionsphilosophie katholischer Theologie,* 67ff. For a history of analogy in treatises and manuals from the sixteenth to the nineteenth century, see Gertz, *Glaubenswelt als Analogie,* 53–86, "a history of an idea which Erich Przywara hardly knew" (87).

44. *Religionsphilosophie katholischer Theologie,* 83. "Why," Gertz asked, "is the first part of *Analogia Entis* published only in 1932? Because first there had to be a reflective encounter with Scheler and Newman, with Kierkegaard and Kant, because 350 essays and reviews and countless lectures and courses took up his time. Why is there no systematic, second volume of *Analogia Entis?* Because time was taken up with writing *Christliche Existenz* and with the structure of the theology of the *Exercises.* Why no 'systematic' theology of the *analogia fidei?* Because Przywara was busy during the war years with pastoral ministry in Munich and his theological work was channeled to evening lectures which are still not published" (Gertz, *Glaubenswelt als Analogie,* 314f.).

45. *Analogia Entis,* 7.

46. Fourth Lateran Council in *Enchiridion Symbolorum, Definitionum et Declarationum,* 26th edition, n. 806. The sources of the articles added later are given in *Analogia Entis,* 18.

47. Przywara, "Die Reichweite der Analogie," 361.

48. *Analogia Entis,* 103.

49. Ibid., 206; for a summary, see Gertz, "Erich Przywara (1889–1972)," 581–88.

50. Przywara, "Die Reichweite der Analogie," 352.

51. Przywara, *Logos,* 129; see Zechmeister, "Admirabile commercium als Konkret-Form der Analogie," *Gottes-Nacht* (Münster: LIT, 1997), 213–18; Karl-Heinz Wiesemann, *Zerspringender Akkord* (Würzburg: Echter, 2000), 280f.

52. "Die Reichweite der Analogie," 352f.

53. Ibid., 362.

54. A theme developed at length in *Deus Semper Maior* (Freiburg: Herder, 1938) to illustrate how Ignatian spirituality is the counterpart to analogy.

55. *Analogia Entis,* 95–97.

56. Przywara, "Katholizismus," in *Ringen der Gegenwart* (Augsburg: Filser, 1929), 2:667.

57. "Die Reichweite der Analogie," 362.

58. *Analogia Entis,* 35ff., 58ff. Przywara mentioned "Schwebe" in the work of his fellow Jesuit, J. B. Lotz ("Sein und Wert," *Zeitschrift für katholische Theologie* 57 [1933]: 557–613); see Otto Muck, "Weiterführung der Philosophie Joseph Maréchals durch Johannes B. Lotz," in *Schule des Denkens. 75 Jahre Philosophische Fakultät der Jesuiten in Pullach und München,* ed. Julius Oswald (Stuttgart: Kohlhammer, 2000), 116–36.

59. *Analogia Entis,* 161ff.

60. Ibid.; Zeitz singles out as the basic themes of the book primal structure, balance in tension leading to a total structure, and createdness (136ff.); on analogy as rhythmic dynamism, see Gertz, "Erich Przywara," 584f. For a survey of first and later reviews and reactions to the work in Europe and the United States, see Terán Dutari, *Christentum und Metaphysik*, 600–609.

61. Terán Dutari, *Christentum und Metaphysik*, 530–63; see Gertz, "Kreuz-Struktur. Zur theologischen Methode Erich Przywaras," 45 (1970): 555–61; Zechmeister, "Karsamstag. Zu einer Theologie des Gott-vermissens," *Vom Wagnis der Nichtidentität* (Münster: LIT, 2000), 64–70.

62. "Laudatio," 270.

63. Typical of the neoscholastic reaction is W. Bange, "Form-Einheit und Philosophie und Theologie?" *Catholica* 3 (1934): 10–20.

64. Schenk, *Die Gnade*, 375–81.

65. Gertz, "Erich Przywara (1889–1972)," 581, 576; see Gertz, *Glaubenswelt als Analogie*, 166ff.

66. Faber, "*Deus semper maior*," *Geist und Leben* 66 (1993): 209.

67. Karl H. Neufeld, "Vertiefte und gelebte Katholizität. Erich Przywara, 100 Jahre," *Theologie und Philosophie* 65 (1990): 165f.; see the summary of Joachim Track, "Analogie," in *Theologische Realenzyklopädie* (Berlin: de Gruyter, 1977), 2:639.

68. Wulf, "Christliches Denken," 356

69. Terán Dutari, *Christentum und Metaphysik*, 95f., 429, 420, 397f. and "Zur philosophisch-theologischen Auffassung der Freiheit bei K. Rahner und E. Przywara," in *Wagnis Theologie. Erfahrungen mit der Theologie Karl Rahners*, ed. H. Vorgrimler (Freiburg: Herder, 1979), 284–98.

70. Terán Dutari, *Christentum und Metaphysik*, 510–16, 622.

71. L. B. Puntel, *Analogie und Geschichtlichkeit* (Freiburg: Herder, 1969), 538ff., 165f.; for further critique, see Erich Naab, *Zur Begründung der analogia entis bei Erich Przywara* (Regensburg: Pustet, 1987). Georges Schrijver concludes: "Actually Przywara appears to admit that the rhythm of the analogy of being, as he conceives it, is capable of ending in a rapprochement with God, but he is not at all disposed to describe it in terms other than differentiation and difference. He will say that in the event of analogy a rapport with God is really established but precisely one shown by the creature in its proper *ontological difference* in the very instance of its approach to God. This is all in virtue of the very reality of its participation as the creature understands better and at what point God is—although in his unsurpassable fullness of a totally other nature than the one created—and when God extends itself in intimacy. In short, the relationship of *analogia entis* is established concretely only under the form of an effective link, but one which is moving, of two profoundly differentiated partners" (Georges de Schrijver, *Le merveilleux accord de l'homme et de Dieu. Étude de l'analogie de l'être chez Hans Urs von Balthasar* [Leuven: University Press, 1983], 269).

72. Stefan Nieborak, *'Homo analogia': Zur philosophisch-theologischen Bedeutung der 'analogia entis' im Rahmen der existentiellen Frage bei Erich Przywara S.J. (1889–1972)* (Frankfurt: Lang, 1994), 557.

73. Zechmeister, *Gottes-Nacht,* 14, 95ff., 300ff.; on this topic and the later Przywara, see Przywara, "Die fünf Wenden," 121.

74. Karl Eschweiler, "Zur Krisis der neuscholastichen Religionsphilosophie," 337.

75. "Katholischer Radikalismus," in *Ringen der Gegenwart,* 1:82.

76. Przywara, "Zwischen Religion und Kultur," in *Weg zu Gott,* 103. In 1952 Niels Nielsen, Methodist theologian at Rice University, began a series of articles on Przywara to show that his theory of analogy marked an extension of neo-Thomism into existentialism, a shift from logic to personal involvement; he saw in the German Jesuit a new approach for metaphysics and a contribution to ecumenism: e.g., "Przywara's Philosophy of the *Analogia Entis,*" *Review of Metaphysics* 5 (1952): 599–620.

77. Aquinas, *De Spiritualibus Creaturis* art. 10, ad 16.

78. "Der Grundsatz 'Gratia non destruit, sed supponit et perficit naturam'. Eine ideengeschichtliche Interpretation," *Scholastik* 17 (1942): 183.

79. Ibid., 184.

80. "Thomas und Hegel," in *Ringen der Gegenwart,* 2:948ff.

81. Gertz, "Erich Przywara (1889–1972)," 586.

82. Duffy, *The Graced Horizon. Nature and Grace in Modern Catholic Thought* (Collegeville: The Liturgical Press, 1992), 8. See Medard Kehl, Werner Löser, "Situation de la théologie systématique en Allemagne," *Revue de théologie et philosophie* 113 (1981): 25–38, and relating this shift in theology to Ignatian spirituality, Karlheinz Ruhstorfer, *Das Prinzip ignatianischen Denkens. Zum geschichtlichen Ort der 'Geistlichen Übungen' des Ignatius von Loyola* (Freiburg: Herder, 1998), 406ff. "In these issues [nature and grace, obediential potency and natural desire] there was particularly in the 1920s a widely held view that something new was needed. There are many names. . . . The most important impetuses came without doubt from Maurice Blondel and Joseph Maréchal; with de Lubac should be named Pierre Rousselot and with Rahner Erich Przywara" (Max Seckler, "Die scholastische 'Potentia Oboedientialis' bei Karl Rahner (1904–1984) und Henri de Lubac (1896–1991). Ein Beitrag zur Metaphysik des endlichen Geistes," in *Die Einheit der Person,* ed. Martin Thurner [Stuttgart: Kohlhammer, 1998], 303). Przywara's interpretation of the natural law from 1923 relates to the discussion after *Humanae Vitae* in 1968, for he points out that in human morality the nature is that of a free person, and that natural law is first nature and then, in some way, law (*Religionsbegründung,* 83); see *Glaubenswelt als Analogie,* 435ff.

83. See Zeitz, 31–38.

84. "Katholizismus," in *Ringen der Gegenwart,* 2:607.

85. Przywara wrote an essay on Newman and the German Romantic theoretician of universal systems, Joseph Görres, contrasting their views on history, the total history of humanity, and God; both linked the historical development of Christianity to the growth of the divine in Christ, to the Pauline growth of the Body of Christ ("Newman und Josef von Görres," *Newman Studien* 6 [1964]: 97–104).

86. *Gottgeheimnis der Welt, Religionsphilosophische Schriften* (Einsiedeln: Johannes, 1962), 2:240. "Wege zu Newman" describes his journey toward Newman and recalls how he had to defend Newman against suspicions of modernism while also showing his fresh originality (*In und Gegen,* 28–32). Interestingly Heinrich Fries in his doctoral and postdoctoral dissertations also chose as lasting figures Newman and Scheler; Heinrich Fries, "Lebensgeschichte im Dialog mit Kardinal Newman. Rückblick eines Fundamentaltheologen," in *Sinnsuche und Lebenswenden: Gewissen als Praxis nach John Henry Newman,* ed. G. Biemer (New York: Lang, 1998), 132–47; Norbert Göttler, "Heinrich Fries. Brückenbauer zwischen Kirche und Welt," in *Theologen unserer Zeit,* ed. Stephan Pauly (Stuttgart: Kohlhammer, 1997), 59–68.

87. Henry Tristram, "A Newman Synthesis," *The Clergy Review* 1 (1931): 129; see Tristram, "J. A. Moehler et J. H. Newman. La Pensée allemande et la renaissance catholique en Angleterre," *Revue des sciences philosophiques et théologiques* 27 (1938): 184ff.

88. Davis, Introduction, in *The Heart of Newman* (Springfield: Templegate, 1963); originally *A Newman Synthesis* (New York: Sheed and Ward, 1930). Maisie Ward praised Przywara's selections from Newman's theology, a thinker "held to be dull by the average Englishman" (*Young Mr. Newman* [New York: Sheed and Ward, 1948], 307).

89. Cited in *Augustinisch* (Einsiedeln: Johannes, 1972), 64.

90. Otto Karrer (1888–1976) pursued his studies for the priesthood with Przywara and taught at Stella Matutina, the Jesuit boarding school. He left the Jesuits and became a Lutheran minister but soon returned to the Catholic church, living in Lucerne as a private scholar and pioneer of ecumenism from 1925. His eight volumes of texts and commentaries, *J. H. Newman: Christentum,* was excerpted for the smaller volume by Przywara; in 1943 he published two volumes on Newman's ecclesiology (V. Conzemius, "Karrer, Otto," in *Lexikon für Theologie und Kirche* [Freiburg: Herder, 1996], 5:1265).

91. "Wege zu Newman," 29; in German the book was *J. H. Newmans Christentum. Ein Aufbau aus seinen Werken,* 8 vols. (Freiburg: Herder, 1922).

92. Przywara, *The Heart of Newman,* xv.

93. Newman, *Gesammelte Werke. Im Auftrage des Verbandes der Vereine Katholischer Akademiker zur Pflege der katholischen Weltanschauung,* ed. Daniel Feuling and Erich Przywara (Mainz: Schmidt, 1931).

94. Terán Dutari, "Erich Przywaras Deutung des religionsphilosophischen Anliegens Newmans," *Newman-Studien* 7 (1957): 250.

95. Przywara, "Zum Newmanschen Denktypus," in *Jahrbuch des Verbandes der Vereine katholischer Akademiker zur Pflege der katholischen Weltanschauung* (Augsburg: Verband der Vereine katholischer Akademiker, 1922), 147, 149.

96. Przywara, "J. H. Newmans Problemstellung," in *Ringen der Gegenwart,* 2:824. Terán Dutari inquires as to whether Przywara's *"Explizitmachung"* is as close to Newman's process of "making explicit" as Przywara thinks (*Christentum und Metaphysik,* 74ff.).

97. "Wege zu Newman," 32.

98. *Religionsbegründung,* 213.

99. Ibid., 159f.

100. *Augustinisch,* 68f.

101. I. T. Ker, Introduction, to J. H. Newman, *An Essay in Aid of a Grammar of Assent* (Oxford: Clarendon, 1985), liv–lv.

102. Terán Dutari, *Christentum und Metaphysik,* 567–72

103. To honor Przywara, Heinrich Fries wrote in 1959 an essay comparing Franz Xaver Kraus with John Henry Newman. Franz Xaver Kraus (1840–1901) was a brilliant and engaging professor of church history and a pioneer in the fields of archaeology and Christian art. He joined the Freiburg theological faculty in 1878, becoming its guiding spirit. He was convinced that the policies of the Curia in the Vatican would severely injure the life of the church in Germany and so advocated pastoral reforms and a distinction between "religious" and "political" Catholicism. In 1904 Bavarian Catholics founded a *Krausgesellschaft,* "a society for the advancement of religion and culture," advocating freedom of scholarly research and anti-Roman renewal. Viewed by some as the creator of a mystical, culture-Catholicism, he advocated a liberal church but a conservative state. Kraus wrote in his diary in 1900: "I became convinced that my treatments of church politics were so uncomfortable to Vatican Pharisaism that they would not stop at forbidding attendance at my lectures but would censure or excommunicate me." Newman, Fries argued, was more a theologian, a theologian of the church—but from a decidedly incarnational point of view. He was not someone to flee "the visible and vital aspects of the church into some form of ecclesiological spiritualism and idealism and to place theological constructions and conceptualities in place of reality" (Fries, "Franz Xaver Kraus and John Henry Newman," in Behn, *Der beständige Aufbruch,* 154; see E. Hauviller, *F. X. Kraus. Ein Lebensbild aus der Zeit des Reformkatholizismus* [Munich: Lehmann, 1905]).

104. Placid Murray, Introduction, in *Newman the Oratorian: His Unpublished Oratory Papers* (Leominster: Fowler Wright Books, 1968), 5; R. Grosche, "Der Wandel des deutschen Newman-Bildes," *Newman-Studien* 4 (1960): 331–44. Mathias Laros, an enthusiast along with Przywara for Newman, was a pioneer in ecumenism as a leader in the Una Sancta movement whose director he

became upon the execution by the Nazis of Max J. Metzger ("Laros, Matthias," in *Lexikon für Theologie und Kirche* [Freiburg: Herder, 1997], 3:653).

105. *Gottgeheimnis der Welt*, 242. "My unchangeableness here below is perserverance in changing" (*Meditations and Devotions of the Late Cardinal Newman* [New York: Longmans, Green, 1903], 508). Gertz notes that the year 1925, in which essays on Aquinas appear, was also a year of crises: the translation of the complete works of Newman appeared as unlikely, while Scheler's stances were becoming peculiar and gnostic (Gertz, *Glaubenswelt als Analogie*, 180).

106. Zechmeister, *Gottes-Nacht*, 111f.; Przywara, "Wege zu Newman," 32.

107. Przywara, "Vorwort," in *Kant Heute* (Munich: Oldenbourg, 1930), iii.

108. *Kant Heute*, 5.

109. Ibid., 47.

110. Ibid., 72f.; on the differences between the two Jesuits, see Terán Dutari, *Christentum und Metaphysik*, 294–308.

111. Ibid., 107f.

112. See "Platonismus. Platon—Baader—Franz Brentano," *Stimmen der Zeit* 114 (1928): 16ff.; also on Brentano and Husserl, *Religionsbegründung*, 2; "Simmel—Husserl—Scheler," in *In und Gegen*, 41ff. Finding a role for Franz Brentano in the thought of Przywara as well as in that of Husserl is Richard Schaeffler, *Die Wechselbeziehung zwischen Philosophie und katholischer Theologie* (Darmstadt: Wissenschaftliche Buchgesellschaft, 1980), 59; Hanna-Barbara Gerl, *Unerbittliches Licht. Edith Stein—Philosophie, Mystik, Leben* (Mainz: Matthias-Grünewald, 1991), 81ff., 87ff.; on Brentano as a student of Schelling and an influence on the Catholic theologian Hermann Schell, see Thomas F. O'Meara, *Church and Culture. German Catholic Theology, 1860–1914* (Notre Dame: University of Notre Dame Press, 1991), 103–5; on Husserl and Scheler, see Richard Schaeffler, "Philosophie und katholische Theologie im 20. Jahrhundert," in *Christliche Philosophie im katholischen Denken des 19. und 20. Jahrhunderts*, ed. Emerich Coreth et al. (Graz: Styria, 1990), 3:56–60.

113. "Simmel—Husserl—Scheler," in *In und Gegen*, 45.

114. *Gott*, 13, 15, 21.

115. *Gottgeheimnis der Welt*, 124. One can see the author describing these turns to the object, to Husserl leading to Aquinas, twenty years later in "Thomas von Aquin Heute," in *Humanitas. Der Mensch gestern und morgen* (Nuremberg: Glock und Lutz, 1952), 735ff.

116. Zechmeister, *Gottes-Nacht*, 104.

117. Przywara, "Drei Richtungen der Phänomenologie" *Stimmen der Zeit* 115 (1928): 253.

118. The thought of Heidegger is a realistic ethics but not a "realogy" which, flowing from Max Scheler's view of the "insurrection of reality," treats and views the real in a sharp distinction to consciousness-content (*Analogia Entis*, 381f.).

119. Przywara, "Drei Richtungen der Phänomenologie," 253.

120. *Gottgeheimnis der Welt,* 133.

121. Przywara, "Drei Richtungen der Phänomenologie," 255.

122. Husserl, *Briefwechsel* (Dordrecht: Kluwer, 1994), 7:87.

123. "Simmel—Husserl—Scheler," 47.

124. Helmut Kuhn, "Scheler, Max," in *Lexikon für Theologie und Kirche* (Freiburg: Herder, 1964), 9:383; see Heinrich M. Schmidinger, "Max Scheler (1874–1928) und sein Einfluss auf das katholische Denken," in *Christliche Philosophie im katholischen Denken des 19. und 20. Jahrhunderts,* ed. Emerich Coreth et al. (Graz: Styria, 1990), 3:89–111.

125. Gertz, *Glaubenswelt als Analogie,* 154, citing Przywara, *Humanitas,* 858. In 1954 Przywara referred to him as "an authentic Christian from the authentic Old Covenant" ("Simmel—Husserl—Scheler," 50).

126. Przywara, "Drei Richtungen der Phänomenologie," 256.

127. Ibid., 257.

128. *Religionsbegründung,* 26; this book offers a positive analysis of how a phenomenology of values can assume an ontological role in leading to religion and faith (20ff., 128ff.).

129. Ibid., 113.

130. Ibid., 15. Scheler wrote in *Krieg und Aufbau* (Leipzig: Weissen Bücher, 1916), 206f., of "the idea of a church beyond states and nations but at the same time a church which is an international and intra-national total person."

131. "Simmel—Husserl—Scheler," 52f.

132. *Religionsbegründung,* 15.

133. Ibid., 219f.

134. Ibid., 119f.

135. *Humanitas,* 857f.; "Vorwort," *In und Gegen,* 8.

136. *Religionsbegründung,* 223, 254ff.

137. *Logos,* 90. The forms of Catholic philosophical theology have been those of particular schools (Cajetan, Suárez) and usually apologetic and historical (Bellarmine and Melchior Cano) (*Logos,* 89).

Chapter 4.   A Theologian's Contemporaries

1. In 1919 the Holy Office had forbidden Catholics from taking part in ecumenical conferences, and the encyclical of Pius XI, *Mortalium animos,* in 1928 (*Acta Apostolicae Sedis* 20), was a stinging critique of the movement itself.

2. Przywara, "Protestantismus II. Beurteilung vom Standpunkt des Katholizismus," in *Religion in Geschichte und Gegenwart,* 2d edition (Tübingen: Mohr, 1928), 3:1602.

3. Ibid., 1603.

4. Przywara, "Neue Theologie? Das Problem protestantischer Theologie," *Stimmen der Zeit* 111 (1925/1926): 349f.

5. Ibid., 350f.

6. For a survey of literature and a perceptive history on the changing image of Luther among Catholics, see Otto Hermann Pesch, "TwentyYears of Catholic Luther Research," *Lutheran World* 13 (1966): 303–16; Thomas Sartory, "Martin Luther in katholischer Sicht," *Una Sancta* 16 (1961): 38–54.

7. Heinrich Denifle, *Luther and Lutherdom* (Somerset: Torch, 1917), 2 vols.; Hartmann Grisar, *Luther* (St. Louis: Herder, 1913–1917), 6 vols.

8. Bernhard Gertz, "Erich Przywara (1889–1972)," in *Christliche Philosophie im katholischen Denken des 19. und 20. Jahrhunderts,* ed. Emerich Coreth (Graz: Styria, 1988), 2:575; see Julio Terán Dutari, *Christentum und Metaphysik. Das Verhältnis beider nach der Analogielehre Erich Przywaras* (Munich: Berchmanskolleg, 1973), 145ff.; on Przywara's study of Luther's theology of the cross during World War II, see K. H. Neufeld, "Vertiefte und gelebte Katholizität. Erich Przywara, 100 Jahre," *Theologie und Philosophie* 65 (1990): 168.

9. Zechmeister, "Durchbruch zum 'eigentlichen' Luther," *Gottes-Nacht* (Münster: LIT, 1997), 206f.

10. Przywara, "Die dialektische Theologie," *Schweizerische Rundschau* 12 (1927/28): 1089–90.

11. Przywara, "Die dialektische Theologie," 1091. As the pages below mention, there was a "dialectical theology" of sorts at work in Jewish thought at that time.

12. Przywara mentioned an article from 1926 by Karl Adam who wrote: "There is no doubt that Protestant theology, which to the outside observer of a few years ago seemed to be in many areas a desert over which the hot wind of limitless criticism blew, now has emerged anew from sources unexpected, [with] a new sense for supernatural realities, for God and his revelation, for miracle and faith. . . . The 'Theology of Crisis' has emerged" ("Die Theologie der Krisis," *Hochland* 23 [1925/26]: 271). The Catholic response to Karl Barth began in the 1920s with studies by Karl Adam, E. Peterson, and Gustav Söhngen, and continued with such French-speaking theologians as Léopold Malévez, Henri Bouillard, and Jérôme Hamer through Hans Urs von Balthasar to its climax in Hans Küng in 1957.

13. Przywara, "Die dialektische Theologie," 1092; there is no mention by name in the article of the dialectical theologian identified with religious socialism, Paul Tillich.

14. *Stimmen der Zeit* 111 (1926): 432; for a list of the articles on Barth and dialectical theology and their themes, see Neuser, *Karl Barth in Münster,* 42ff.

15. See W. H. Neuser, *Karl Barth in Münster, 1925–1930* (Zurich: TVZ, 1985), 38.

16. Letter of February 9, 1929, in *Karl Barth–Eduard Thurneysen. Brief-wechsel* (Zurich: Theologischer Verlag, 1974), 2:651.

17. *Gespräch zwischen den Kirchen* (Nuremberg: Glock und Lutz, 1956), 7.

18. Letter of September 30, 1923, in *Karl Barth–Eduard Thurneysen. Brief-wechsel,* 2:190.

19. Barth, Preface to the Fourth Edition, in *The Epistle to the Romans* (London: Oxford University Press, 1933), 21. Barth is referring to Przywara's article, "Gott in uns und Gott über uns?" *Stimmen der Zeit* 105 (1923): 343ff.

20. "Das katholische Kirchenprinzip," *Zwischen den Zeiten* 7 (1929): 302; that lecture was published along with articles by Bultmann and Brunner and a response by Barth in *Zwischen den Zeiten.* The theme of the meeting in Münster was touched on again in a radio talk of 1961, "Una Sancta," in *Kathol-ische Krise* (Düsseldorf: Patmos, 1967), 211–17; see Philip Rosato, "The Influ-ence of Karl Barth on Catholic Theology," *Gregorianum* 67 (1986): 668.

21. *Karl Barth—Eduard Thurneysen. Briefwechsel,* 2:652. "Son of a Baltic Pole and on his mother's side from an oriental princely line" (652).

22. Barth cited by Przywara, "Evangelische Katholizität—Katholische Evangelizität," in *Katholische Krise,* 199.

23. Karl Gerhard Steck, "Über das ekklesiologische Gespräch zwischen Karl Barth und Erich Przywara 1927/29," in *Antwort Karl Barth zum 70. Geburtstag* (Zollikon: Evangelischer Verlag, 1956), 250.

24. *Karl Barth—Eduard Thurneysen. Briefwechsel,* 2:652. Barth observed in a letter to Thurneysen that in private conversations Przywara flowed over like grace in the Catholic Church and saw the analogy of being as solving all modern and Protestant contradictions about transcendence and immanence (*Briefwechsel,* 2:652). In 1930, Barth wrote that in the following week he would hear "the magician Przywara" lecture on Kierkegaard in Basel (Letter of January 12, 1930, in *Karl Barth—Eduard Thurneysen. Briefwechsel,* 2:698).

25. "Przywara, Erich, SJ," in *Lexikon für Theologie und Kirche,* 3d ed. (Freiburg: Herder, 1999), 8:688.

26. Barth, *The Doctrine of the Word of God,* Church Dogmatics I:1 (Edinburgh: T. & T. Clark, 1936), x. A few years later Barth wrote sympatheti-cally of the many Catholic attempts to reconsider and explain analogy (*The Doctrine of God,* Church Dogmatics II [Edinburgh: T. & T. Clark, 1957], 80–84). Przywara for his part wrote that in the years of fruitful conversation with Barth he developed further his own form for analogy (*Analogia Entis* [Einsiedeln: Johannes, 1962], 8).

27. See *Humanitas* (Nuremberg: Glock und Lutz, 1952), 172ff.

28. Eberhard Mechels, *Analogie bei Erich Przywara und Karl Barth. Das Verhältnis von Offenbarungstheologie und Metaphysik* (Neukirchen-Vluyn: Neukirchener Verlag, 1974), 14, 17.

29. Steck, 261.

30. Barth's response to Przywara's lecture in *Zwischen den Zeiten* 7 (1929): 300. After Przywara left, Barth wrote to Thurneyssen: "A living Jesuit . . . , with a friendliness that was highly attractive. Yes, Eduard, what was that? And what is with Catholicism, which despite all our Reformation anniversaries is so alert in the public forum? Was it an angel of the anti-Christ or an elected instrument of the Lord? The grand inquisitor or truly a disciple of the Apostle of the Gentiles?" (*Karl Barth—Eduard Thurneysen. Briefwechsel*, 2:654).

31. *Alter und Neuer Bund. Theologie der Stunde* (Munich: Herold, 1956), 11f.

32. *Weg zu Gott*, in *Religionsphilosophische Schriften* (Einsiedeln: Johannes, 1962), 88.

33. *Analogia Entis*, 64ff.

34. Ibid., 72.

35. Mechels, "Das Problem der Denkform in der Theologie," in *Analogie bei Erich Przywara und Karl Barth*, 247; see Mechel's insightful and extensive comparison of the two thinkers and the confessional reasons for their differences (159–250).

36. Karl Barth, "Grüsswort an Erich Przywara," in Siegfried Behn, *Der beständige Aufbruch*, 48.

37. Cited in Werner Schüssler, "Die Berliner Jahre (1919–1924)," in *Paul Tillich. Sein Leben* (New York: Lang, 1993).

38. *Die religiöse Lage der Gegenwart* (Berlin: Ullstein, 1926), 40.

39. Ibid., 43.

40. Ibid., 105.

41. Ibid., 103.

42. Ibid., 20; see 108–10, 116.

43. Ibid., 43. America and its representative William James are limited, "confessional" (44).

44. Ibid., 123.

45. Ibid., 128–29. "Within the direct transcendental grounding realization of spirit Przywara uncovered a transparency and inwardly an opacity; directed to these were two inseparable fundamental intentions broadly distinguished as culture and religion. This level of treatment of religion and culture in Przywara corresponds to the original levels of unseparated 'theonomy. . . ,' along which an autonomy of profane culture and a heteronomy of the specifically religious sphere unfold" (Terán Dutari, *Christentum und Metaphysik,* 153f.). Przywara found the term "correlation" in dialectical theology, noticing that the word had already appeared in Hermann Cohen ("Neue Theologie? Das Problem protestantischer Theologie," 359). All this breaks up the old philosophical pantheism, and for Protestantism includes sin as a presence, a force which Tillich named the demonic.

46. Przywara, "Kairos," *Stimmen der Zeit* 119 (1930): 230. Sections from Tillich's books reviewed at that time appeared in English translation in *The*

Protestant Era and *The Interpretation of History*. On Przywara's view of *Kairos,* "the lightning-like moment of illumination of kindness" ("Dienst," *Laby-rinth* [September, 1960]: 70), see Gertz, *Glaubenswelt als Analogie* (Düsseldorf: Patmos, 1969), 398–403.

47. "Kairos," 230. Thomas Corbishley sees Przywara's thought as resem-bling at times the form and language of Tillich but expressing a fuller and more religious expression and content; Introduction, *The Divine Majesty* (London: Collins, 1971), 13f.

48. "Kairos," 231.

49. Gustav Wilhelmy, "Vita Erich Przywara. Ein Überblick," in *Erich Przy-wara. 1889–1969. Eine Festgabe* (Düsseldorf: Patmos, 1969), 17. Reporting on the beginnings of these meetings is "Über die Davoser Hochschulkurse," *Davoser Revue* 4 (1929): 102–4; Marguerite Siegrist, "Die Davoser Hochschulkurse 1928–1931," in *Davos. Profil eines Phänomens,* ed. Ernst Halter (Zurich: Offizin, 1994), 161–66. On Ernst Cassirer and Heidegger at Davos, see *The Existentialist Tradition: Selected Writings,* ed. Nino Langiulli (Garden City: Doubleday, 1971), 192–203.

50. Kuhlmann, "Allmächtigkeit oder Alleinwirksamkeit der Gnade. Ein theologisches Nachwort zu den Davoser internationalen Hochschulkursen," *Theologische Blätter* 7 (May 1928): 122.

51. Ibid.

52. Tillich, "Zum 'Theologischen Nachwort zu den Davoser interna-tionalen Hochschulkursen," *Theologische Blätter* 7 (July 1928): 177. Kuhlmann then responded to this with "Radikaler Protestantismus? Antwort an Paul Tillich," *Theologische Blätter* 7 (September 1928): 225–26. Przywara reacted to Tillich's view of the demonic in publications before 1927 in "Tragische Welt," in *Ringen der Gegenwart* (Augsburg: Filsen, 1929), 1:356–59. "Przywara thought he always had to find in Tillich the shadow of the sole divine omnipotency, sometimes in a rather idiosyncratic, Schellingian approach.... Culture as employed in Tillich's *Religionsphilosophie,* which Przywara said in 1959 had influenced him, ... is seen too much, and perhaps misunderstood, against the background of Schelling" (Teràn Dutari, *Christentum und Meta-physik,* 588f.).

53. Przywara, "Protestantische und katholische Ur-Einstellung. Zur Aus-sprache zwischen Paul Tillich und Gerhardt Kuhlmann," *Theologische Blätter* 7 (1928): 226f.

54. "Christian Root-Terms: Kerygma, Mysterium, Kairos, Oikonomia," in *Paul Tillich in Catholic Thought* (Dubuque: The Priory Press, 1964), 197–214; this was published first in *Religion and Culture: Essays in Honor of Paul Tillich,* ed. Walter Leibrecht (New York: Harper and Brothers, 1959) and reprinted in German in *Analogia Entis* (1962); some of the material may have been developed later in Przywara's *Logos. Logos, Abendland, Reich, Com-mercium* (Düsseldorf: Patmos, 1963). Leibrecht published a study of Johann

Georg Hamman and *Being a Christian in Today's World* (Philadelphia: Muhlenberg, 1962). On the relationship between Przywara and the volume of essays by Catholics on Tillich, see Thomas F. O'Meara, "Paul Tillich in Catholic Thought: The Past and the Future," in *Paul Tillich: A New Catholic Assessment,* ed. Raymond Bulman and Frederick Parella (Collegeville: Liturgical Press, 1994), 9–32.

55. Review of *Religion and Culture,* in *Les Études philosophiques* 14 (1959): 384.

56. "Protestantische und katholische Ur-Einstellung," 227.

57. "Christian Root-Terms . . . ," 204; on *oikonomia* in the Jesuit's theology, see Gertz, *Glaubenswelt als Analogie,* 402–5.

58. "Neue Theologie? Das Problem protestantischer Theologie," 360.

59. "Der Ruf von Heute," in *Katholische Krise,* 91. Eberhard Jüngel studies Przywara briefly in *Gott als Geheimnis der Welt* (Tübingen: Mohr, 1978).

60. "Judentum und Christentum," in *Ringen der Gegenwart* (Augsburg: Filser, 1929), 2:624; this chapter contains some sections from the article in *Stimmen der Zeit* with the same name; the ideas are repeated in 1954 ("Simmel—Husserl—Scheler," *In und Gegen* [Nuremberg: Glock und Lutz, 1955], 33ff.).

61. "Judentum und Christentum. Zwischen Orient und Okzident," *Stimmen der Zeit* 110 (1925–1926): 81–99. For Cohen, Kant was the philosopher of Judaism as Aquinas was for Catholicism. That modern situation, however, should not obscure the fact that Jewish scholars in the early Middle Ages had found in Aristotle a means of presenting the Torah.

62. "Begegnungen," in Hans Jürgen Schultz, *Juden, Christen, Deutsche* (Stuttgart: Kreuz, 1961), 239–42

63. Przywara, "Judentum und Christentum. Zwischen Orient und Okzident," 82ff.

64. Judentum und Christentum," *Ringen der Gegenwart,* 2:625.

65. Eugene Borowitz, "Religious Consciousness: Leo Baeck," in *Choices in Modern Jewish Thought. A Partisan Guide* (West Orange, N. J.: Behrman House, 1995), 68.

66. A. E. S., "Baeck, Leo," in *Encyclopedia Judaica* 4 (Jerusalem: Macmillan, 1971), 78. Eugene Borowitz explains, "Cohen's God is the logical ground of our worldview who integrates the divergent aspects of our rational activity into a coherent system. Such a God, Baeck felt, is too abstract to elicit piety and hardly provides a reason for expanding ethics into a broader pattern of religious observance. . . . For the devout there remains an unbearable distance between what philosophy says God is and what the religious life discloses" (Eugene Borowitz, "Religious Consciousness: Leo Baeck," 58); see Albert Friedlander, *Leo Baeck: Teacher of Theresienstadt* (Woodstock: Overlook Press, 1991).

67. "Judentum und Christentum. Zwischen Orient und Okzident," 86.

68. Ibid., 86, 91.

69. Baeck, *Das Wesen des Judentums,* 2d ed. (Frankfurt: Kaufmann, 1923), 174.

70. Judentum und Christentum," in *Ringen der Gegenwart,* 2:655.

71. *Wege im Judentum* (Berlin: Schocken, 1933), 21, cited in Przywara, "Jude und Christ," *Stimmen der Zeit* 126 (1934): 51.

72. *Wege im Judentum,* 65f., cited in Przywara, "Jude und Christ," 53.

73. *Leo Baeck: Teacher of Theresienstadt* (Woodstock: The Overlook Press, 1991), 193.

74. Judentum und Christentum," in *Ringen der Gegenwart,* 2:658

75. Przywara, "Jude, Heide, Christ," *Europäische Revue* 8 (1932): 470–76.

76. Ibid., 476.

77. In 1933, as Hitler was assuming political control, Przywara published a review of Hans Joachim Schoeps' work on "Jewish faith in this age," a kind of systematic theology for Judaism. Schoeps was born in Berlin and became a prominent intellectual and a prolific writer, and yet one not fully acceptable to either liberal or orthodox Jews. His "radical dialectical Jewish theology excluded all nomistic as well as national-cultural elements, bringing Judaism very close to Christianity but stopping short of baptism" (L. H. S., "Schoeps, Hans Joachim," in *Encyclopedia Judaica* [Jerusalem: Macmillan, 1971], 14:991). He thought it possible in 1933 for the German Jews, as distinguished from other Jews living in Germany, to come to terms with the Nazis. In Przywara's view Schoeps has something of a Barthian mentality—the Jesuit observed that from studying Jewish writers he had learned how much Protestantism is from the Old Testament—but also recalls Heidegger, "in the concrete existential situation of a people wanting to understand their existence in light of the ideas and terms of the Jewish faith." His approach moves away from the rational religious approach of Moses Mendelssohn and looks at the traditions of the synagogue, away from the Enlightenment to the vocation of Israel as something effective now in each member. The time of the diaspora, the trend of Jews moving from a religion of law through an ignorance of their tradition to secularization, is finished. Schoeps' book is an unveiling of the mystery between God and Israel, but as a covenant understood biologically, in terms of blood. Judaism is simply Jews. But is this not what the prophets, "the truest and sharpest anti-Semites," criticized? ("Theologie des Judentums," 342). Is not identifying Judaism with land and blood, "in a foundation of the biologically sacral" (to use Schoeps' phrase), a kind of paganism? Does it set aside both original sin and grace? ("Theologie des Judentums," 342). After the war Przywara mentioned Schoeps' ideas and their parallel to Prussian directions, e.g., the rejection of electoral democracy ("Um Preussen," in *In und Gegen,* 243). For Schoeps' views on the prophets, see *Die jüdischen Prophetenmorde* (Uppsala: Ohlssons, 1943). Schoeps' *An Intel-*

ligent Person's Guide to the Religions of Mankind (London: Gollancz, 1967) is a survey of data on the various religions with little on Judaism and ending in a plea for tolerance.

78. "Jude und Christ," 54.

79. "Judentum und Christentum," *Ringen der Gegenwart,* 2: 660.

80. Baeck, *Wesen des Judentums,* 292.

81. "Judentum und Christentum. Zwischen Orient und Okzident," 99.

82. Ibid. In a review of *Europa und Asien. Untergang der Erde am Geist* by Theodor Lessing, a Jewish theoretician of Jewish life in touch with nature amid a failing Europe filled with Christian hate, and a victim of Nazi assasination in 1933, Przywara seemed to see at the center of turbulent Europe a cultural, non-Jewish, wandering nonbeliever ("Ahasver," *Stimmen der Zeit* 121 [1931]: 153).

83. "Römische Katholizität—allchristliche Ökumenizität," in *Katholische Krise,* 248.

84. *Leo Baeck: Teacher of Theresienstadt,* 195.

85. *Alter und Neuer Bund.*

86. Wilhelmy, 20; see review of B. Cohn in *Stimmen der Zeit* (1934); the Jesuit cited the *Talmud* in "Ahasver," *Stimmen der Zeit* 121 (1931): 153. Georges Schrijver presents in detail similarities between Przywara's thought on the prophetic element in the Bible and those of Abraham Heschel (Georges de Schrijver, *Le merveilleux accord de l'homme et de Dieu. Étude de l'analogie de l'être chez Hans Urs von Balthasar* [Leuven: University Press, 1983], 279–81).

87. *Mein Göttinger Semester* (Nuremberg: Glock und Lutz, 1979), 5, 10.

88. Edith Stein, "Husserls transzendentale Phänomenologie," *Werke* (Freiburg: Herder, 1962), 6:33.

89. Husserl, "Letter to Rudolf Otto (1919)," in Thomas Sheehan, *Heidegger. The Man and the Thinker* (Chicago: Precedent, 1981), 24.

90. "Ein sehr begabtes kleines Mädchen" (Stein, *Aus dem Leben einer jüdischen Familie,* in *Werke* [Freiburg: Herder, 1965], 7:289).

91. Edith Stein, *Brief an Roman Ingarden 1917–1938* (Freiburg: Herder, 1991), 36; on Stein and Heidegger, see Otto Pöggeler, "Heidegger und die Religionsphänomenologie," in *Heidegger in seiner Zeit* (Munich: Fink, 1999), 250–54.

92. Przywara, "Edith Stein. Zu ihrem zehnten Todestag," in *In und Gegen,* 65. Husserl thought that the Catholic church should employ his philosophy as Aquinas had employed Aristotle. Not valuing French neo-Thomism highly, he said "Catholic philosophy must grow beyond that" (cited in Hanna-Barbara Gerl, *Unerbittliches Licht* [Mainz: Matthias Grünewald, 1991], 148); see Przywara, "Edith Stein," in *Ignis Ardens* (Barcelona, 1950); see too Przywara, "Edith Stein," *Die Besinnung* 7 (1952): 238–42.

93. "Die Frage Edith Stein," *In und Gegen,* 72. Przywara reviewed a *Festschrift* for Hedwig Conrad-Martius, "Zwischen Metaphysik und Christentum," *Philosophisches Jahrbuch* 66 (1958): 181–93.

94. Przywara, "Edith Stein. Zu ihrem zehnten Todestag," 61; Beate Imhof, *Edith Steins philosophische Entwicklung* (Basel: Birkhäuser, 1987), 1:234; Hildebrand, "Selbstdarstellung" in *Philosophie in Selbstdarstellungen,* ed. L. Pongratz (Hamburg: Meiner, 1975), 2:77–127.

95. Josephine Koeppel, *Edith Stein: Philosopher and Mystic* (Collegeville: Liturgical Press, 1990), 24.

96. Przywara, "Edith Stein. Zu ihrem zehnten Todestag," in *In und Gegen,* 61.

97. Ibid.

98. Imhof, 108–17; for favorable and unfavorable reviews, see Imhof, 279.

99. See Gerl, *Unerbittliches Licht,* 86, and Imhof, 281. Daniel Feuling (1882–1947), O. S. B., was an expert in spirituality and Aquinas, and a professor of theology and philosophy in Salzburg. He wrote basic studies on metaphysics and Catholic dogmatics ("Das Wesen des katholischen Glaubens und Lebens," *Benediktinische Monatschrift* 4 [1922]: 1ff). His *Das Wesen des Katholizismus* in 1920 came not long after Karl Adam's book by the same name; Edith Stein cited him in *Endliches und Ewiges Sein.*

100. "Vorwort" to *Endliches und Ewiges Sein* (Freiburg: Herder, 1950), viii.

101. Grabmann, "Geleitwort," to Edith Stein, *Des hl. Thomas von Aquin Untersuchungen über die Wahrheit,* 5. On the phenomenologist's study, appreciation, and limited appropriation of Aquinas, see Beate Imhof, 108–15.

102. Grabmann, "Geleitwort," 5. In an unusually irenic (in contrast to the neo-Thomist schools at that time) overview, the historian sketched the variety of efforts from L. Noël at Louvain, Rousselot, Maritain, and Gilson as well as "the pioneering work of J. Maréchal." "In Germany Przywara has often pointed out the characteristics of scholasticism and Thomism in modern thought and vice-versa" ("Geleitwort," 4); see *Credo ut intelligam. Martin Grabmann zum 50. Todestag,* ed. Thomas Prügl (St. Ottilien: EOS, 1999).

103. Przywara, "Edith Stein, Thomas von Aquin, deutsch," *Stimmen der Zeit* 121 (1931): 386. Some German Dominicans expressed the view that the translation was not always exact. "A sharp critique was the provincial Laurentius Siemer, O. P. His letter of criticism no longer exists — she was a Carmelite when she received it — but her response . . . still exists. Siemer informed her that she had a meager or nonexistent knowledge of Thomism. That was painful for her but she does not at all lose her composure and does not at all betray that she was insulted, indignant, or bitter" (Maria Adele Herrmann, *Die Speyerer Jahre von Edith Stein* [Speyer: Pilger, 1990], 111). She told other critics that she expected to miss some of Aquinas' nuances but that it was preferable to have a faulty translation than to have none.

104. Wilhelmy, 17.

105. "Vorwort" to *Endliches und Ewiges Sein*, x.

106. See the dense, brief description of their different approaches in "Vorwort" to *Endliches und Ewiges Sein*, x–xii.

107. "Edith Stein. Zu ihrem zehnten Todestag," 61.

108. *Endliches und Ewiges Sein*, 7.

109. Przywara, "Husserl et Heidegger," *Les Études philosophiques*" 16 (1961): 55. "This was done in the most penetrating way for the Husserl *Festschrift*, a conversation, one with a certain artistic style, between E. Husserl and Thomas Aquinas, which she unfortunately at the request of Martin Heidegger had to change into a so-called 'neutral' article" ("Edith Stein," 240). Heidegger thought it was "insufficiently 'serious'" (Przywara, "Husserl et Heidegger," in *Les Études philosophiques*, 55).

110. "Husserls Phänomenologie und die Philosophie des hl. Thomas von Aquino. Versuch einer Gegenüberstellung," in *Jahrbuch für Philosophie und phänomenologische Forschung* (*Festschrift Husserl*) (Halle, 1929), 315ff.

111. "Metaphysik der Gemeinschaft" (review of Dietrich von Hildebrand, *Metaphysik der Gemeinschaft*) in *Mädchenbildung auf christlicher Grundlage* 24 (1932): 695.

112. Philibert Secrétan, "Le Recours à une scolastique non Thomiste," in Edith Stein, *Phénoménologie et philosophie chrétienne* (Paris: Cerf, 1987), 165–73; "Edith Stein au carrefour de la Phénoménologie et de la scolastique," 151ff. Jacques Maritain spoke of her Thomism as being "not very orthodox" ("Edith Stein," *Nova et Vetera* 25 [1951]: 116).

113. "Edith Stein. Zu ihrem zehnten Todestag," 63.

114. "Die Frage Edith Stein," 69.

115. Florent Gaboriau, *Edith Stein philosophe* (Paris: FAC, 1989), 78.

116. See Przywara, "'Die Heilige unserer Zeit'" *Stimmen der Zeit* 127 (1934): 352f.

117. Nicholas J. Meyerhofer, *Gertrud von le Fort* (Berlin: Morgenbuch, 1993), 52–53; see Edith Stein, *Essays on Woman*, The Collected Works of Edith Stein 2 (Washington: ICS, 1986); Gerl, "Im Spannungsfeld der Frauenfrage," in *Unerbittliches Licht*, 43–80.

118. Przywara, "Edith Stein und Simone Weil—Zwei philosophische Grund-Motive," in *Edith Stein—eine grosse Glaubenzeugin*, ed. W. Herbstrith (Anweiler: Thomas Plöger, 1986), 231, 233. This is Przywara's German text previously unpublished; the article was originally published as "Edith Stein et Simone Weil. Essentialisme, Existentialisme, Analogie," *Les Études Philoso-phiques* 11:3 (1956): 458–72.

119. "Edith Stein und Simone Weil," 239–41.

120. Ibid., 243. Josephine Koeppel sees Przywara as having a role in the writing of *Kreuzwissenschaft* (Koeppel, 167).

121. "Edith Stein. Zum ihren zehnten Todestag," 66.
122. Ibid., 62.
123. Ibid.
124. "Die Frage Edith Stein," 71.
125. Ibid., 67.
126. "Edith Stein. Zu ihrem zehnten Todestag," 66.
127. Ibid., 66f. In light of the partial and unclear presentations by John Paul II at her beatification and canonization, ignoring much of who Edith Stein was as a woman, a modern philosopher, a teacher, and a laywoman, this may be still true.
128. "Die Frage Edith Stein," 68.
129. Stein's words on the way to Auschwitz given by James Carroll, "The Saint and the Holocaust," *The New Yorker* 75 (June 7, 1999): 57.
130. See Theodore Kisiel, "Theo-Logical Beginnings: Toward a Phenomenology of Christianity," in *The Genesis of Heidegger's Being & Time* (Berkeley: University of California Press, 1995). Kierkegaard, like Nietzsche, saw the world and the age as bankrupt, and Przywara found in both thinkers "the atmosphere of Lutheran theology," the contradiction of the fallen person not only over against the church but against God. They express the lack of resolution in the guilt of Luther and the penance of Luther, of faith over against any renewal. Both Kierkegaard and Nietzsche could in their Lutheran spirit lead to "the liquidation of the Reformation" (Przywara, "End-Zeit," *Stimmen der Zeit* 119 [1930]: 353).
131. *Das Geheimnis Kierkegaards* (Munich: Oldenbourg, 1929), vi.
132. Diem's evaluation in "Zwischen den Zeiten" 1932, cited in *Erich Przywara, 1889–1969. Ein Festgabe* (Düsseldorf: Patmos, 1969), 54. On the conversation between Diem and Przywara over analogy, see Téran Dutari, *Christentum und Metaphysik,* 279f.
133. *Das Geheimnis Kierkegaards,* v–viii; see Téran Dutari, *Christentum und Metaphysik,* 352ff.
134. *Das Geheimnis Kierkegaards,* 22, 61, 15.
135. Ibid., 19; see Zechmeister, "Kierkegaard—'Unglückliche Liebe' als Metapher des Gott-Verhältnisses," *Gottes-Nacht,* 222–56.
136. *Das Geheimnis Kierkegaards,* 22–26.
137. "Theologische Motive," 56.
138. A review of *Sein und Zeit* opens the article "Drei Richtungen der Phänomenologie," *Stimmen der Zeit* 115 (1928): 252–64.
139. Ibid., 259.
140. Ibid., 252–64. For other writings touching on Heidegger, see "Wende zum Menschen," *Stimmen der Zeit* 119 (1930): 1–13 (on the book on Kant); "Der Mensch des Abgrundes," *Stimmen der Zeit* 120 (1931): 252–66; "Theologische Motive," 55ff.
141. See Zechmeister, *Gottes-Nacht,* 101.

142. "Essenz- und Existenz-Philosophie.Tragische Identität oder Distanz der Geduld," *Scholastik* 14 (1939): 531, 541. "It was not for nothing that Heidegger was in the Jesuit novitiate (and there for a short time) in this active order, and then [becoming] a clear follower of Scotus . . . who sees the world and people as 'dynamic'" ("Theologische Motive," 60).

143. "Tradition," *In und Gegen*, 173; see Gertz, *Glaubenswelt als Analogie*, 158–61. Przywara mentions that conversations with Heidegger, when the Jesuit was giving lectures at Davos in 1929 and Freiburg in 1930, "clarified the idea of creatureliness" (*Analogia Entis*, 8).

144. "Theologische Motive," 59f.; *Humanitas*, 477f.

145. *Christliche Existenz* (Leipzig: Hegner, 1934), 13.

146. Przywara,"Husserl et Heidegger," *Les Études philosophiques* 16 (1961): 61; Przywara, "Drei Richtungen," 261.

147. Przywara, "Neuer Thomismus," *Stimmen der Zeit* 138 (1914): 301.

148. Przywara, review of Gustav Siewerth, *Das Schicksal der Metaphysik. Von Thomas zu Heidegger*, in *Les Études philosophiques* 17 (1962): 288.

149. "Reichweite der Analogie als katholischer Grundform," *Scholastik* 15 (1940): 340. For a balanced view of Maréchal and Thomism, see Johannes B. Lotz, "Zur Thomas-Rezeption in der Maréchal-Schule," in *Thomas von Aquin* (Darmstadt:Wissenschaftliche Buchgesellschaft, 1981), 2:433–55.

150. "Theologische Motive," 60.

151. Przywara, review of Gustav Siewerth, *Das Schicksal der Metaphysik. Von Thomas zu Heidegger*, in *Die Furche* 49 (December 3, 1960): 12.

152. Przywara,"Husserl et Heidegger," *Les Études philosophiques* 16 (1961): 62; "Die Frage Edith Stein," 70; *Analogiae Entis*, 107, 113; review of Walter Schulz, *Der Gott der neuzeitlichen Metaphysik*, in *Die Fürche* (March 8, 1959): 11. Przywara pointed out in 1955 that Heidegger's address as rector was a kind of secular eschatology, a nihilist adventism, but he misinterpreted Heidegger as positive toward technology, American and Russian ("Theologische Motive," 56).

153. Review of Heidegger, *Der Satz von Grund*, in *Les Études philosophiques* 12 (1957): 408.

154. Przywara, "Husserl et Heidegger," *Les Études philosophiques* 16 (1961): 62.

155. "Theologische Motive," 55ff.

156. Przywara,"Husserl et Heidegger," *Les Études philosophiques* 16 (1961): 61. Roman Bleistein writes of Alfred Delp's enthusiasm for Heidegger: "The reason for this interest may lie in a search for a philosophy linked to the current times which he missed in many neo-scholastic theses; for the philosophical works of J. Maréchal S.J. (1878–1944) and E. Przywara S.J. (1889–1972) up until that time exerted only a modest influence on the content and form of that traditional mode of philosophizing." Roman Bleistein, "Lebensbild Alfred Delp," in Alfred Delp, *Gesammelte Schriften*, ed. Roman

Bleistein (Frankfurt: Knecht, 1982), 1:16f. His dissertation of 1935, *Tragische Existenz* (Freiburg: Herder, 1935), cites the older Jesuit's writings on analogy, Kierkegaard, and Heidegger. In July 1939 Delp joined the editorial staff of *Stimmen der Zeit* where Przywara was at work.

157. L.B. Puntel, *Analogie und Geschichtlichkeit* (Freiburg: Herder, 1969), 534–40; Emilio Brito, *Heidegger et l'hymne du sacré* (Leuven: University Press, 1999), 249.

158. Hans Urs von Balthasar, "Erich Przywara," in *Erich Przywara. Sein Schrifttum 1912–1962* (Einsiedeln: Johannes, 1963), 5–18; Hans Urs von Balthasar, "Erich Przywara," in *Tendenzen der Theologie im 20. Jahrhundert. Eine Geschichte in Porträts,* ed. Hans Jürgen Schulz (Stuttgart: Kreuz, 1966), 354–59.

159. "Erich Przywara," *Erich Przywara. Sein Schrifttum,* 5.

160. Articles in *Divus Thomas* and "Die Metaphysik Erich Przywaras," *Schweizer Rundschau* 33 (1933): 489–99. Balthasar repeatedly stressed the thought of Barth, while Przywara throughout his life expressed a clear distance from all that was Protestant, and in his first meetings with Barth he showed only a sympathy for Christian directions beyond the secular, but not for the inner theology of Barth. Neufeld concludes: "his judgement and his view is different from the position of Przywara. . . . It was no longer the same Barth with whom Przywara had discussed in the 1920s" (Neufeld, "Kategorien," 309); see James Zeitz, "Przywara and von Balthasar on Analogy," *The Thomist* 52 (1988): 473ff. "Balthasar was attracted to Barth's Christocentrism and sought to interpret his theology in a favorable light. Balthasar went so far as to seek to integrate the analogy of being into the analogy of faith. Nonetheless, he retained the view that the analogy of being was a necessary presupposition for the analogy of faith, since only through the analogy of being could one preserve the liberty of the creature without which a genuine covenant would be impossible" (John J. O'Donnell, *Hans Urs von Balthasar* [Collegeville: Glazier, 1992], 5). Georges de Schrijver makes the observation that the theme of analogy, although later Balthasar holds it up as opposing idealism, has some affinity to Balthasar's writings on Romantic idealism (*Le merveilleux accord de l'homme et de Dieu. Étude de l'analogie de l'être chez Hans Urs von Balthasar* [Leuven: University Press, 1983], 32f.).

161. Manfred Lochbrunner, "Daten zum Lebenswerk von Hans Urs von Balthasar," in *Analogia Caritatis. Darstellung und Deutung der Theologie Hans Urs von Balthasars* (Freiburg: Herder, 1981), 323ff.

162. Wilhelmy, 22.

163. Neufeld, "Kategorien," 310.

164. "Es stellt sich vor," *Das neue Buch* 7 (1945): 43–46. Balthasar called the book on the church year from 1923 "a small masterpiece," although most of the great figures of the liturgical movement saw it as representative of a previous attitude toward prayer during the liturgy and lacking an under-

standing of the renewal needed by the liturgical cycles of the year and of the saints (Balthasar, *Das Ganze im Fragment* [Einsiedeln: Johannes, 1963], 323); see Gertz, "Katholische Krise und Konzil," in *Katholische Krise,* 258.

165. Balthasar, "Erich Przywara," in *Tendenzen der Theologie,* 354.

166. For instance, it is not clear that Przywara's work culminates in an "encompassing anthropology . . . of a universal mode of classification" (Balthasar, "Erich Przywara," 359); what Przywara published in 1953 was a large collection of random and disconnected segments titled *Humanitas.* Przywara's later books did resemble Balthasar's collections. "His work is a kind of universal classification where everything is observed and ordered: a comparison with Hegel, whose titanic philosophy is also anthropology, and even more with the Sybilline late Schelling is inevitable" (Balthasar, "Erich Przywara," 359).

167. Balthasar, "Erich Przywara," 357.

168. "Erich Przywara," *Erich Przywara. Sein Schrifttum,* 8; Balthasar, "Erich Przywara," 354. Balthasar emphasizes similarities to Hegel, perhaps because of his own work from the 1930s on German Romanticism, but it is not clear that Hegel has such a place in Przywara's sources (see "Thomas und Hegel," *Ringen der Gegenwart,* 2:930–57).

169. *Weg zu Gott,* chapter 5.

170. See Balthasar's treatment of Mary, Peter, Paul, John, and James in *The Office of Peter (Der antirömische Effekt)* (San Francisco: Ignatius, 1986).

171. See Przywara, "Das Dogma von der Kirche. Ein Aufbau," in *Katholische Krise,* 191–95; Eva-Maria Faber, *Kirche zwischen Identität und Differenz* (Würzburg: Echter, 1993), 298ff.

172. Balthasar, "Erich Przywara," 357. "The work of Erich Przywara is from its beginning up to the final writings a *closed philosophical-theological total plan* which in its individual components is already completed in the early Whylen lectures just as it is present in the [later] books like *Humanitas* and *Mensch.* The lecture series of the years 1923–1926 form in their thoroughly constructed pattern a structure of relations upon which the structure and content of subsequent works of Przywara are based. At the center of this entire opus stands the creature's experience of the reality manifest in oppositions and the consequent direction of the human person toward the knowledge of the primal ground of life" (Stefan Nieborak, *'Homo analogia': Zur philosophisch-theologischen Bedeutung der 'analogia entis' im Rahmen der existentiellen Frage bei Erich Przywara S. J. (1889–1972)* [Frankfurt: Lang, 1994], 551); see the extensive presentation of analogy as a theme from the earliest works on by Julio Terán Dutari, *Christentum und Metaphysik,* 446ff. and the writings of Gertz.

173. Schrijver, "Différence avec Przywara," in *Le Merveilleux,* 284f.

174. "Erich Przywara," *Erich Przywara. Sein Schrifttum,* 5.

175. The following is stimulating but is it precise? "What in patristic theology lies together, unexplained, in a great vision—nature and supernature—

explains itself through differentiation under the influence of Aquinas and the post-Tridentine scholasticism; but as much as Przywara sees Thomas thereby as the beginning of modernity he still ultimately reads him in light of Dionysius" (Balthasar, "Erich Przywara," in *Erich Przywara. Sein Schrifttum*, 12).When he mentioned Ignatius, Newman, or Scheler as Przywara's sources, Balthasar described less their influential ideas than their symbolic roles. "Thomas, next to Augustine, is the other pole of the Christian thinking of order, since he even more strongly grasps the balancing swing of the relative oppositions of the world *before* the Absolute and gives a philosophical correction to Augustine, which gift brought forth the religious Newman" (Balthasar, "Erich Przywara," 355). Newman "is presented by Przywara as a patristic figure revivified" ("Die Metaphysik Erich Przywaras," *Schweizer Rundschau* 33 [1933]: 493).

176. Schrijver, *Le Merveilleux*, 258; Schrijver offers analytic sections on the thought of Przywara, its presence in Balthasar, and the differences between them (255–81; 284–88).

177. Ibid., 258.

178. Ibid., 284.

179. Ibid., 287. Edward Oakes describes well the shift of Przywara's analogy from Greek and medieval logic to the reality of tension and interplay between the Creator and creature ("Erich Przywara and the Analogy of Being," in *Pattern of Redemption. The Theology of Hans Urs von Balthasar* [New York: Continuum, 1994], 35).

180. Ibid., 266; agreeing is Gertz, *Glaubenswelt als Analogie*, 271.

181. Lochbrunner, *Analogia Caritatis*, 284, 288f.

182. Ibid., 298; he asserts without supporting passages that the extrapolation of the analogy of love can be found in Przywara (299). If the "Barthian" or "Protestant" force in Przywara's thought is the role of the cross in incarnational analogy, that more likely came from the early study of Luther than from Barth. The Jesuit was clear about the essential identity of Catholicism over against the later forms of Protestantism. "In Catholicism there is no either/or between quest and tradition and it is erroneous when one exalts one of the two as the Catholic position. Being in tradition is the discipline and ethos of the Catholic quest, and the religious quest is the inner life of Catholic tradition. The separation of either is Protestant, whether it is a Protestantism of the absolutized seeker or that of the divinized authority" ("Custos, quid de nocte?" in *Ringen der Gegenwart*, 1:44).

183. Sturmius—M. Wittschier, *Kreuz, Trinität, Analogie. Trinitarische Ontologie unter dem Leitbild des Kreuzes, dargestellt als ästhetische Theologie* (Würzburg: Echter, 1987), 80.

184. "Hans Urs von Balthasars formaler und inhaltlicher Naturbegriff." Terán Dutari, *Christentum und Metaphysik*, 578–80.

185. Zimny, 8. See the studies by Hans Otmar Meuffels and Carlos Casale Rolle as well as Jacques Servais, *Théologie des Exercices Spirituels. H. U. von*

Balthasar interprète saint Ignace (Paris: Culture et Verité, 1996), 90. In the later decades of Przywara's life, Balthasar thought he saw a move away from "Ignatian obedience" as the foundation of his thought and as too firm a line from God to the individual ("Erich Przywara," 359).

186. Balthasar, "Erich Przywara," 354.

187. "Erich Pryzwara," in *Erich Przywara. Sein Schrifttum,* 11.

188. See Heinrich Fries, "Erich Przywara," *Catholica* 28 (1973): 69; Oakes, 45–71; Schrijver, 141ff. 288ff.

189. Balthasar cited Przywara to discredit Rahner's central explanatory form of categorical and transcendental ("Anspruch auf Katholizität," *Pneuma und Institution* [Einsiedeln: Johannes, 1974], 70–73, and *Der antirömische Affekt* [Freiburg: Herder, 1974], 97), although one can find in Przywara, for instance, in his view of the triune God, of grace, and of the Body of Christ, not a few indications of that central distinction between divine ground and objective realizations; indeed one could argue that this is central to Przywara. In his book on Kant, Przywara, anxious over the union of transcendental Thomism with Heidegger, had distanced himself from Maréchal, although his respect for figures like Rahner and Lotz as well as for the originality of Maréchal remained (see Lochbrunner, *Analogia Caritatis,* 127–31). James Zeitz says that Rahner and Balthasar developed after Przywara concrete theologies of nature and grace. Certainly Rahner does, but it is not clear that the aesthetic spirituality presented in the most varied philosophical, theological, and artistic systems directly continues the realism of grace in human existence ("Erich Przywara, Visionary Theologian," *Thought* 58 [1983]: 148). Balthasar joined Przywara with Blondel and Maréchal as "the three most vital attempts to link modernity and scholasticism" (Zimny, 3), but he often evaluated the Belgian Jesuit negatively: "a so-called Thomistic Kant holding a 'more redemptive' dynamism of knowledge, [a position] which today dominates almost the entire field of Catholic thinking but which for Przywara approached too closely a rejected Augustinianism" (Balthasar, "Erich Przywara," 356). Przywara wrote: "The Thomist writer who was the first to have tried the challenging enterprise of 'transposing' Kant and Hegel to the plane of Aquinas" (review of Gustav Siewerth, *Das Schicksal der Metaphysik. Von Thomas zu Heidegger,* in *Les Études philosophiques* 17 [1962]: 288). Przywara separates himself clearly from the general directions of the thinking of both Maréchal and Balthasar ("Trinität. Gespräch," in *In und Gegen,* 311).

190. Balthasar, "Erich Przywara," 359.

191. "Laudatio auf Erich Przywara," *Gnade als Freiheit* (Freiburg: Herder, 1968), 271.

192. Peter Hebblethwaite wrote that, prior to the pontificate of John Paul II, Balthasar "had played no role in international church life. He was not a *peritus* at Vatican II. To judge by his later criticisms of the Council, he would

have chafed under its 'committee theology.' He believed that its theological weakness was that it neglected the 'hierarchy of problems,' devoting itself to the shallows of 'second-order' questions summed up under the slogan *aggiornamento* instead of launching into the deep waters of Father, Son and Holy Spirit. He wanted to set the absolute claim of Christ against the reductionist Christ who was little more than 'the man for others.' Meantime he pursued his own *oeuvre.*" (Hebblethwaite, "Between Lucerne and Krakow: European Pluralism and the *Magisterium,*" in *Hans Küng. New Horizons for Faith and Thought,* ed. K.-J. Kuschel [New York: Continuum, 1993], 71). Max Seckler wrote recently: "Certainly with Balthasar it is very much a question less of factual arguments which one can pin down in texts . . . as, much more, of offering an alternative thought-form in a particular area which, however, tolerates no other gods before it" (Seckler, "Die scholastische 'Potentia Oboedientialis' bei Karl Rahner [1904–1984] und Henri de Lubac [1896–1991]. Ein Beitrag zur Metaphysik des endlichen Geistes," in *Die Einheit der Person* [Stuttgart: Kohlhammer, 1998], 312).

193. Paul Imhof, ed., *Karl Rahner in Dialogue. Conversations and Interviews, 1965–1985* (New York: Crossroad, 1986), 14.

194. Ibid., 191. Peter Lippert S. J. (1899–1936) was well known as a radio preacher. He wrote on dogmatic theology and more frequently on spirituality, including a book on the psychology of the Society of Jesus; his book *Die Weltanschauung des Katholizismus* (Leipzig: Reinicke, 1927) would be interesting to compare with Przywara's approach at the same time as it treats the structure, sin, renewal, and end of the world, and Catholicism as a metaphysics, a religion, an ethos. See Hannes Schwander, *Peter Lippert. Sprache und Weltbild* (Fribourg: University Press, 1948); Josef Kreitmaier, *Peter Lippert, der Mann und sein Werk* (Freiburg: Herder, 1938); Oskar Köhler, "Peter Lippert," *Stimmen der Zeit* 208 (1990): 745–51; Julius Oswald, "Lippert, Peter, SJ (1899)," in *Lexikon für Theologie und Kirche* (Freiburg: Herder, 1996), 6:949.

195. Neufeld, "Kategorien," 310.

196. Neufeld, *Die Brüder Rahner* (Freiburg: Herder, 1994), 82.

197. "Laudatio," 266.

198. Ibid., 268.

199. Ibid., 270.

200. Ibid., 272; see Heinrich Fries, "Erich Przywara," *Catholica* 17 (1973): 69ff. and Neufeld, "Vertiefte und gelebte Katholizität. Erich Przywara, 100 Jahre," 161ff.

201. See M. Schneider, *"Unterscheidung der Geister." Die ignatianischen Exerzitien in der Deutung von E. Przywara, K. Rahner und G. Fessard* (Innsbruck: Tyrolia, 1983); on Przywara's spiritual theology, see Wulf, 361–64.

202. *Logos* (Düsseldorf: Patmos, 1964), 94.

203. *Gott* (Munich: Oratoriums-Verlag, 1926), 23

204. Ibid., 23.

205. Rahner, *Belief Today* (New York: Sheed and Ward, 1967), 81.

206. *Religionsphilosophie katholischer Theologie* (Munich: Oldenburg, 1927), 52ff. "Only God alone is the totality of simplicity, while the creature is essentially that which is partial, the becoming, the fashioned . . . , [presented] to give itself ceaselessly into God to an extent which the creature recognizes humbly corresponds to the very limits of his creatureliness" (Przywara, "Der Ruf von heute (1930)," in *Katholische Krise*, 99).

207. "Wohin?" in *Ringen der Gegenwart*, 1:128; for a similarity between Rahner and Przywara in terms of the reemphasis upon grace as a modification of the formal acts and objects of the person (in contrast to actual grace), see Terán Dutari, "Zur Frage des übernatürlichen Formalobjekts" in *Christentum und Metaphysik*, 590–93.

208. *Religionsphilosophie katholischer Theologie*, 94.

209. Rahner, "Jesus Christus," in *Kleines Theologisches Wörterbuch* (Freiburg: Herder, 1963), 188.

210. *Gott*, 59.

211. Przywara, "Die religiöse Krisis in der Gegenwart und der Katholizismus," 52–53.

212. "Protestantische und katholische Ur-Einstellung," 227; see Fischer, *Der Mensch als Geheimnis. Die Anthropologie Karl Rahners* (Freiburg: Herder, 1974), 85–89; 366–69; 381–84; and Richard Schenk, *Die Gnade vollendeter Endlichkeit: Zur tranzendentaltheologischen Auslegung der thomanischen Anthropologie* (Freiburg: Herder, 1989) 378–80.

213. Fischer says that Przywara suggested indirectly to Rahner the study of Carmelite mysticism and Kierkegaard as coming from Przywara (36). Rahner, "The Logic of Concrete Individual Knowledge in Ignatius Loyola," in *The Dynamic Element in the Church* (New York: Herder and Herder, 1964), 84ff.

214. Fischer, *Der Mensch als Geheimnis*, 36, 83; on the two Jesuits as interpreters of the *Exercises*, see 34–37, 55–61, 83–90.

215. Fischer, *Der Mensch als Geheimnis*, 56.

216. "Katholizismus," in *Ringen der Gegenwart*, 2:607.

217. Fischer, *Der Mensch als Geheimnis*, 59.

218. "Edith Stein. Zu ihrem zehnten Todestag," 66.

219. "Umschau," *Stimmen der Zeit* 138 (1941): 302.

220. Przywara, "Die Reichweite der Analogie als katholischer Grundform," 341.

221. Rahner, "Nature and Grace," in *Nature and Grace. Dilemmas in the Modern Church* (New York: Sheed and Ward, 1964), 119.

222. Rahner, "The Importance of Thomas Aquinas," in *Faith in a Wintry Season* (New York: Crossroad, 1989), 15ff., 43ff.

223. Przywara, "Liquidierung von Reformation und Gegenreformation" (1961), in *Katholische Krise,* 236; speaking of Edith Stein in 1954 as someone who offered a better approach, Przywara wrote with nostalgia for decades past: "For the intellectual mentality of the German postwar period is unfortunately still an imitation, without critique, of the great phenomenologies (Husserl, Scheler, Heidegger) or an easy baptizing without reflection of a so-called Catholic phenomenology, like the work of Joseph Maréchal or the circle, empty of ideas, dependent upon a mix of Heidegger and Maréchal" ("Edith Stein. Zu ihrem zehnten Todestag," 66).

224. "Dialectical Analogy: the Oscillating Center of Rahner's Thought," *Gregorianum* 75 (1994): 679.

225. *Foundations of Christian Faith. An Introduction to the Idea of Christianity* (New York: Crossroad, 1978), 141. Rahner's theology has its own sources for letting the supernatural provide the ground for the natural, sources independent of Barth (699f.).

226. "Dialectical Analogy," 700.

227. "Liquidierung," 239 (reviewing Rahner's *Sendung und Gnade* of 1959).

228. Przywara, "Liquidierung," 239. Walter Birnbaum sees Rahner continuing Przywara's ideas on the importance of the liturgy of the word in the Eucharist (*Das Kultusproblem und die liturgischen Bewegungen des 20. Jahrhunderts,* 1, *Die deutsche katholische liturgische Bewegung* [Tübingen: Katzmann, 1966], 140ff.).

229. Przywara, "Liquidierung," 240. Przywara in 1952 seems to disagree with Rahner's later call for a deeper identity of the divine and economic Trinity, but this may be only an effort to understand the differences between the "Being-Trinity" and its revelation to human beings ("Trinität. Gespräch," in *In und Gegen,* 309).

230. Przywara, "Liquidierung," 241.

231. "Katholische Ökumenizität," in *Ringen der Gegenwart,* 2:612. See Richard Schaeffler, "Philosophie und katholische Theologie im 20. Jahrhundert," in *Christliche Philosophie im katholischen Denken des 19. und 20. Jahrhunderts,* ed. Emerich Coreth et al. (Graz: Styria, 1990), 3:60–64.

Chapter 5.   The Christian in the Church

1. "Neue Theologie? Das Problem katholischer Theologie," *Stimmen der Zeit* 111 (1926): 443.

2. "Einheit von Natur und Übernatur?" *Stimmen der Zeit* 105 (1923): 428–40.

3. Rahner, "Laudatio auf Erich Przywara," in *Gnade als Freiheit* (Freiburg: Herder, 1968), 270.

4. "Thomas von Aquin, Ignatius von Loyola, Friedrich Nietzsche," *Zeitschrift für Aszese und Mystik* 11 (1936): 257ff.

5. *Religionsbegründung. Max Scheler—J. H. Newman* (Freiburg: Herder, 1923), 275.

6. Introduction, to the English translation of *Majestas Divina: The Divine Majesty* (London: Collins, 1971); unfortunately this edition omits the final essay of the original edition mentioned in the following note. Contrasting Franciscan with Ignatian spirituality is *Weg zu Gott, Religionsphilosophische Schriften* (Einsiedeln: Johannes, 1962), 55.

7. *Maiestas Divina* (Augsburg: Filser, 1925), 69. These words from the concluding meditative essay sound like a poet cited by Przywara (*Gott* [Munich: Oratorium, 1926], 9, 167), Rainer Maria Rilke, a writer of detachment before the autumnal fall of dying leaves (see Rilke, "Herbst").

8. "Being alone is not for all. Therefore Ignatian spirituality is almost impossible for converts or for Catholics who find themselves coming back from the icey wilderness of a modern atomized individualism to enter the war room of ecclesial community" (72). Przywara devoted some pages to the interesting theme of converts. There is a distinct psychology of the convert; Paul and Augustine had it, a fiery enthusiasm. "Religion is for the convert the conscious and reflexive content of his or her life, so strong that the changing contradictions of life which play out for born Catholics in the profane sphere of daily life (because they 'rest' in a kind of possession of God) are for the convert change and opposition in religion, a religious life which is the total absolutism of religion. In other words: the danger of the convert is religious fanaticism" (Przywara, "Konvertiten," in *Ringen der Gegenwart* [Augsburg: Filser, 1929], 1:147). For instance, one does not find sharp antitheses between the younger and older Aquinas although his theological career includes upheavals. "The problem of the convert can reach tragic proportions when two converts oppose each other like Newman and Manning" (149). Some converts are too demanding of what they see as religious and too critical of what is profane. "While the born Catholic rests in the security of his or her faith and in an authentic discipleship to the teaching coming from God and sees a reference of the entirety of creation to God, and so is drawn into the real world and is at home there, the Catholic convert who has just torn away from an idolatrous world has the vague insecurity of a convalescent" (153). She has a more difficult time living between modernism and integralism, and finds herself at home not in the church but only with other converts. The convert has to get used to the "holy ordinariness" of Catholicism, the family with its many movements, the ordinary life of graced human beings (153).

9. "Seelsorge," *In und Gegen* (Nuremberg: Glock und Lutz, 1955), 391.

10. Gertz, *Glaubenswelt als Analogie* (Düsseldorf: Patmos, 1969), 347.

11. Fischer, *Der Mensch als Geheimnis. Die Anthropologie Karl Rahners* (Freiburg: Herder, 1974), 34.

12. James Zeitz, *Spirituality and Analogia Entis according to Erich Przywara* (New York: University Press of America, 1982), 186. Zeitz offers a summary exposition of Ignatian material in *Spirituality and Analogia Entis,* chapter 4; see also Karlheinz Ruhstorfer, "Das moderne und das postmoderne Interesse an den Geistlichen Übungen," in *Das Prinzip ignatianischen Denkens. Zum geschichtlichen Ort der 'Geistlichen Übungen' des Ignatius von Loyola* (Freiburg: Herder, 1998), 14ff. On the history of the interpretation of the *Spiritual Exercises* at the time of Przywara, see Klaus Fischer, *Der Mensch als Geheimnis,* 31–33; for an extensive treatment of Przywara on the *Exercises,* and on his relationship to Rahner, see Fischer, *Der Mensch als Geheimnis,* 34–37, 55–61, 83–90. Balthasar refers to the insight of Przywara, along with Rahner and Gaston Fessard, in drawing out a theology of the *Exercises* from the detailed formalism of the Baroque ("Theologie und Herrlichkeit," in *Verbum Caro. Skizzen zur Theologie* [Einsiedeln: Johannes, 1960], 1:204). Josef Sudbrack offers a later look at the development of these interpretations of the *Spiritual Exercises* in "Fragestellung und Infragestellung der ignatianischen Exerzitien," *Geist und Leben* 43 (1970): 206–26.

13. *Deus Semper Maior. Theologie der Exerzitien* (Freiburg: Herder, 1938), iv. "Appearing in 1938, its first edition was almost completely destroyed by bombing raids" (Martha Zechmeister, *Gottes-Nacht* [Münster: LIT, 1997], 142).

14. "Thomas von Aquin, Ignatius von Loyola, Friedrich Nietzsche," 269–73.

15. Schneider, *"Unterscheidung der Geister"* (Innsbruck: Tyrolia, 1983), 26, 27.

16. Karl Rahner's *Spiritual Exercises* (London: Sheed and Ward, 1967) illustrates a variant, perhaps further, transformation of the *Spiritual Exercises* into a spirituality of being and transcendental personality. Rahner spoke of the *Spiritual Exercises* as theological mystagogy: "[they] concern themselves not merely and not primarily with an extrinsic indoctrination stemming from dogmatic, moral, and ascetical insights, but rather evoke and actualize *the* humanity and *the* Christ-directedness which, through transcendentality and grace (in unity), are always given as an intrinsic, total thrust of the one whole person into 'loving mystery.' To be sure, this inner thrust anticipates, corresponds to, and is fulfilled by the history of salvation which encounters man from the outside" (Rahner, Foreword to Harvey D. Egan, *The Spiritual Exercises and the Ignatian Mystical Horizon* (St. Louis: Institute of Jesuit Sources, 1976), xivf. Hugo Rahner said that Przywara had made an "exemplary contribution" to understanding the theological Ignatius (*Ignatius the Theologian* [New York: Herder and Herder, 1968], 2).

17. "Alltag," in *Ringen der Gegenwart,* 1:164ff; see Schneider, 28f.

18. This English word does not quite do justice to the German word *Erfahrung,* which is a knowing experiential contact with general realms of

culture like the economics or arts of a time, and not an emotional experience caused by a person or an object. To confuse this with *Erlebnis*—some English-speaking theologians fall into this mistake—which stands close to the English word "experience," is to gain a skewed stance on modern German Catholic theology.

19. Friedrich Wulf, "Christliches Denken. Eine Einführung in das theologische Werk von Erich Przywara (1889–1972)," in *Gottes Nähe*, ed. Peter Imhof (Würzburg: Echter, 1990), 361.

20. *Deus Semper Maior*, 1:363; see J. Solá, "Przywara. Su teologia de la pasión," *Revista de espiritualidad* 23 (1964): 210–28; L. Arostegui, "La gloria de la Cruz en Erich Przywara," *Revista de espiritualidad* 35 (1976): 275–300; Bernhard Gertz, "Kreuz-Struktur. Zur theologischen Methode Erich Przywaras," *Theologie und Philosophie* 45 (1970): 553ff.

21. Wulf, "Christliches Denken," 364.

22. *Wandlung, Frühe Religiöse Schriften* (Einsiedeln: Johannes, 1962), 384.

23. "Die Idee des Jesuiten nach der Liturgie des Festes Allerheiligen der Gesellschaft Jesu," *Zeitschrift für Aszese und Mystik* 8 (1933): 252ff.

24. "Katholizität," in *Katholische Krise* (Düsseldorf: Patmos, 1967), 25; see the early "Geheimis der Frau," *Das neue Reich* 12 (1930): 709ff., 730ff.

25. "Katholizität," in *Katholische Krise*, 25.

26. Ibid., 33f.

27. "Wohin?" in *Ringen der Gegenwart*, 1:128.

28. Przywara, *Demut, Geduld, Liebe. Die drei christlichen Tugenden* (Düsseldorf: Patmos, 1960), 8.

29. Maréchal, *Studies in the Psychology of the Mystics* (Albany: Magi, 1964).

30. "Katholische Totalität," in *Ringen der Gegenwart* (Augsburg: Filser, 1929), 2:607. Karl Neufeld writes: "More and more existential experiences with people, even with an unshakeable confidence in the ever greater God, led to a greater reserve toward human possibilities and capabilities . . . , to the disclosure of the limitation, weakness and meanness of people who therein concretely influenced the course of history" (Neufeld, "Vertiefte und gelebte Katholizität. Erich Przywara, 100 Jahre," *Theologie und Philosophie* 65 [1990]: 168f.).

31. The Bible and the liturgy went together: the liturgy presented the Bible, while the liturgical year represented biblical history. Both Bible and liturgy were extrametaphysical, signs and stories where God's grace presented itself not in theories of being and consciousness but in the concreteness of life or of aesthetic pattern. Przywara liked to draw the Bible into dialogue with theology and spirituality, and to write poetic paraphrases of Scripture. Studies on the Bible appeared after World War II, books on the old and new covenant, and the Gospel according to John. The work on the covenants began as a series of talks given during the war in Munich, Berlin, and Vienna and was published in 1955; the work on John was begun in 1947

and appeared in 1954. Parable and story and textual genres serve narrative and ontology, allowing the message of revelation to nourish and inspire individuals. The Word speaks in parables to explain his own life. The stories are not irrational but logos-centered; even the cross finds illumination in a parable like that of the good Samaritan. Beneath biblical-historical images lies the analogy of being. Both the orders of being and cosmos, and that of revelation and salvation exist in a tension, in an emergence, in a movement. The Bible is the living revelation of God at the intersection of human history, salvation-history, and God himself. Against Protestant theologians he asserted repeatedly that the Bible speaks its message noetically and ontically. A biblical theology already has examples from the past to show that it must avoid both rationalism and gnosticism, the extremes of Platonism and of the Reformation. A Catholic approach to Scripture underlies dogma precisely as at the same time it stimulates devotion and spirituality.

32. "Verklärung oder Polarität," in *Ringen der Gegenwart*, 2:26.

33. See Pius Parsch, *The Church's Year of Grace* (Collegeville: Liturgical Press, 1953–1959), 5 vols.; Gertz, "Kirchenjahr," in *Glaubenswelt als Analogie*, 123–26; his view was criticized for focusing too much on the soul by figures in the liturgical movement such as Athanasius Wintersig who called attention to the fact that the liturgical year was not first about personal devotion but was the temporal prayer of the church. The Jesuit theologian responded to this in "Verklärung oder Polarität," in *Ringen der Gegenwart*, 2:26ff.; see also their theological discussion in articles in the *Sonntagsbeilage der Augsburger Postzeitung* # 48–50 (1923) and # 4 (1924).

34. See Walter Birnbaum, *Das Kultusproblem und die liturgischen Bewegungen des 20. Jahrhunderts*: 1, *Die deutsche katholische liturgische Bewegung* (Tübingen: Katzmann, 1966).

35. "Liquidierung von Reformation und Gegenreformation" (1961), in *Katholische Krise*, 234 (original article from 1960 in *Die Furche*).

36. Przywara, "Liturgische Erneuerung," 71; see *Humanitas* (Nuremberg: Glock und Lutz, 1952), 235. See too *The Legacy of the Tübingen School*, ed. Michael Himes, D. Dietrich (New York: Crossroad, 1997), 173–91. Przywara wrote an essay on Newman and the German Romantic theoretician of universal systems, Joseph Görres, on their views of history, humanity, and God; both linked the historical development of Christianity to the growth of the Pauline Body of Christ; "Newman und Josef von Görres," *Newman Studien* 6 (1964): 97–104.

37. *Humanitas*, 577. He objected to Karl Eschweiler describing his theology as more or less Romantic ("Vorwort," in *Ringen der Gegenwart*, 1:VIII).

38. Przywara, "Verklärung oder Polarität," 13; *Weg zu Gott*, chapters 4 and 5.

39. *Gottgeheimnis der Welt, Religionsphilosophische Schriften* (Einsiedeln: Johannes, 1962), 24; "Liturgische Erneurung" (1930), in *Katholische Krise* (Düsseldorf: Patmos, 1967), 71.

40. Eva-Maria Faber, *Kirche zwischen Identität und Differenz: Die ekklesiologischen Entwürfe von Romano Guardini und Erich Przywara* (Würzburg: Echter, 1993), 71f., 123, 194 (see also Faber, "*Deus semper maior,*" *Geist und Leben* 66 [1993]: 208–27).

41. Przywara, "Liturgische Erneuerung," 80.

42. Gertz, "Katholische Krise und Konzil," in *Katholische Krise,* 258.

43. Przywara, "Verklärung oder Polarität" (1924), in *Katholische Krise* (Düsseldorf: Patmos, 1967), 12; "Ringen um Gott," in *Ringen der Gegewart,* 1:248–51 which reviews Guardini's *Liturgische Bildung* (1923) and *Von heiligen Zeichen* (1922); see the reviews of Guardini's books on Pascal and Dostoyevsky in *Stimmen der Zeit* 30 (1935–36): 56ff. In 1952 he wrote that Guardini had taken over his theme of opposition from Georg Simmel but left it at the level of style and aphorism ("Simmel—Scheler—Husserl" (*In und Gegen,* 36).

44. Przywara, "Liturgische Erneuerung," 85; see Hanna-Barbara Gerl, *Romano Guardini, 1885–1968* (Mainz: Matthias-Grünewald, 1985), 150f.

45. Przywara, "Vorwort," in *Das Geheimnis Kierkegaards* (Munich: Oldenbourg, 1929), v. On Przywara's views on the basic structure of opposition in Guardini before the publication of Guardini's *Der Gegensatz* in 1925, see Alfons Knoll, *Glaube und Kultur bei Romano Guardini* (Paderborn: Schöningh, 1993), 232.

46. Przywara, "Corpus Christi Mysticum—Eine Bilanz" (1940), in *Katholische Krise,* 133; the mission of the church and its uniqueness under Christ is weakened by the writings which relate it too extensively to the world and its religions. Przywara linked Guardini to Karl Adam (133). In a review of Maritain's book on Christian philosophy and Guardini's collection of essays he saw both of them empty of a final synthesis that could be drawn from the missions of the Trinity where God does not disdain the human or the secular but draws from true disciples service as well as prayer ("Das Christliche im Denken," *Stimmen der Zeit* 130 [1935–36]: 493ff.); see *Mensch* (Nuremberg: Glock & Lutz, 1959), 319f.

47. Faber, 178.

48. Review of Cipriano Vagaggini, *Theologie der Liturgie,* in *Die Furche* (March 7, 1960), 23.

49. "The authenticity and health of the liturgical renewal depends above all on the ultimate comportment of *service*" (Przywara, "Liturgische Erneuerung," 85).

50. Yves Congar, *L'Église de saint Augustin à l'époque moderne* (Paris: Cerf, 1970); "Situation ecclésiologique au moment de 'Ecclesiam suam' et passage à une église dans l'itinéraire des hommes," *Le Concile de Vatican II* (Paris: Beauchesne, 1984), 8ff.; "'Lumen Gentium No. 7,' L'Eglise, Corps mystique du Christ, vu au terme de huit siècles d'histoire de la théologie du Corps mystique," in *Le Concile de Vatican II,* 148f.

51. *Religionsphilosophie katholischer Theologie* (Munich: Oldenbourg, 1927), 32.

52. *Gott*, 90.

53. *Religionsphilosophie katholischer Theologie*, 41ff.

54. See Przywara's response to this enterprise, "Wesen des Katholizismus," *Stimmen der Zeit* 108 (1924): 47–67.

55. "Protestantische und katholische Ur-Einstellung," 227.

56. "Das katholische Kirchenprinzip," *Zwischen den Zeiten* 7 (1929): 277, 285.

57. *Religionsphilosophie*, 30; see 32.

58. *Gott*, 96; see Faber, 166ff.; on this period of ecclesiology in the twentieth century, see Congar, *L'Église de saint Augustin*, 461–71.

59. *Gott*, 126.

60. "Das katholische Kirchenprinzip," 254.

61. "Custos, quid de nocte?" in *Ringen der Gegenwart*, 1:44. On the Ignatian characteristic of feeling with the church, see Schneider, 68.

62. "Corpus Christi Mysticum—eine Bilanz," 123–52; see Mannes Dominikus Koster, *Ekklesiologie im Werden* (Paderborn: Bonifacius-Druckerei, 1940), and L. Deimel, *Leib Christi. Sinn und Grenzen einer Deutung des innerkirchlichen Lebens* (Freiburg: Herder, 1940).

63. See Rudolf Michael Schmitz, *Aufbruch zum Geheimnis der Kirche Jesu Christi. Aspekte der katholischen Ekklesiologie des deutschen Sprachraumes von 1918 bis 1943* (St. Ottilien: Eos, 1991).

64. "Die Reichweite der Analogie als katholischer Grundform," *Scholastik* 15 (1940): 510.

65. Przywara, "Theologie der Kirche. Ekklesiologie" (1941), in *Katholische Krise*, 154–57.

66. Scheler, "Soziologische Neuorientierung und die Aufgaben der deutschen Katholiken nach dem Krieg," *Hochland* 13 (1915/16): 385–406; 682–700.

67. Przywara, "Gottesgemeinschaft und Kirche," in *Religionsbegründung*, 174–88.

68. See *Katholische Krise*, 71f. 123, 194; see Faber, "Rechtskirche und Liebeskirche," 229–33.

69. Congar, *L'Église de saint Augustin à l'époque moderne*, 469.

70. Przywara, "Das Dogma von der Kirche–Ein Aufbau" (1944), in *Katholische Krise*, 194.

71. Przywara, "Das Dogma von der Kirche—Ein Aufbau," 194.

72. "Theologie der Kirche," 192–94; *Was Ist Gott? Summula* (Nuremberg: Glock und Lutz, 1947), 58. Gertz sees this fundamental theology as anticipating Vatican II's documents on the church (*Glaubenswelt als Analogie*, 340, 345).

73. Faber, 234; 417ff.

74. *Katholische Krise,* 84, 151; on the Ignatian aspect, Faber, 238ff.

75. Przywara, "Theologie der Kirche," 165; "Corpus Christi Mysticum—eine Bilanz," 149. In 1935 Maritain's book on Christian philosophy was criticized because it made the secular transparent to religion at the expense of the secular itself. The world lost its own identity and maturity, something which weakened creation and incarnation and became too much a mental pathway to God. ("Das Christliche im Denken," *Stimmen der Zeit* 130 [1935–1936]: 497).

76. The phrase of Gertz, *Glaubenswelt als Analogie,* 344.

77. *Gespräch zwischen den Kirchen* (Nuremberg: Glock und Lutz, 1956), 56.

78. "Theologie der Kirche," in *Katholische Krise.*

79. See Faber, 220–23. After the proclamation of the Assumption in 1950 Przywara's composed a subtle reflection noting that the melange of neo-scholasticism and papal prose stood outside the tradition of pondering the fathers of the church. At the same time the dogma was a balance to an overbearing presentation of Christian revelation in terms of father figures and men; it reaffirmed salvation-history and eschatology. It was, too, a restoration of the papal magisterium consulting the world-wide episcopacy and the laity and liturgy, also aspects of tradition ("Um Maria," in *In und Gegen,* 331–39, published originally under the pseudonym Franz-S. Tharser); see Gertz, "Kreuz-Struktur. Zur theologischen Methode Erich Przywaras," 555.

80. "Custos, quid de nocte?" in *Ringen der Gegenwart,* 1:39.

81. Faber, 223.

82. Zeitz, *Spirituality,* 319.

83. Faber, 209.

84. *Alter und Neuer Bund,* 290; see Faber, 213f. It seems inaccurate to understand Przywara's critique of the controversial Joseph Wittig as supportive of extreme or unjust ecclesial censorship (Otto Weiss, *Der Modernismus in Deutschland* [Regensburg: Pustet, 1995], 523ff.).

85. *Was ist Gott? Summula,* 56f; see *Kirche in Gegensätzen* (Düsseldorf: Patmos, 1962), 23.

86. Przywara, "Papst-König," *Stimmen der Zeit* 117 (1929): 1–2.

87. Przywara, *Kirche in Gegensätzen,* 30.

88. Cited in Faber, 219.

89. Przywara, "Papst-König," *Stimmen der Zeit* 117 (1929): 7.

90. Ibid. "Pius X," in *In und Gegen,* 87ff.

91. Przywara, "Papst-König," *Stimmen der Zeit* 117 (1929): 11. The newly established feast of Christ the King is not to be an asylum for the monarchs of Europe but a liturgical statement that God is not the captive of time. Przywara seems to limit the motif of prophet, priest, and king to the hierarchy ("Theologie der Kirche. Ekklesiologie," 164). Around 1960 Przywara gave a lecture on the radio about his meetings with Nuncio Pacelli, later to be Pope

Pius XII, who in 1928 had asked him to go on a mission to Rome to see cardinals Frühwirth and Merry del Val; he did not disclose the purpose but only that he received Pius XII's autographed picture as a sign of thanks. As cardinal secretary of state, Pacelli met with Przywara in Berlin in Cardinal Preysing's residence to discuss the Jesuit's lecture on the so-called "cultural turn" which Pacelli had attended; see Gustav Wilhelmy, "Erich Przywara. Ein Überblick," in *Erich Przywara, 1889–1969. Eine Festgabe* (Düsseldorf: Patmos, 1969), 21.

92. Przywara, "Papst-König," *Stimmen der Zeit* 117 (1929): 7, 8.

93. "Corpus Christi Mysticum—Eine Bilanz," 146.

94. Wilhelmy reports that Przywara from the beginning had problems with church and Jesuit censors required before Vatican II for every published piece; this led him to add, sometimes, unnecessary patristic and papal citations (Wilhelmy, 12).

95. *Gespräch zwischen den Kirchen,* 56; he interpreted the transposition of the angelic hierarchy of Pseudo-Dionysius into the church as an impetus to service.

96. *In und Gegen,* 405; *Deus Semper Major,* 337. Przywara distanced himself from the common German name for a priest, a *Geistlicher,* since all Christians lead a spiritual life and are of the Spirit (*Geist*) (*In und Gegen,* 407). There is a general priesthood of the baptized which is not in competition with the priesthood of the ordained (*Kirche in Gegensätzen,* 28f.).

97. Przywara, "Theologie der Kirche. Ekklesiologie," 160–62; "Seelsorge," *In und Gegen,* 407; *Katholische Krise,* 194, 57.

98. *Gespräche zwischen den Kirchen,* 47.

99. Przywara, "Liquidierung von Reformation und Gegenreformation" (1961), in *Katholische Krise,* 235.

100. Semmelroth, *Church and Sacrament* (Notre Dame: Fides, 1965 [originally published in Germany in 1953]); Przywara, "Die Kirche als Ursakrament (1953)," in *Katholische Krise,* 196–98.

101. Przywara, "Theologie der Kirche. Ekklesiologie," 164.

102. Ibid., 165.

103. Ibid., 163.

104. See Gertz, *Glaubenswelt als Analogie,* 346–49; Faber, "Der Laie in der Kirche," 226–30.

105. Przywara, "Evangelische Katholizität—Katholische Evangelizität" (1960), 199.

106. Przywara, "Alter und neuer Katholizismus" (1961), 182.

107. "Una Sancta" (1961), in *Katholische Krise,* 211ff.; *Begegnung der Christen,* ed. Oscar Cullmann (Stuttgart: Evangelisches Verlagswerk, 1959).

108. See the essays "Alter und Neuer Katholizismus" and "Römische Katholizität—Allchristliche Ökumenizität," in *Katholische Krise.*

109. Przywara, "Liquidierung von Reformation und Gegenreformation," 226.

110. Ibid., 221–23.

111. *Religionsbegründung*, 87.

112. For a survey of theologies of grace outside of explicit faith and baptism, see S. Harent, "Infidèles (Salut des)," in *Dictionnaire de Théologie Catholique* (Paris: Letouzey et Ané, 1927), 7:2:1860–1930.

113. "Katholische Ökumenizität," *Ringen der Gegenwart*, 2:611.

114. Ibid., 611.

115. Ibid., 612.

116. Ibid., 616. It is interesting to see Przywara's critique of Alois Dempf's philosophy of religion of 1937 that described a unity of religious worldviews but in its presentation of the commonality and universality in religions and religious drives lacked the concreteness of incarnation and community (review of Alois Dempf, *Religionsphilosophie* [Vienna: Thomas, 1937], in *Stimmen der Zeit* 134 [1938]: 338).

117. Przywara, "Alter und neuer Katholizismus," 179.

118. This may explain why Thomas Ruster (*Die verlorene Nützlichkeit der Religion. Katholizismus und Moderne in der Weimarer Republik* [Paderborn: Schöningh, 1994], 285ff.) thought that he excluded salvation from those outside Christianity. The passage Ruster cites about how the church enters powerfully into the act of faith of a Catholic is not developed by Przywara even to exclude Protestants (who have a different theology and a different kind of church) but to describe what is characteristic of the Catholic perspective: indeed here there is a struggle to show how different kinds of divine faith are ecclesial ("Neue Theologie," in *Ringen der Gegenwart*, 2:705).

119. "Wohin?" in *Ringen der Gegenwart*, 1:128.

120. *Religionsphilosophie katholischer Theologie*, 104.

121. "Katholizismus der Kirche und Katholizismus der Stunde," *Stimmen der Zeit* 110 (1926): 260–70.

122. *Vier Predigten über das Abendland* (Einsiedeln: Johannes, 1948): 39–45.

123. Przywara, *Kirche in Gegensätzen*, 6.

124. Ibid., 13, 18.

125. Ibid., 30. Yves Congar had brought back into public view in the 1930s the work of Möhler (See Thomas O'Meara, "Beyond 'Hierarchology': Johann Adam Möhler and Yves Congar," in *The Legacy of the Tübingen School*, 173–91).

126. Przywara, review of *Die eine Kirche. Zum Gedenken J. A. Möhlers 1838–1938*, ed. H. Tüchle (Paderborn: Schöningh, 1939), in *Scholastik* 15 (1940): 241.

127. Przywara, *Kirche in Gegensätzen*, 54.

128. Gertz, "Katholische Krise und Konzil," in *Katholische Krise*, 257; on the church, 262–65.

129. See Gertz, *Glaubenswelt als Analogie*, 422–27, 340–44.

130. "Laudatio," 270.

131. Schmitz, *Aufbruch zum Geheimnis,* 210.

132. "Alter und neuer Katholizismus," 188.

133. Gertz, "Kreuz-Struktur," 561. In the 1920s the German bishops published a catechism toward which Przywara expressed reservations. The text had been begun under Cardinal Faulhaber and reflected new catechetical directions. It is more biblical than speculative, more an ecclesiology of the mystical body than one of institution and hierarchy. Pryzwara thinks that following the liturgical movement there is too great a stress on memory and presence rather than on sacrifice. The primacy of Peter is bound more to the Easter appearances than to the handing over of the keys. The style of the catechism is more that of "a Christian humanism" missing the cross, and missing Marian devotions (Przywara, "Liquidierung von Reformation und Gegenreformation," in *Katholische Krise,* 230–32).

134. *Christliche Existenz* (Leipzig: Hegner, 1934), 119.

135. See Karl Neufeld, "Kategorien des Katholischen. P. Erich Przywara—100 Jahre," *Catholica* 43 (1989): 306f.

136. Przywara, "Evangelische Katholizität—Katholische Evangelizität" (1960), 205ff.; manifesting a similar anxiety over conforming to the world and renewing Catholicism, rejecting both modernism and integralism (for which the papacy found no middle position), is his response to an inquiry in 1961 as to what he expected from the council ("Was Erwarten Sie vom Konzil? Eine Rundfrage unter Katholiken Deutschlands, Österreichs und der Schweiz," *Wort und Wahrheit* 16 [1961]: 656).

137. *Logos* (Düsseldorf: Patmos, 1964), 100.

Conclusion

1. Zechmeister, "Karsamstag. Zu einer Theologie des Gott-vermissens," *Vom Wagnis der Nichtidentität* (Münster: LIT, 2000) 70.

2. *Gottgeheimnis der Welt, Schriften* (Einsiedeln: Johannes, 1962), 2:215.

3. Gertz, "Kreuz-Struktur. Zur theologischen Methode Erich Przywaras," *Theologie und Philosophie* 45 (1970): 557.

4. Przywara, "Augustin Wibbelt, Ein Heimatbuch," *Literarischer Handweiser* 5 (1916): 178.

5. Rahner, "Laudatio auf Erich Przywara," in *Gnade als Freiheit* (Freiburg: Herder, 1968), 269. An unpublished short article from 1966 singled out the theme of people and people of God as fundamental to the work of Vatican II; Przywara described Paul VI as a pilgrim pope between the princely pope, Pius XII, and the people's pope, John XXIII ("Kirche als Volk und Volk asl Kirche. Der Sinn des Zweiten Vatikanischen Konzils [1966]," *Katholische Krise,* 251–53).

6. Karl Neufeld, "Kategorien des Katholischen. P. Erich Przywara—100 Jahre," *Catholica* 43 (1989): 297.

7. Przywara, "Christian Root-Terms: Kerygma, Mysterium, Kairos, Oikonomia," in *Paul Tillich in Catholic Thought* (Dubuque: The Priory Press, 1964), 204.

8. "My unchangeableness here below is perserverance in changing" (*Meditations and Devotions of the Late Cardinal Newman* [New York: Longmans, Green, 1903], 508); this phrase was used for a volume honoring Przywara, *Der beständige Aufbruch* (Nuremberg: Glock und Lutz, 1959).

9. Julio Terán Dutari, *Christentum und Metaphysik. Das Verhältnis beider nach der Analogielehre Erich Przywaras* (Munich: Berchmanskolleg, 1973), 34–39; 558–68.

10. Rahner, "Laudatio," 271.

11. *In und Gegen. Stellungnahmen zur Zeit* (Nuremberg: Glock und Lutz, 1955), 35.

12. "La pensée d'Erich Przywara," *Nouvelle Revue Théologique* 121 (1999): 253.

13. Martha Zechmeister, *Gottes-Nacht* (Münster: LIT, 1997), 16.

14. *Logos* (Düsseldorf: Patmos, 1964), 100.

15. See Zechmeister, "Thomas als Durchgang," in *Gottes-Nacht,* 139f.

16. *Ignatianisch* (Frankfurt: Knecht, 1956), 65f.

17. Cited in *Augustinisch* (Einsiedeln: Johannes, 1972), 64.

Bibliographic Resources

There is an extensive bibliography of Erich Przywara's publications published as a small book, Leo Zimny, *Erich Przywara: Sein Schrifttum, 1912–1962* (Einsiedeln: Johannes, 1963). The writings are arranged chronologically and include book reviews. At the end the author promised a second part of the bibliography which would include unpublished works, new editions, writings, and inaccessible publications; this did not appear. The Przywara *Festschrift, Erich Przywara: 1889–1969: Eine Festgabe* (Düsseldorf: Patmos, 1969) offers a section on his writings with the most basic books up to 1962 followed by further entries taken from Zimny's planned second part as well as a number of translations from the 1960s. This is followed by a bibliography of secondary literature compiled by Julio Terán Dutari reaching from 1922 to 1969 (eighty-nine works are cited). There is then a list of reviews and articles touching on Przywara's writings over the years, and a sample of those texts.

No extensive bibliography of writings on Przywara has appeared. Much of the literature can be found by consulting the bibliographies in Martha Zechmeister. *Gottes-Nacht: Erich Przywaras Weg negativer Theologie* (Münster: LIT, 1997), 320–32, and Stefan Nieborak, *'Homo Analogia': Zur philosophisch-theologischen Bedeutung der 'analogia entis' im Rahmen der existentiellen Frage bei Erich Przywara, S.J. (1889–1997)* (New York: Peter Lang, 1994), 596–613; see too László Polgár, *Bibliographie sur l'histoire de la compagnie de Jésus 1901–1980: III, Les Personnes* (Rome: Institutum Historicum S. J. 1990), 709–11.

There are not many studies of Przywara in English, and very few apart from those concerned with analogy.

Translations into English of Works by Przywara

The Divine Majesty. Translated by Thomas Corbishley. London: Collins, 1971.
Polarity: A German Catholic's Interpretation of Religion. Translated by A. C. Bouquet. London: Oxford University Press, 1935.
"St. Augustine and the Modern World." In *A Monument to Saint Augustine: Essays on Some Aspects of His Thought Written in Commemoration of His 15th Centenary.* London: Sheed and Ward, 1930. Reprint: *Saint Augustine.* Cleveland: World Publishing Co., 1964.

Works Edited by Przywara

An Augustine Synthesis: Arranged by Erich Przywara, S.J. Introduction by C. C. Martindale, S. J. New York: Sheed and Ward, 1936. Reprints: *An Augustine Synthesis.* New York: Harper Torchbook, 1958; *An Augustine Synthesis.* Philadelphia: Ridgeway Books, 1989.
A Newman Synthesis: Arranged by Erich Przywara, S.J. New York: Longmans, Green, 1931. Reprints: *A Newman Synthesis.* New York: Sheed and Ward, 1945; *The Heart of Newman: A Synthesis Arranged by Erich Przywara.* Springfield: Templegate, 1963; *The Heart of Newman.* San Francisco: Ignatius Press, 1997.

Secondary Literature on Przywara in English

Collins, James. "Przywara's '*Analogia Entis*'" *Thought* 17 (1942): 119–35.
Kevern, John R. "A Future for Anglican Catholic Theology." *Anglican Theological Review* 76 (1994): 246–61.
McDermott, John M. "Dialectical Analogy: The Oscillating Center of Rahner's Thought." *Gregorianum* 75 (1994): 675–703.
Nielsen, Niels C. "'*Analogia Entis*' as the Basis of Buddhist-Christian Dialogue." *Modern Theology* 3 (1987): 345–57.
———. "Analogy and the Knowledge of God: An Ecumenical Appraisal (Roman Catholic and Protestant Interpretations in Relation to the Debate about the Analogy of Being between Erich Przywara, S. J., and K. Barth)" *Rice University Studies* 60 (1974): 21–102.
———. *The Debate between Karl Barth and Erich Przywara: A New Evaluation of Protestant and Roman Catholic Differences.* Rice Institute Pamphlet 40. Houston: Rice Institute, 1953.
———. "Przywara's Philosophy of the '*Analogia Entis*.'" *Review of Metaphysics* 5 (1952): 599–620.

Palakeel, Joseph. *The Use of Analogy in Theological Discourse: An Investigation in Ecumenical Perspective*. Rome: Pontificia Universita Gregoriana, 1995.

Zeitz, James V. *Spirituality and Analogia Entis According to Erich Przywara, S.J.: Metaphysics and Religious Experience, the Ignatian Exercises, the Balance in Rhythm in 'Similarity' and 'Greater Dissimilarity' According to Lateran IV*. Washington, D. C.: University Press of America, 1982.

————. "Erich Przywara on Ultimate Reality and Meaning: '*Deus Semper Major*,' 'God Ever Greater.'" *Ultimate Reality and Meaning* 12 (1989): 192–201.

————. "Erich Przywara: Visionary Theologian." *Thought* 58 (1983): 145–57.

————. "God's Mystery in Christ: Reflections on Erich Przywara and Eberhard Jüngel [The Analogy of Being]." *Communio* 12 (1985): 158–72.

————. "Przywara and von Balthasar on Analogy." *Thomist* 52 (1988): 473–98.

Index